P9-DCV-504

Rick Steves'
Italian
Phrase Book & Dictionary
Fifth Edition

AVALON
TRAVEL

Avalon Travel Publishing, 1400 65th Street, Suite 250, Emeryville, CA 94608, USA

AVALON
publishing group incorporated

Avalon Travel Publishing is an imprint of Avalon Publishing Group, Inc.

Text © 2003 by Rick Steves
Cover © 2003 by Avalon Travel Publishing, Inc.
  All rights reserved.
Maps © 2003 by Europe Through the Back Door

Printed in the United States of America by Worzalla.
Fifth edition. Eleventh printing March 2007.

ISBN-10: 1-56691-520-1
ISBN-13: 978-1-56691-520-5

Europe Through the Back Door Managing Editor:
  Risa Laib
Europe Through the Back Door Editors:
  Cameron Hewitt, Jill Hodges
Avalon Travel Publishing Editor: Matt Orendorff
Translation: Giulia Fiorini, Manfredo Guerzoni,
  Simona Bondavalli, Heidi Sewell
Phonetics: Risa Laib, Cameron Hewitt
Production & Typesetting: Matt Orendorff
Cover Design: Kari Gim
Maps & Graphics: David C. Hoerlein, Zoey Platt
Photography: Rick Steves, Dominic Bonuccelli,
  Julie Coen, Andrea Johnson
Front cover photos:
  foreground–Piazza San Marc, Venice; © Getty
Images/Digital Vision/2003; background–The
Colosseum, Rome; © Royalty-Free/CORBIS

Distributed to the book trade by Publishers Group West, Berkeley, California

Other ATP travel guidebooks by Rick Steves

Rick Steves' Best of Europe
Rick Steves' Europe 101: History and Art for the Traveler
  (with Gene Openshaw)
Rick Steves' Europe Through the Back Door
Rick Steves' Best European City Walks & Museums
  (with Gene Openshaw)
Rick Steves' Postcards from Europe
Rick Steves' France (with Steve Smith)
Rick Steves' Germany & Austria
Rick Steves' Great Britain
Rick Steves' Ireland (with Pat O'Connor)
Rick Steves' Italy
Rick Steves' Portugal
Rick Steves' Scandinavia
Rick Steves' Spain
Rick Steves Switzerland
Rick Steves' Provence & the French Riviera
Rick Steves' Amsterdam, Bruges & Brussels
  (with Gene Openshaw)
Rick Steves' Florence & Tuscany (with Gene Openshaw)
Rick Steves' London (with Gene Openshaw)
Rick Steves' Paris
  (with Steve Smith and Gene Openshaw)
Rick Steves' Rome (with Gene Openshaw)
Rick Steves' Venice (with Gene Openshaw)
Rick Steves' Phrase Books: German, Italian, Portuguese,
Spanish, and French/Italian/German

For the latest on Rick's lectures, guidebooks, tours, and public
television series, contact Europe Through the Back Door, Box
2009, Edmonds, WA 98020, tel. 425/771-8303, fax 425/771-
0833, www.ricksteves.com, or e-mail: rick@ricksteves.com.

Although the author and publisher have made every effort to provide
accurate, up-to-date information, they accept no responsibility for
loss, injury, bad crêpes, or inconvenience sustained by any person
using this book.

CONTENTS

Hi, I'm Rick Steves.

I'm the only monolingual speaker I know who's had the nerve to design a series of European phrase books. But that's one of the things that makes them better. You see, after 25 summers of travel through Europe, I've learned first-hand (1) what's essential for communication in another country, and (2) what's not. I've assembled these important words and phrases in a logical, no-frills format, and I've worked with native Europeans and seasoned travelers to give you the simplest, clearest translations possible.

But this book is more than just a pocket translator. The words and phrases have been carefully selected to help you have a smarter, smoother trip in my favorite country without going broke. Italy used to be cheap and chaotic. These days it's neither. It's better organized than ever — and often more expensive than France or Germany. The key to getting more out of every travel dollar is to get closer to the local people, and to rely less on entertainment, restaurants, and hotels that cater only to foreign tourists. This book will not only help you order a meal at a locals-only Venetian restaurant — it'll help you talk to the family that runs the place . . . about their kids, social issues, travel dreams, and favorite flavors of *gelati*. Long after your memories of museums have faded, you'll still treasure the personal encounters you had with your new Italian friends.

A good phrase book should help you enjoy your Italian experience — not just survive it — so I've added a healthy dose of humor. A few phrases are just for fun and aren't meant to be used at all. Most of the phrases are for real and should be used with "please" (*per favore*). I know you can tell the difference.

To get the most out of this book, take the time to internalize and put into practice my Italian pronunciation tips. Remember that Italians, more than their European neighbors, are forgiving of your linguistic fumbling. Don't worry too much about memorizing grammatical rules, like which gender a particular noun is—the important thing is to rise above sex . . . and communicate!

This book has a dictionary and a nifty menu decoder. You'll also find Italian telephone tips and a handy tear-out cheat sheet. Tear it out and keep it in your pocket so you can easily use it to memorize key phrases during idle moments. As you prepare for your trip, you may want to read this year's edition of my *Rick Steves' Italy* guidebook.

Italy can be the most intense, difficult, and rewarding destination in Europe. Travelers either love it—or they quickly see the big sights and flee to Switzerland. To me, someone's love of Italy is a sign of a good traveler—thoughtful, confident, and extroverted. If this phrase book helps make that happen, or if you have suggestions for making it better, I'd love to hear from you. I personally read and value all feedback. My address is Europe Through the Back Door, P.O. Box 2009, Edmonds, WA 98020, tel. 425/771-8303, fax 425/771-0833, e-mail: rick@ricksteves.com.

Happy travels, and **buona fortuna** (good luck) as you hurdle the language barrier!

Rick Steves

GETTING
STARTED

User-friendly Italian

...is easy to get the hang of. Some Italian words are so
familiar, you'd think they were English. If you can say
pizza, lasagna, and spaghetti, you can speak Italian.

There are a few unusual twists to its pronunciation:

C usually sounds like C in cat.
    But C followed by E or I sounds like CH in chance.
CH sounds like C in cat.
E often sounds like AY in play.
G usually sounds like G in get.
    But G followed by E or I sounds like G in gentle.
GH sounds like G in spaghetti.
GLI sounds like LI in million. The G is silent.
GN sounds like GN in lasagna.
H is never pronounced.
I sounds like EE in seed.
R is rolled as in brrravo!
SC usually sounds like SK in skip.
    But SC followed by E or I sounds like SH in shape.
Z usually sounds like TS in hits, and sometimes like the
    sound of DZ in kids.

Have you ever noticed that most Italian words end in a vowel? It's *o* if the word is masculine and *a* if it's feminine. So a *bambino* gets blue and a *bambina* gets pink. A man is *generoso* (generous), a woman is *generosa*. A man will say, "*Sono sposato*" (I am married). A woman will say, "*Sono sposata*." In this book, we show gender-bender words like this: *generoso[a]*. If you are speaking of a woman (which includes women speaking about themselves), use the *a* ending. It's always pronounced "ah." If a noun or adjective ends in *e*, such as *cantante* (singer) or *gentile* (kind), the same word applies to either sex.

Adjective endings agree with the noun. It's *cara amica* (a dear female friend) and *caro amico* (a dear male friend). Sometimes the adjective comes after the noun, as in *vino rosso* (red wine).

Plurals are formed by changing the final letter of the noun: *a* becomes *e*, and *o* becomes *i*. So it's one pizza and two *pizze*, and one cup of *cappuccino* and two cups of *cappuccini*. If you're describing any group of people that includes at least one male, the adjective should end with *i*. But if the group is female, the adjective ends with *e*. A handsome man is *bello* and an attractive group of men (or men and women) is *belli*. A beautiful woman is *bella* and a bevy of beauties is *belle*. In this book, you'll see plural adjective endings depicted like this: *belli[e]*.

Italians usually pronounce every letter in a word, so *due* (two) is **doo**-ay. Sometimes two vowels share one syllable. *Piano* sounds like peeah-noh. The "pee**ah**" is one syllable. When one vowel in a pair should be emphasized, it will appear in bold letters: *Italiano* is ee-tah-lee**ah**-noh.

The key to Italian inflection is to remember this simple rule: most Italian words have their accent on the second-to-last syllable. To override this rule, Italians sometimes insert an accent: *città* (city) is pronounced chee-**tah**.

Italians are animated. You may think two Italians are arguing when in reality they're agreeing enthusiastically. Be confident and have fun communicating in Italian. The Italians really do want to understand you, and are forgiving of a yankee-fied version of their language.

Here's a quick guide to the phonetics used in this book:

ah like A in father.
ay like AY in play.
eh like E in let.
ee like EE in seed.
ehr sounds like "air."
g like G in go.
oh like O in note.
oo like OO in too.
or like OR in core.
ow like OW in now.
s like S in sun.
ts like TS in hits. It's a small explosive sound.
Think of pizza (**pee**-tsah).

ITALIAN
BASICS

In 800, Charlemagne traveled to Rome and became the Holy Roman Emperor using only these phrases.

Meeting and Greeting

Good day.	*Buon giorno.*	bwohn **jor**-noh
Good morning.	*Buon giorno.*	bwohn **jor**-noh
Good evening.	*Buona sera.*	**bwoh**-nah **say**-rah
Good night.	*Buona notte.*	**bwoh**-nah **noh**-tay
Hi / Bye. (informal)	*Ciao.*	chow
Welcome.	*Benvenuto. /*	behn-vay-**noo**-toh /
(said to male /	*Benvenuta. /*	behn-vay-**noo**-tah /
female / group)	*Benvenuti.*	behn-vay-**noo**-tee
Mr. / Mrs.	*Signore / Signora*	seen-**yoh**-ray / seen-**yoh**-rah
Miss	*Signorina*	seen-yoh-**ree**-nah
How are you?	*Come sta?*	**koh**-may stah
Very well.	*Molto bene.*	**mohl**-toh **behn**-ay
Thank you.	*Grazie.*	**graht**-seeay
And you?	*E lei?*	ay **leh**ee
My name is ___.	*Mi chiamo ___.*	mee kee**ah**-moh
What's your name?	*Come si chiama?*	**koh**-may see kee**ah**-mah
Pleased to meet you.	*Piacere.*	peeah-**chay**-ray
Where are you from?	*Di dove è?*	dee **doh**-vay eh

4

I am / We are / Are you...?	Sono / Siamo / È...?	**soh**-noh / see**ah**-moh / eh
...on vacation	...in vacanza	een vah-**kahnt**-sah
...on business	...qui per lavoro	kwee pehr lah-**voh**-roh
See you later.	A più tardi.	ah pew **tar**-dee
Goodbye.	Arrivederci.	ah-ree-vay-**dehr**-chee
Good luck!	Buona fortuna!	**bwoh**-nah for-**too**-nah
Have a good trip!	Buon viaggio!	bwohn vee**ah**-joh

The greeting *"Buon giorno"* (Good day) turns to *"Buona sera"* (Good evening) in the late afternoon.

Essentials

Hello.	Buon giorno.	bwohn **jor**-noh
Do you speak English?	Parla inglese?	**par**-lah een-**glay**-zay
Yes. / No.	Sì. / No.	see / noh
I don't speak Italian.	Non parlo l'italiano.	nohn **par**-loh lee-tah-lee**ah**-noh
I'm sorry.	Mi dispiace.	mee dee-spee**ah**-chay
Please.	Per favore.	pehr fah-**voh**-ray
Thank you.	Grazie.	**graht**-seeay
Thank you very much.	Grazie mille.	**graht**-seeay **mee**-lay
It's (not) a problem.	(Non) c'è una problema.	(nohn) cheh **oo**-nah proh-**blay**-mah
Good. / Great. / Excellent.	Bene. / Benissimo. / Perfetto.	**behn**-ay / behn-**ee**-see-moh / pehr-**feht**-toh
It's good.	Va bene.	vah **behn**-ay
You are very kind.	Lei è molto gentile.	**leh**ee eh **mohl**-toh jehn-**tee**-lay
Excuse me. (to get attention)	Mi scusi.	mee **skoo**-zee
Excuse me. (to pass)	Permesso.	pehr-**may**-soh

It doesn't matter.	Non importa.	nohn eem-**por**-tah
You're welcome.	Prego.	**pray**-goh
Sure.	Certo.	**chehr**-toh
O.K.	Va bene.	vah **behn**-ay
Let's go.	Andiamo.	ahn-dee**ah**-moh
Goodbye!	Arrivederci!	ah-ree-vay-**dehr**-chee

Where?

Where is...?	Dov'è...?	doh-**veh**
...the tourist	...l'ufficio	loo-**fee**-choh
information office	informazioni	een-for-maht-see**oh**-nee
...a cash machine	...un bancomat	oon **bahnk**-oh-maht
...the train station	...la stazione	lah staht-see**oh**-nay
...the bus station	...la stazione	lah staht-see**oh**-nay
	degli autobus	**dayl**-yee **ow**-toh-boos
...the toilet	...la toilette	lah twah-**leht**-tay
men	uomini,	**woh**-mee-nee
	signori	seen-**yoh**-ree
women	donne, signore	**doh**-nay, seen-**yoh**-ray

You'll find some Italian words are similar to English if you're looking for a *banca, farmacia, hotel, ristorante,* or *supermercato.*

How Much?

How much is it?	Quanto costa?	**kwahn**-toh **koh**-stah
Write it?	Me lo scrive?	may loh **skree**-vay
Is it free?	È gratis?	eh **grah**-tees
Is it included?	È incluso?	eh een-**kloo**-zoh
Do you have...?	Ha...?	ah
Where can	Dove posso	**doh**-vay **poh**-soh
I buy...?	comprare...?	kohm-**prah**-ray
I would like...	Vorrei....	vor-**rehe**e
We would like...	Vorremmo...	vor-**ray**-moh

...this.	*...questo.*	**kweh**-stoh
...just a little.	*...un pochino.*	oon poh-**kee**-noh
...more.	*...di più.*	dee pew
...a ticket.	*...un biglietto.*	oon beel-**yay**-toh
...a room.	*...una camera.*	**oo**-nah kah-may-rah
...the bill.	*...il conto.*	eel **kohn**-toh

How Many?

one	*uno*	**oo**-noh
two	*due*	**doo**-ay
three	*tre*	tray
four	*quattro*	**kwah**-troh
five	*cinque*	**cheeng**-kway
six	*sei*	**seh**ee
seven	*sette*	**seht**-tay
eight	*otto*	**oh**-toh
nine	*nove*	**noh**-vay
ten	*dieci*	dee**ay**-chee

You'll find more to count on in the Numbers section (page 15).

When?

At what time?	*A che ora?*	ah kay **oh**-rah
open / closed	*aperto / chiuso*	ah-**pehr**-toh / kee**oo**-zoh
Just a moment.	*Un momento.*	oon moh-**mayn**-toh
Now.	*Adesso.*	ah-**dehs**-soh
Soon.	*Presto.*	**prehs**-toh
Later.	*Più tardi.*	pew **tar**-dee
Today.	*Oggi.*	**oh**-jee
Tomorrow.	*Domani.*	doh-**mah**-nee

BASICS

Be creative! You can combine these phrases to say: "Two, please," or "No, thank you," or "Open tomorrow?" or "Please, where can I buy a ticket?" Please is a magic word in any language. If you want something and you don't know the word for it, just point and say *"Per favore"* (Please). If you know the word for what you want, such as the bill, simply say, *"Il conto, per favore"* (The bill, please).

Struggling with Italian

Do you speak English?	*Parla inglese?*	**par**-lah een-**glay**-zay
A teeny weeny bit?	*Nemmeno un pochino?*	nehm-**may**-noh oon poh-**kee**-noh
Please speak English.	*Parli inglese, per favore.*	**par**-lee een-**glay**-zay pehr fah-**voh**-ray
You speak English well.	*Lei parla bene l'inglese.*	**leh**ee par-lah **behn**-ay leen-**glay**-zay
I don't speak Italian.	*Non parlo l'italiano.*	nohn **par**-loh lee-tah-lee**ah**-noh
We don't speak Italian.	*Non parliamo l'italiano.*	nohn par-lee**ah**-moh lee-tah-lee**ah**-noh
I speak a little Italian.	*Parlo un po' d'italiano.*	**par**-loh oon poh dee-tah-lee**ah**-noh
Sorry, I speak only English.	*Mi dispiace, parlo solo inglese.*	mee dee-spee**ah**-chay **par**-loh **soh**-loh een-**glay**-zay
Sorry, we speak only English.	*Mi dispiace, parliamo solo inglese.*	mee dee-spee**ah**-chay par-lee**ah**-moh **soh**-loh een-**glay**-zay
Does somebody nearby speak English?	*C'è qualcuno qui che parla inglese?*	cheh kwal-**koo**-noh kwee kay **par**-lah een-**glay**-zay
Who speaks English?	*Chi parla inglese?*	kee **par**-lah een-**glay**-zay

What does this mean?	Cosa significa?	**koh**-zah seen-**yee**-fee-kah
What is this in Italian / English?	Come si dice questo in italiano / inglese?	**koh**-may see **dee**-chay **kweh**-stoh een ee-tah-lee**ah**-noh / een-**glay**-zay
Repeat?	Ripeta?	ree-**pay**-tah
Speak slowly.	Parli lentamente.	**par**-lee layn-tah-**mayn**-tay
Slower.	Più lentamente.	pew layn-tah-**mayn**-tay
I understand.	Capisco.	kah-**pees**-koh
I don't understand.	Non capisco.	nohn kah-**pees**-koh
Do you understand?	Capisce?	kah-**pee**-shay
Write it?	Me lo scrive?	may loh **skree**-vay

BASICS

Handy Questions

How much?	Quanto?	**kwahn**-toh
How many?	Quanti?	**kwahn**-tee
How long...?	Quanto tempo...?	**kwahn**-toh **tehm**-poh
How long is the trip?	Quanto dura il viaggio?	**kwahn**-toh **doo**-rah eel vee**ah**-joh
How many minutes?	Quanti minuti?	**kwahn**-tee mee-**noo**-tee
How many hours?	Quante ore?	**kwahn**-tay **oh**-ray
How far?	Quanto dista?	**kwahn**-toh **dee**-stah
How?	Come?	**koh**-may
Can you help me?	Può aiutarmi?	pwoh ah-yoo-**tar**-mee
Can you help us?	Può aiutarci?	pwoh ah-yoo-**tar**-chee
Can I / Can we...?	Posso / Possiamo...?	**poh**-soh / poh-see**ah**-moh
...have one	...averne uno	ah-**vehr**-nay **oo**-noh
...go free	...andare senza pagare	ahn-**dah**-ray **sehn**-sah pah-**gah**-ray
...borrow that for a moment / an hour	...prenderlo in prestito per un momento / un'ora	prehn-**dehr**-loh een preh-**stee**-toh pehr oon moh-**mehn**-toh / oon-**oh**-rah

BASICS

...use the toilet	...usare la toilette	oo-**zah**-ray lah twah-**leht**-tay
What? (didn't hear)	Che cosa?	kay **koh**-zah
What is this / that?	Che cos'è questo / quello?	kay koh-**zeh** **kweh**-stoh / **kway**-loh
What is better?	Quale è meglio?	**kwah**-lay eh **mehl**-yoh
What's going on?	Cosa succede?	**koh**-zah soo-**chay**-day
When?	Quando?	**kwahn**-doh
What time is it?	Che ora è?	kay **oh**-rah eh
At what time?	A che ora?	ah kay **oh**-rah
On time?	Puntuale?	poon-too**ah**-lay
Late?	In ritardo?	een ree-**tar**-doh
How long will it take?	Quanto ci vuole?	**kwahn**-toh chee voo**oh**-lay
When does this open / close?	A che ora apre / chiude?	ah kay **oh**-rah **ah**-pray / keeoo-day
Is this open daily?	È aperto tutti i giorni?	eh ah-**pehr**-toh **too**-tee ee **jor**-nee
What day is this closed?	Che giorno chiudete?	kay **jor**-noh keeoo-**day**-tay
Do you have...?	Ha...?	ah
Where is...?	Dov'è...?	doh-**veh**
Where are...?	Dove sono...?	**doh**-vay **soh**-noh
Where can I find / buy...?	Dove posso trovare / comprare...?	**doh**-vay **poh**-soh troh-**vah**-ray / kohm-**prah**-ray
Where can we find / buy...?	Dove possiamo trovare / comprare...?	**doh**-vay poh-see**ah**-moh troh-**vah**-ray / kohm-**prah**-ray
Is it necessary?	È necessario?	eh nay-say-**sah**-reeoh
Is it possible...?	È possibile...?	eh poh-**see**-bee-lay
...to enter	...entrare	ehn-**trah**-ray
...to picnic here	...mangiare al sacco qui	mahn-**jah**-ray ahl **sah**-koh kwee
...to sit here	...sedersi qui	say-**dehr**-see kwee
...to look	...guardare	gwar-**dah**-ray
...to take a photo	...fare una foto	**fah**-ray oo-nah **foh**-toh

...to see this room	...vedere questa camera	vay-**day**-ray **kweh**-stah **kah**-may-rah
Who?	Chi?	kee
Why?	Perchè?	pehr-**keh**
Why not?	Perchè no?	pehr-**keh** noh
Yes or no?	Si o no?	see oh noh

To prompt a simple answer, ask, "*Si o no?*" (Yes or no?). To turn a word or sentence into a question, ask it in a questioning tone. "*Va bene*" (It's good) becomes "*Va bene?*" (Is it good?). An easy way to say, "Where is the toilet?" is to ask, "*Toilette?*"

Yin e Yang

cheap / expensive	economico / caro	ay-koh-**noh**-mee-koh / **kah**-roh
big / small	grande / piccolo	**grahn**-day / **pee**-koh-loh
hot / cold	caldo / freddo	**kahl**-doh / **fray**-doh
warm / cool	caldo / fresco	**kahl**-doh / **fray**-skoh
open / closed	aperto / chiuso	ah-**pehr**-toh / kee**oo**-zoh
entrance / exit	entrata / uscita	ehn-**trah**-tah / oo-**shee**-tah
push / pull	spingere / tirare	**speen**-jay-ray / tee-**rah**-ray
arrive / depart	arrivare / partire	ah-ree-**vah**-ray / par-**tee**-ray
early / late	presto / tardi	**prehs**-toh / **tar**-dee
soon / later	presto / più tardi	**prehs**-toh / pew **tar**-dee
fast / slow	veloce / lento	vay-**loh**-chay / **lehn**-toh
here / there	qui / lì	kwee / lee
near / far	vicino / lontano	vee-**chee**-noh / lohn-**tah**-noh
indoors / outdoors	dentro / fuori	**dehn**-troh / foo-**oh**-ree
good / bad	buono / cattivo	**bwoh**-noh / kah-**tee**-voh

best / worst	*il migliore / il peggiore*	eel meel-**yoh**-ray / eel pay-**joh**-ray
a little / lots	*poco / tanto*	**poh**-koh / **tahn**-toh
more / less	*più / meno*	pew / **may**-noh
mine / yours	*mio / suo*	**mee**-oh / **soo**-oh
this / that	*questo / quello*	**kweh**-stoh / **kweh**-loh
everybody / nobody	*tutti / nessuno*	**too**-tee / nehs-**soo**-noh
easy / difficult	*facile / difficile*	**fah**-chee-lay / dee-**fee**-chee-lay
left / right	*sinistra / destra*	see-**nee**-strah / **dehs**-trah
up / down	*su / giú*	soo / joo
above / below	*sopra / sotto*	**soh**-prah / **soh**-toh
young / old	*giovane / anziano*	joh-**vah**-nay / ahnt-seeah-noh
new / old	*nuovo / vecchio*	**nwoh**-voh / **vehk**-eeoh
heavy / light	*pesante / leggero*	pay-**zahn**-tay / lay-**jay**-roh
dark / light	*scuro / chiaro*	**skoo**-roh / keeah-roh
happy / sad	*felice / triste*	fee-**lee**-chay / **tree**-stay
beautiful / ugly	*bello[a] / brutto[a]*	**behl**-loh / **broo**-toh
nice / mean	*carino[a] / cattivo[a]*	kah-**ree**-noh / kah-**tee**-voh
smart / stupid	*intelligente / stupido[a]*	een-tehl-ee-**jayn**-tay / **stoo**-pee-doh
vacant / occupied	*libero / occupato*	**lee**-bay-roh / oh-koo-**pah**-toh
with / without	*con / senza*	kohn / **sehn**-sah

Italian words marked with an [a] end with "a" if used to describe a female. A handsome man is *bello*, a beautiful woman is *bella*.

Big Little Words

I	*io*	**ee**oh
you (formal)	*Lei*	**leh**ee
you (informal)	*tu*	too

we	*noi*	**noh**ee
he	*lui*	lwee
she	*lei*	**leh**ee
they	*loro*	**loh**-roh
and	*e*	ay
at	*a*	ah
because	*perchè*	pehr-**keh**
but	*ma*	mah
by (via)	*in*	een
for	*per*	pehr
from	*da*	dah
here	*qui*	kwee
if	*se*	say
in	*in*	een
it	*esso*	**ehs**-soh
not	*non*	nohn
now	*adesso*	ah-**dehs**-soh
only	*solo*	**soh**-loh
or	*o*	oh
that	*quello*	**kweh**-loh
this	*questo*	**kweh**-stoh
to	*a*	ah
very	*molto*	**mohl**-toh

BASICS

Very Italian Expressions

Prego.	**pray**-goh	You're welcome. / Please. / All right. / Can I help you?
Pronto.	**prohn**-toh	Hello. (answering phone) / Ready. (other situations)
Ecco.	**ay**-koh	Here it is.
Dica.	**dee**-kah	Tell me.
Allora...	ah-**loh**-rah	Well…
(like our "uh" before a sentence)		
Senta.	**sayn**-tah	Listen.
Tutto va bene.	**too**-toh vah **behn**-ay	Everything's fine.

Basta.	**bah**-stah	That's enough.
È tutto.	eh **too**-toh	That's all.
la dolce vita	lah **dohl**-chay **vee**-tah	the sweet life
il dolce far	eel **dohl**-chay far	the sweetness of
niente	nee**ehn**-tay	doing nothing
...issimo[a]	...**ee**-see-moh	very

("bravo" means good, "bravissimo" means very good)

COUNTING

Numbers

0	*zero*	**zay**-roh
1	*uno*	**oo**-noh
2	*due*	**doo**-ay
3	*tre*	tray
4	*quattro*	**kwah**-troh
5	*cinque*	**cheeng**-kway
6	*sei*	**seh**ee
7	*sette*	**seht**-tay
8	*otto*	**oh**-toh
9	*nove*	**noh**-vay
10	*dieci*	dee**ay**-chee
11	*undici*	**oon**-dee-chee
12	*dodici*	**doh**-dee-chee
13	*tredici*	**tray**-dee-chee
14	*quattordici*	kwah-**tor**-dee-chee
15	*quindici*	**kween**-dee-chee
16	*sedici*	**say**-dee-chee
17	*diciassette*	dee-chah-**seht**-tay
18	*diciotto*	dee-**choh**-toh
19	*diciannove*	dee-chahn-**noh**-vay
20	*venti*	**vayn**-tee

15

21	*ventuno*	vayn-**too**-noh
22	*ventidue*	vayn-tee-**doo**-ay
23	*ventitrè*	vayn-tee-**tray**
30	*trenta*	**trayn**-tah
31	*trentuno*	trayn-**too**-noh
40	*quaranta*	kwah-**rahn**-tah
41	*quarantuno*	kwah-rahn-**too**-noh
50	*cinquanta*	cheeng-**kwahn**-tah
60	*sessanta*	say-**sahn**-tah
70	*settanta*	say-**tahn**-tah
80	*ottanta*	oh-**tahn**-tah
90	*novanta*	noh-**vahn**-tah
100	*cento*	**chehn**-toh
101	*centouno*	chehn-toh-**oo**-noh
102	*centodue*	chehn-toh-**doo**-ay
200	*duecento*	doo-ay-**chehn**-toh
1000	*mille*	**mee**-lay
2000	*duemila*	doo-ay-**mee**-lah
2001	*duemilauno*	doo-ay-mee-lah-**oo**-noh
2002	*duemiladue*	doo-ay-mee-lah-**doo**-ay
2003	*duemilatre*	doo-ay-mee-lah-**tray**
2004	*duemila- quattro*	doo-ay-mee-lah- **kwah**-troh
2005	*duemila- cinque*	doo-ay-mee-lah- **cheeng**-kway
2006	*duemilasei*	doo-ay-mee-lah-**seh**ee
2007	*duemilasette*	doo-ay-mee-lah-**seht**-tay
2008	*duemilaotto*	doo-ay-mee-lah-**oh**-toh
2009	*duemilanove*	doo-ay-mee-lah-**noh**-vay
2010	*duemila- dieci*	doo-ay-mee-lah- dee**ay**-chee
million	*milione*	mee-lee**oh**-nay
billion	*miliardo*	meel-**yar**-doh
number one	*numero uno*	**noo**-may-roh **oo**-noh
first	*primo*	**pree**-moh
second	*secondo*	say-**kohn**-doh
third	*terzo*	**tehrt**-soh

once / twice	*una volta / due volte*	**oo**-nah **vohl**-tah / **doo**-ay **vohl**-tay
a quarter	*un quarto*	oon **kwar**-toh
a third	*un terzo*	oon **tehrt**-soh
half	*mezzo*	**mehd**-zoh
this much	*tanto così*	**tahn**-toh koh-**zee**
a dozen	*una dozzina*	**oo**-nah dohd-**zee**-nah
some	*un po'*	oon poh
enough	*abbastanza*	ah-bah-**stahnt**-sah
a handful	*una manciata*	**oo**-nah mahn-**chah**-tah
50%	*cinquanta per cento*	cheeng-**kwahn**-tah pehr **chehn**-toh
100%	*cento per cento*	**chehn**-toh pehr **chehn**-toh

Money

Where is a cash machine?	*Dov'è un bancomat?*	doh-**veh** oon **bahnk**-oh-maht
My ATM card has been...	*La mia tessera bancomat è stata...*	lah **mee**-ah teh-**say**-rah **bahnk**-oh-maht eh **stah**-tah
...demagnetized.	*...demagnetizzata.*	day-man-yeht-eed-**zah**-tah
...stolen.	*...rubata.*	roo-**bah**-tah

KEY PHRASES: MONEY

euro (€)	*euro*	ay-**oo**-roh
money	*soldi, denaro*	**sohl**-dee, day-**nah**-roh
cash	*contante*	kohn-**tahn**-tay
credit card	*carta di credito*	**kar**-tah dee **kray**-dee-toh
bank	*banca*	**bahn**-kah
cash machine	*bancomat*	**bahnk**-oh-maht
Where is a cash machine?	*Dov'è un bancomat?*	doh-**veh** oon **bahnk**-oh-maht
Do you accept credit cards?	*Accettate carte di credito?*	ah-chay-**tah**-tay **kar**-tay dee **kray**-dee-toh

COUNTING

...eaten by the machine.	...trattenuta dal bancomat.	trah-tay-**noo**-tah dahl **bahnk**-oh-maht
Do you accept credit cards?	Accettate carte di credito?	ah-chay-**tah**-tay **kar**-tay dee **kray**-dee-toh
Can you change dollars?	Può cambiare dollari?	pwoh kahm-bee**ah**-ray **dol**-lah-ree
What is your exchange rate for dollars...?	Qual'è il cambio del dollaro...?	kwah-**leh** eel **kahm**-beeoh dayl **dol**-lah-roh
...in traveler's checks	...per traveler's checks	pehr "traveler's checks"
What is the commission?	Quant'è la commissione?	kwahn-**teh** lah koh-mee-see**oh**-nay
Any extra fee?	C'è un sovrapprezzo?	cheh oon soh-vrah-**prehd**-zoh
Can you break this? (big bill into smaller bills)	Mi può cambiare questo?	mee pwoh kahm-bee**ah**-ray **kweh**-stoh
I would like...	Vorrei....	vor-**reh**ee
...small bills.	...banconote di piccolo taglio.	bahn-koh-**noh**-tay dee **pee**-koh-loh **tahl**-yoh
...large bills.	...banconote di grosso taglio.	bahn-koh-**noh**-tay dee **groh**-soh **tahl**-yoh
...coins.	...monete.	moh-**nay**-tay
€ 50	cinquanta euro	cheeng-**kwahn**-tah ay-**oo**-roh
Is this a mistake?	Questo è un errore?	**kweh**-stoh eh oon eh-**roh**-ray
This is incorrect.	Questo non e' corretto.	**kweh**-stoh nohn eh kor-**reht**-toh
Did you print these today?	Le ha stampate oggi?	lay ah stahm-**pah**-tay **oh**-jee
I'm broke.	Sono al verde.	**soh**-noh ahl **vehr**-day
I'm poor.	Sono povero[a].	**soh**-noh **poh**-vay-roh
I'm rich.	Sono ricco[a].	**soh**-noh **ree**-koh
I'm Bill Gates.	Sono Bill Gates.	**soh**-noh "Bill Gates"

| **Where is the nearest casino?** | *Dov'è il casinò più vicino?* | doh-**veh** eel kah-zee-**noh** pew vee-**chee**-noh |

Italy uses the euro currency. Euros (€) are divided into 100 cents. Use your common cents—cents are like pennies, and the euro has coins like nickels, dimes, and quarters.

Money Words

euro (€)	*euro*	ay-**oo**-roh
cents	*centesimi*	chehn-**tay**-zee-mee
money	*soldi, denaro*	**sohl**-dee, day-**nah**-roh
cash	*contante*	kohn-**tahn**-tay
cash machine	*bancomat*	**bahnk**-oh-maht
bank	*banca*	**bahn**-kah
credit card	*carta di credito*	**kar**-tah dee **kray**-dee-toh
change money	*cambiare dei soldi*	kahm-beeah-ray **deh**ee **sohl**-dee
exchange	*cambio*	**kahm**-beeoh
buy / sell	*comprare / vendere*	kohm-**prah**-ray / vehn-**day**-ray
commission	*commissione*	koh-mee-seeoh-nay
traveler's check	*traveler's check*	"traveler's check"
cash advance	*prelievo*	pray-leeay-voh
cashier	*cassiere*	kah-seeay-ray
bills	*banconote*	bahn-koh-**noh**-tay
coins	*monete*	moh-**nay**-tay
receipt	*ricevuta*	ree-chay-**voo**-tah

Commissions for changing traveler's checks can be steep in Italy—cash machines are a good bet. All machines are multilingual. On the small chance you'd need to conduct your transaction in Italian, you'd use these buttons: *esatto* (correct), *conferma* (confirm), and *annullare* (cancel). Your PIN number is a *codice segreto*.

Time

What time is it?	*Che ore sono?*	kay **oh**-ray **soh**-noh
It's...	*Sono...*	**soh**-noh
...8:00 in the morning.	*...le otto di mattina.*	lay **oh**-toh dee mah-**tee**-nah
...16:00.	*...le sedici.*	lay **say**-dee-chee
...4:00 in the afternoon.	*...le quattro del pomeriggio.*	lay **kwah**-troh dayl poh-may-**ree**-joh
...10:30 in the evening.	*...le dieci e mezza di sera.*	lay deeay-chee ay **mehd**-zah dee **say**-rah
...a quarter past nine.	*...le nove e un quarto.*	lay **noh**-vay ay oon **kwar**-toh
...a quarter to eleven.	*...le undici meno un quarto.*	lay **oon**-dee-chee **may**-noh oon **kwar**-toh
It's...	*È...*	eh
...noon.	*...mezzogiorno.*	mehd-zoh-**jor**-noh
...midnight.	*...mezzanotte.*	mehd-zah-**noh**-tay
...early / late.	*...presto / tardi.*	**prehs**-toh / **tar**-dee
...on time.	*...puntuale.*	poon-tooah-lay
...sunrise.	*...alba.*	**ahl**-bah
...sunset.	*...tramonto.*	trah-**mohn**-toh
It's my bedtime.	*Per me è ora di andare a dormire.*	pehr may eh **oh**-rah dee ahn-**dah**-ray ah dor-**mee**-ray

KEY PHRASES: TIME		
minute	*minuto*	mee-**noo**-toh
hour	*ora*	**oh**-rah
day	*giorno*	**jor**-noh
week	*settimana*	say-tee-**mah**-nah
What time is it?	*Che ore sono?*	kay **oh**-ray **soh**-noh
It's...	*Sono...*	**soh**-noh
...8:00.	*...le otto.*	lay **oh**-toh
...16:00.	*...le sedici.*	lay **say**-dee-chee
When does this open / close?	*A che ora apre / chiude?*	ah kay **oh**-rah **ah**-pray / keeoo-day

Timely Expressions

I'll return / We'll return...	Torno / Torniamo...	**tor**-noh / tor-nee**ah**-moh
...at 11:20.	...alle undici e venti.	**ah**-lay **oon**-dee-chee ay **vayn**-tee
I'll arrive / We'll arrive...	Arrivo / Arriviamo...	ah-**ree**-voh / ah-ree-vee**ah**-moh
...by 18:00.	...per le diciotto.	pehr lay dee-**choh**-toh
When is checkout time?	A che ora bisogna liberare la camera?	ah kay **oh**-rah bee-**sohn**-yah lee-bay-**rah**-ray lah **kah**-may-rah
At what time...?	A che ora...?	ah kay **oh**-rah
...does this open / close	...apre / chiude	**ah**-pray / kee**oo**-day
...does the train / bus leave for ___	...parte il treno / l'autobus per ___	**par**-tay eel **tray**-noh / **low**-toh-boos pehr
...the next train / the bus leave for ___	...parte il prossimo treno / autobus per ___	**par**-tay eel **proh**-see-moh **tray**-noh / **ow**-toh-boos pehr
...the train / the bus arrive in ___	...arriva a ___ il treno / l'autobus?	ah-**ree**-vah ah ___ eel **tray**-noh / **low**-toh-boos
I / We want to take the 16:30 train.	Vorrei / Vorremmo prendere il treno delle sedici e trenta.	vor-**reh**ee / vor-**ray**-moh **prehn**-day-ray eel **tray**-noh **dehl**-lay **say**-dee-chee ay **trayn**-tah
Is the train / the bus...?	È... il treno / l'autobus?	eh... eel **tray**-noh / **low**-toh-boos
...early / late	...in anticipo / in ritardo	een ahn-tee-**chee**-poh / een ree-**tar**-doh
...on time	...in orario	een oh-**rah**-reeoh

In Italy, the 24-hour clock (or military time) is used by hotels, for opening/closing hours of stores, and for train, bus, and ferry schedules. Friends use the same "clock" we do. You'd meet a friend at 3:00 in the afternoon (*tre del pomeriggio*) to catch a train that leaves at 15:15. In Italy, the *pomeriggio* (afternoon) turns to *sera* (evening) generally about 5:00 p.m. (5:30 p.m. is *cinque e mezza di sera*).

More Time

COUNTING

minute	*minuto*	mee-**noo**-toh
hour	*ora*	**oh**-rah
in the morning	*di mattina*	dee mah-**tee**-nah
in the afternoon	*di pomeriggio*	dee poh-may-**ree**-joh
in the evening	*di sera*	dee **say**-rah
night	*notte*	**noh**-tay
at 6:00 sharp	*alle sei in punto*	**ah**-lay **seh**ee een **poon**-toh
from 8:00 to 10:00	*dalle otto alle dieci*	**dah**-lay **oh**-toh **ah**-lay dee**ay**-chee
in half an hour	*tra mezz'ora*	trah mehd-**zoh**-rah
in one hour	*tra un'ora*	trah oon-**oh**-rah
in three hours	*tra tre ore*	trah tray **oh**-ray
anytime	*a qualsiasi ora*	ah kwahl-see**ah**-zee **oh**-rah
immediately	*immediata- mente*	ee-may-deeah-tah- **mayn**-tay
every hour	*ogni ora*	**ohn**-yee **oh**-rah
every day	*ogni giorno*	**ohn**-yee **jor**-noh
last	*passato*	pah-**sah**-toh
this	*questo*	**kweh**-stoh
next	*prossimo*	**proh**-see-moh
May 15	*il quindici maggio*	eel **kween**-dee-chee **mah**-joh
high season	*alta stagione*	**ahl**-tah stah-jee**oh**-nee
low season	*bassa stagione*	**bah**-sah stah-jee**oh**-nee
in the future	*in futuro*	een foo-**too**-roh
in the past	*nel passato*	nehl pah-**sah**-toh

The Day

day	*giorno*	**jor**-noh
today	*oggi*	**oh**-jee
yesterday	*ieri*	**yay**-ree
tomorrow	*domani*	doh-**mah**-nee
tomorrow morning	*domani mattina*	doh-**mah**-nee mah-**tee**-nah
day after tomorrow	*dopodomani*	doh-poh-doh-**mah**-nee

The Week

week	*settimana*	say-tee-**mah**-nah
last week	*la settimana scorsa*	lah say-tee-**mah**-nah **skor**-sah
this week	*questa settimana*	**kweh**-stah say-tee-**mah**-nah
next week	*la settimana prossima*	lah say-tee-**mah**-nah **proh**-see-mah
Monday	*lunedì*	loo-nay-**dee**
Tuesday	*martedì*	mar-tay-**dee**
Wednesday	*mercoledì*	mehr-koh-lay-**dee**
Thursday	*giovedì*	joh-vay-**dee**
Friday	*venerdì*	vay-nehr-**dee**
Saturday	*sabato*	**sah**-bah-toh
Sunday	*domenica*	doh-**may**-nee-kah

The Month

month	*mese*	**may**-zay
January	*gennaio*	jay-**nah**-yoh
February	*febbraio*	fay-**brah**-yoh
March	*marzo*	**mart**-soh
April	*aprile*	ah-**pree**-lay
May	*maggio*	**mah**-joh
June	*giugno*	**joon**-yoh

July	*luglio*	**lool**-yoh
August	*agosto*	ah-**goh**-stoh
September	*settembre*	say-**tehm**-bray
October	*ottobre*	oh-**toh**-bray
November	*novembre*	noh-**vehm**-bray
December	*dicembre*	dee-**chehm**-bray

The Year

year	*anno*	**ahn**-noh
spring	*primavera*	pree-mah-**vay**-rah
summer	*estate*	ay-**stah**-tay
fall	*autunno*	ow-**too**-noh
winter	*inverno*	een-**vehr**-noh

Holidays and Happy Days

holiday	*festa*	**fehs**-tah
national holiday	*festa*	**fehs**-tah
	nazionale	naht-seeoh-**nah**-lay
religious holiday	*festa religiosa*	**fehs**-tah ray-lee-**joh**-zah
Is today / tomorrow	*Oggi / Domani*	**oh**-jee / doh-**mah**-nee
a holiday?	*è festa?*	eh **fehs**-tah
Is a holiday coming	*Siamo vicini*	see**ah**-moh vee-**chee**-nee
up soon? When?	*a una festa?*	ah **oo**-nah **fehs**-tah
	Quand'è?	kwahn-**deh**
What is the holiday?	*Che festa è?*	kay **fehs**-tah eh
Merry Christmas!	*Buon Natale!*	bwohn nah-**tah**-lay
Happy new year!	*Felice anno*	fay-**lee**-chay **ahn**-noh
	nuovo!	**nwoh**-voh
Easter	*Pasqua*	**pahs**-kwah
Happy (wedding)	*Buon*	bwohn
anniversary!	*anniversario*	ah-nee-vehr-**sah**-reeoh
	(di matrimonio).	(dee mah-tree-**moh**-neeoh)
Happy birthday!	*Buon compleanno!*	bwohn kohm-play-**ahn**-noh

COUNTING

Italians celebrate birthdays with the same "Happy Birthday" tune that we use. The Italian words mean "Best wishes to you": *"Tanti auguri a te, tanti auguri a te, tanti auguri, caro[a] ___ , tanti auguri a te!"*

Holidays which strike during tourist season are April 25 (Liberation Day), May 1 (Labor Day), June 24th (*San Giovanni,* northern Italy), August 15 (*Ferragosto,* or Assumption of Mary), and November 1 (All Saints Day). In Italy, every saint gets a holiday—these are sprinkled throughout the year and celebrated in local communities with flair.

COUNTIN

TRAVELING

Flights

All airports have bilingual signage with the local language and always English. Also, nearly all airport service personnel and travel agents speak English these days. Still, these words and phrases could conceivably come in handy.

Making a Reservation

I'd like to... my	Vorrei... la mia	vor-**reh**ee... lah **mee**-ah
reservation /	prenotazione /	pray-noh-taht-seeoh-nay /
my ticket.	il mio biglietto.	eel **mee**-oh beel-**yay**-toh
We'd like to... our	Vorremmo... la nostra	vor-**ray**-moh... lah **noh**-strah
reservation /	prenotazione /	pray-noh-taht-seeoh-nay /
our tickets.	i nostro biglietti.	ee **noh**-stroh beel-**yay**-tee
...confirm	...confermare	kohn-fehr-**mah**-ray
...change	...cambiare	kahm-beeah-ray
...cancel	...cancellare	kahn-cheh-**lah**-ray
seat...	posto...	**poh**-stoh
...by the window	...vicino al	vee-**chee**-noh ahl
	finestrino	fee-nay-**stree**-noh
...on the aisle	...vicino al	vee-**chee**-noh ahl
	corridoio	koh-ree-**doh**-yoh

At the Airport

Which terminal?	*Quale terminal?*	kwah-lay tehr-mee-**nahl**
international flights	*voli internazionali*	**voh**-lee een-tehr-naht-seeoh-**nah**-lee
domestic flights	*voli interni*	**voh**-lee een-**tehr**-nee
arrival	*arrivo*	ah-**ree**-voh
departure	*partenza*	par-**tehn**-zah
baggage check	*check-in bagagli*	"check-in" bah-**gahl**-yee
baggage claim	*ritiro bagagli*	ree-**tee**-roh bah-**gahl**-yee
Nothing to declare.	*Niente da dichiarare.*	nee-**ehn**-tay dah dee-keeah-**rah**-ray
I have only carry-on luggage.	*Ho solo bagaglio a mano.*	oh **soh**-loh bah-**gahl**-yoh ah **mah**-noh
flight number	*numero del volo*	**noo**-may-roh dehl **voh**-loh
departure gate	*cancello di imbarco*	kahn-**chehl**-loh dee eem-**bar**-koh
duty free	*duty free*	"duty free"
luggage cart	*carrello per i bagagli*	kar-**ehl**-loh pehr ee bah-**gahl**-yee
jet lag	*fus'orario*	fooz-oh-**rah**-reeoh

Getting to/from the Airport

Approximately how much is a taxi ride...?	*Quanto costa più o meno un viaggio in taxi fino...?*	**kwahn**-toh **koh**-stah pew oh **may**-noh oon veeah-joh een **tahk**-see **fee**-noh
...to downtown	*...al centro*	ahl **chehn**-troh
...to the train station	*...alla stazione*	**ah**-lah staht-seeoh-**nay**
...to the airport	*...all'aeroporto*	ah-lah-ay-roh-**por**-toh
Does a bus (or train) run...?	*C'è un autobus (o treno) che va...?*	cheh oon **ow**-toh-boos (oh **tray**-noh) kay vah

TRAVELING

...from the airport to downtown	...dall'aeroporto al centro	dah-lah-ay-roh-**por**-toh ahl **chehn**-troh
...to the airport from downtown	...dal centro all'aeroporto	dahl **chehn**-troh ah-lah-ay-roh-**por**-toh
How much is it?	Quanto costa?	**kwahn**-toh **koh**-stah
Where does it leave from...?	Da dove parte...?	dah **doh**-vay **par**-tay
Where does it arrive...?	Dove arriva...?	**doh**-vay ah-**ree**-vah
...at the airport	...all'aeroporto	ah-lah-ay-roh-**por**-toh
...downtown	...in centro	een **chehn**-troh
How often does it run?	Ogni quanto passa?	**ohn**-yee **kwahn**-toh **pah**-sah

Trains

The Train Station

Where is the...?	Dov'è la...?	doh-**veh** lah
...train station	...stazione	staht-see**oh**-nay
Italian State Railways	Ferrovie dello Stato (FS)	fay-**roh**-veeay **dehl**-loh **stah**-toh
train information	informazioni sui treni	een-for-maht-see**oh**-nee **soo**ee **tray**-nee
train	treno	**tray**-noh
fast train	inter-city (IC, EC)	"inter-city"
fastest train	Eurostar (ES)	**yoo**-roh-star
fast / faster	veloce / più veloce	vay-**loh**-chay / pew vay-**loh**-chay
arrival	arrivo	ah-**ree**-voh
departure	partenza	par-**tehnt**-sah
delay	ritardo	ree-**tar**-doh
toilet	toilette	twah-**leht**-tay

KEY PHRASES: TRAINS

train station	*stazione*	staht-see**oh**-nay
train	*treno*	**tray**-noh
ticket	*biglietto*	beel-**yay**-toh
transfer (verb)	*cambiare*	kahm-bee**ah**-ray
supplement	*supplemento*	soo-play-**mehn**-toh
arrival	*arrivo*	ah-**ree**-voh
departure	*partenza*	par-**tehnt**-sah
platform or track	*binario*	bee-**nah**-reeoh
train car	*vagone*	vah-**goh**-nay
A ticket to ___.	*Un biglietto per ___.*	oon beel-**yay**-toh pehr
Two tickets to ___.	*Due biglietti per ___.*	doo-ay beel-**yay**-tee pehr
When is the	*Quando è il*	**kwahn**-doh eh eel
next train?	*prossimo treno?*	**proh**-see-moh **tray**-noh
Where does the	*Da dove parte*	dah **doh**-vay **par**-tay
train leave from?	*il treno?*	eel **tray**-noh
Which train to ___?	*Quale treno per ___?*	**kwah**-lay **tray**-noh pehr

waiting room	*sala di attesa,*	**sah**-lah dee ah-**tay**-zah,
	sala d'aspetto	**sah**-lah dah-**spay**-toh
lockers	*armadietti*	ar-mah-dee**ay**-tee
baggage check	*deposito*	day-**poh**-zee-toh
room	*bagagli,*	bah-**gahl**-yee,
	consegna	kohn-**sayn**-yah
lost and found	*ufficio oggetti*	oo-**fee**-choh oh-**jeht**-tee
office	*smarriti*	smah-**ree**-tee
tourist information	*informazioni*	een-for-maht-see**oh**-nee
	per turisti	pehr too-**ree**-stee
to the platforms	*ai binari*	**ah**ee bee-**nah**-ree
platform or track	*binario*	bee-**nah**-reeoh
to the trains	*ai treni*	**ah**ee **tray**-nee
train car	*vagone*	vah-**goh**-nay
dining car	*carrozza*	kar-**rohd**-zah
	ristorante	ree-stoh-**rahn**-tay
sleeper car	*carrozza letto*	kar-**rohd**-zah **leht**-toh
conductor	*capotreno*	kah-poh-**tray**-noh

TRAVELING

Some Italian train stations have wonderful (and fun)
schedule computers. Once you've mastered these (start
by punching the "English" button), you'll save lots of time
figuring out the right train connections.

You'll encounter several types of trains in Italy. Along
with the various local and milk-run (*locale*) trains, there are:
- the slow *diretto* trains
- the medium-speed *espresso* and *InterRegionale* trains
- the fast *rapido* trains such as the *IC* and *IC Plus*
  (*InterCity*, domestic routes) and *EC* (*EuroCity*, international routes)
- the super-fast *Cisalpino* trains (from Florence, Milan, or
  Venice to Switzerland and Stuttgart)
- the super-duper-fast *Eurostar Italia,* Italy's bullet train

Even If you have a railpass, you will need to pay a
reservation fee for the *Eurostar Italia, Cisalpino,* and *IC
Plus* trains, as well as some *IC* and *EC* trains (check
schedules).

Getting a Ticket

Where can I buy a ticket?	*Dove posso comprare un biglietto?*	**doh**-vay **poh**-soh kohm-**prah**-ray oon beel-**yay**-toh
A ticket to ___.	*Un biglietto per ___.*	oon beel-**yay**-toh pehr ___
Where can we buy tickets?	*Dove possiamo comprare i biglietti?*	**doh**-vay poh-seeah-moh kohm-**prah**-ray ee beel-**yay**-tee
Two tickets to ___.	*Due biglietti per ___.*	**doo**-ay beel-**yay**-tee pehr ___
Is this the line for...?	*È questa la fila per...?*	eh **kweh**-stah lah **fee**-lah pehr
...tickets	*...biglietti*	beel-**yay**-tee
...reservations	*...prenotazioni*	pray-noh-taht-see**oh**-nee
How much is the fare to ___?	*Quant'è la tariffa per___?*	kwahn-**teh** lah tah-**ree**-fah pehr

Is this ticket valid for ___?	Questo biglietto è valido per ___?	**kwehs**-toh beel-**yay**-toh eh **vah**-lee-doh pehr
How long is this ticket valid?	Per quanto tempo è valido questo biglietto?	pehr **kwahn**-toh **tehm**-poh eh **vah**-lee-doh **kwehs**-toh beel-**yay**-toh
When is the next train?	Quando è il prossimo treno?	**kwahn**-doh eh eel **proh**-see-moh **tray**-noh
Do you have a schedule for all trains departing for ___ today / tomorrow?	Ha un orario di tutti i treni in partenza per ___ oggi / domani?	ah oon oh-**rah**-reeoh dee **too**-tee ee **tray**-nee een par-**tehnt**-sah pehr ___ **oh**-jee / doh-**mah**-nee
I'd like to leave...	Vorrei partire...	vor-**reh**ee par-**tee**-ray
We'd like to leave...	Vorremmo partire...	vor-**ray**-moh par-**tee**-ray
I'd like to arrive...	Vorrei arrivare...	vor-**reh**ee ah-ree-**vah**-ray
We'd like to arrive...	Vorremmo arrivare...	vor-**ray**-moh ah-ree-**vah**-ray
...by ___.	...per le ___.	pehr lay
...in the morning.	...di mattina.	dee mah-**tee**-nah
...in the afternoon.	...di pomeriggio.	dee poh-may-**ree**-joh
...in the evening.	...di sera.	dee **say**-rah
Is there a...?	C'è un...?	cheh oon
...earlier train	...treno prima	**tray**-noh **pree**-mah
...later train	...treno più tardi	**tray**-noh pew **tar**-dee
...overnight train	...treno notturno	**tray**-noh noh-**toor**-noh
...cheaper train	...treno più economico	**tray**-noh pew ay-koh-**noh**-mee-koh
...a cheaper option	...una possibilità più economica	**oo**-nah poh-see-bee-lee-**tah** pew ay-koh-**noh**-mee-kah
...local train	...treno locale	**tray**-noh loh-**kah**-lay
...express train	...treno espresso	**tray**-noh ehs-**pray**-soh
What track does it leave from?	Da che binario parte?	dah kay bee-**nah**-reeoh **par**-tay
What track?	Quale binario?	**kwah**-lay bee-**nah**-reeoh
On time?	È puntuale?	eh poon-too**ah**-lay
Late?	In ritardo?	een ree-**tar**-doh

Reservations, Supplements, and Discounts

Is a reservation required?	*Ci vuole la prenotazione?*	chee **vwoh**-lay lah pray-noh-taht-see**oh**-nay
I'd like to reserve...	*Vorrei prenotare...*	vor-**reh**ee pray-noh-**tah**-ray
...a seat.	*...un posto.*	oon **poh**-stoh
...a couchette.	*...una cuccetta.*	**oo**-nah koo-**chay**-tah
...a sleeper.	*...un posto in vagone letto.*	oon **poh**-stoh een vah-**goh**-nay **leht**-toh
...the entire train.	*...tutto il treno.*	**too**-toh eel **tray**-noh
We'd like to reserve...	*Vorremmo prenotare...*	vor-**ray**-moh pray-noh-**tah**-ray
...two seats.	*...due posti.*	**doo**-ay **poh**-stee
...two couchettes.	*...due cuccette.*	**doo**-ay koo-**chay**-tay
...a sleeper compartment with two beds.	*...un vagone letto da due letti.*	oon vah-**goh**-nay **leht**-toh dah doo-ay **leht**-tee
Is there a supplement?	*C'è un supplemento?*	cheh oon soo-play-**mehn**-toh
Does my railpass cover the supplement?	*Il mio railpass include il supplemento?*	eel **mee**-oh **rayl**-pahs een-**kloo**-day eel soo-play-**mehn**-toh
Is there a discount for...?	*Fate sconti per...?*	**fah**-tay **skohn**-tee pehr
...youth	*...giovani*	joh-**vah**-nee
...seniors	*...anziani*	ahnt-seeah-nee
...families	*...famiglie*	fah-**meel**-yay

Ticket Talk

ticket window	*Biglietteria*	beel-yeht-ay-**ree**-ah
reservations window	*Prenotazioni*	pray-noh-taht-see**oh**-nay
national	*nazionali*	naht-seeoh-**nah**-lee

TRAVELING

international	internazio-nali	een-tehr-naht-seeoh-**nah**-lee
ticket	biglietto	beel-**yay**-toh
one way	andata	ahn-**dah**-tah
roundtrip	andata e ritorno	ahn-**dah**-tah ay ree-**tor**-noh
first class	prima classe	**pree**-mah **klah**-say
second class	seconda classe	say-**kohn**-dah **klah**-say
non-smoking	non fumatori, non fumare	nohn foo-mah-**toh**-ree, nohn foo-**mah**-ray
validate	timbrare, obliterare	teem-**brah**-ray, oh-blee-tay-**rah**-ray
schedule	orario	oh-**rah**-reeoh
departure	partenza	par-**tehnt**-sah
direct	diretto	dee-**reht**-toh
transfer (verb)	cambiare	kahm-bee**ah**-ray
connection	coincidenza	koh-een-chee-**dehnt**-sah
with supplement	con supplemento	kohn soo-play-**mehn**-toh
reservation	prenotazione	pray-noh-taht-see**oh**-nay
seat...	posto...	**poh**-stoh
...by the window	...vicino al finestrino	vee-**chee**-noh ahl fee-nay-**stree**-noh
...on the aisle	...vicino al corridoio	vee-**chee**-noh ahl koh-ree-**doh**-yoh
berth...	cuccetta...	koo-**chay**-tah
...upper	...di sopra	dee **soh**-prah
...middle	...in mezzo	een **mehd**-zoh
...lower	...di sotto	dee **soh**-toh
refund	rimborso	reem-**bor**-soh
reduced fare	tariffa ridotta	tah-**ree**-fah ree-**doh**-tah

Changing Trains

Is it direct?	È diretto?	eh dee-**reht**-toh
Must I transfer?	Devo cambiare?	**day**-voh kahm-bee**ah**-ray
Must we transfer?	Dobbiamo cambiare?	doh-bee**ah**-moh kahm-bee**ah**-ray
When? Where?	Quando? Dove?	**kwahn**-doh **doh**-vay

Do I change / Do we change here for ___?	Cambio / Cambiamo qui per ___?	**kahm**-beeoh / kahm-bee**ah**-moh kwee pehr ___
Where do I change / do we change for ___?	Dove cambio / cambiamo per ___?	**doh**-vay **kahm**-beeoh / kahm-bee**ah**-moh pehr ___
At what time?	A che ora?	ah kay **oh**-rah
From what track does my / our connecting train leave?	Da che binario parte la mia / la nostra coincidenza?	dah kay bee-**nah**-reeoh **par**-tay lah **mee**-ah / lah **noh**-strah koh-een-chee-**dehnt**-sah
How many minutes in ___ to change trains?	Quanti minuti a ___ per prendere coincidenza?	**kwahn**-tee mee-**noo**-tee ah ___ pehr **prehn**-day-ray lah koh-een-chee-**dehnt**-sah

On the Platform

Where is...?	Dov'è...?	doh-**veh**
Is this...?	Questo è...?	**kwehs**-toh eh
...the train to ___	...il treno per ___	eel **tray**-noh pehr
Which train to ___?	Quale treno per ___?	**kwah**-lay **tray**-noh pehr
Which train car for ___?	Quale vagone per ___?	**kwah**-lay vah-**goh**-nay pehr
Where is first class?	Dov'è la prima classe?	doh-**veh** lah **pree**-mah **klah**-say
...front / middle / back	...in testa / in centro / in coda	een **tehs**-tah / een **chehn**-troh / een **koh**-dah
Where can I validate my ticket?	Dove posso timbrare il biglietto?	**doh**-vay **poh**-soh teem-**brah**-ray eel beel-**yay**-toh

You must validate (*timbrare*) your train ticket prior to boarding the train. Look for the yellow machines on the platform and insert your ticket—watch others and imitate.

On the Train

Is this (seat) free?	È libero?	eh **lee**-bay-roh
May I / May we...?	Posso / Possiamo...?	**poh**-soh / poh-see**ah**-moh
...sit here (me / we)	...sedermi / sederci qui	say-**dehr**-mee / say-**dehr**-chee kwee
...open the window	...aprire il finestrino	ah-**pree**-ray eel fee-nay-**stree**-noh
...eat your food	...mangiare il suo cibo	mahn-**jah**-ray eel **soo**-oh **chee**-boh
Save my place?	Mi tiene il posto?	mee tee**ay**-nay eel **poh**-stoh
Save our places?	Ci tiene il posto?	chee tee**ay**-nay eel **poh**-stoh
That's my seat.	È il mio posto.	eh eel **mee**-oh **poh**-stoh
These are our seats.	Sono i nostri posti.	**soh**-noh ee **noh**-stree **poh**-stee
Where are you going?	Dove va?	**doh**-vay vah
I'm going to ___.	Vado a ___.	**vah**-doh ah
We're going to ___.	Andiamo a ___.	ahn-dee**ah**-moh ah
Tell me when to get off?	Mi dice quando devo scendere?	mee **dee**-chay **kwahn**-doh **day**-voh **shehn**-day-ray
Tell us when to get off?	Ci dice quando dobbiamo scendere?	chee **dee**-chay **kwahn**-doh doh-bee**ah**-moh **shehn**-day-ray
Where is a (good looking) conductor?	Dov'è un (bel) capotreno?	doh-**veh** oon (behl) kah-poh-**tray**-noh
Does this train stop in ___?	Questo treno si ferma a ___?	**kwehs**-toh **tray**-noh see **fehr**-mah ah
When will it arrive in ___?	Quando arriva a ___?	**kwahn**-doh ah-**ree**-vah ah
When will it arrive?	Quando arriva?	**kwahn**-doh ah-**ree**-vah

Strikes

Is there a strike?	C'è lo sciopero?	cheh loh **shoh**-peh-roh
Only for today?	È solo per oggi?	eh **soh**-loh pehr **oh**-jee
Tomorrow, too?	Anche domani?	**ahn**-kay doh-**mah**-nee
Are there some trains today?	Ci sono qualcuni treni oggi?	chee **soh**-noh kwahl-**koo**-nee **tray**-nee **oh**-jee
I'm going to ___.	Vado a ___.	**vah**-doh ah

In Italy, train strikes (*scioperi*) are not unusual. They often last a day and a few trains still run, particularly the long-distance routes.

Reading Train and Bus Schedules

a	to
arrivi	arrivals
arrivo	arrival (also abbreviated "a")
binario	track
da	from
destinazione	destination
domenica	Sunday
eccetto	except
feriali	weekdays including Saturday
ferma a tutte le stazioni	stops at all the stations
festivi	Sundays and holidays
fino	until
giorni	days
giornaliero	daily
in ritardo	late
non ferma a ___	doesn't stop in ___
ogni	every
partenza	departure (also abbreviated "p")
partenze	departures

Major Rail Lines In Italy

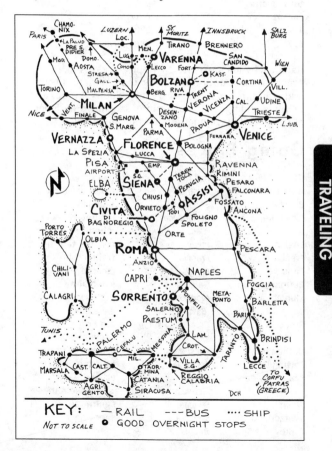

KEY: — RAIL   --- BUS   ···· SHIP
NOT TO SCALE   ● GOOD OVERNIGHT STOPS

per	for	
sabato	Saturday	
si effettua anche ___	it also runs ___	
solo	only	
tutti i giorni	daily	
vacanza	holiday	
1-5	Monday-Friday	
6, 7	Saturday, Sunday	

Italian schedules use the 24-hour clock. It's like American time until noon. After that, subtract twelve and add p.m. So 13:00 is 1 p.m., 20:00 is 8 p.m., and 24:00 is midnight. If your train is scheduled to depart at 00:01, it'll leave one minute after midnight.

Going Places

Italy	*Italia*	ee-**tahl**-yah
Austria	*Austria*	**ow**-streeah
Belgium	*Belgio*	**behl**-joh
Czech Republic	*Repubblica Ceca*	reh-**poo**-blee-kah **cheh**-kah
England	*Inghilterra*	een-geel-**tehr**-rah
France	*Francia*	**frahn**-chah
Paris	*Parigi*	pah-**ree**-jee
Germany	*Germania*	jehr-**mahn**-yah
Munich	*Monaco di Baviera*	**moh**-nah-koh dee bah-veeay-rah
Greece	*Grecia*	**gray**-chah
Ireland	*Irlanda*	eer-**lahn**-dah
Netherlands	*Paesi Bassi*	pah-**ay**-zee **bah**-see
Portugal	*Portogallo*	por-toh-**gah**-loh
Scandinavia	*Paesi Scandinavi*	pah-**ay**-zee skahn-dee-**nah**-vee
Spain	*Spagna*	**spahn**-yah
Switzerland	*Svizzera*	**sveet**-say-rah
Turkey	*Turchia*	**toor**-keeah

TRAVELING

Europe	Europa	ay-oo-**roh**-pah
EU	UE	oo ay
(European	(Unione	(oon-ee-**ohn**-ay
Union)	Europeo)	ay-oo-roh-**pay**-oh)
Russia	Russia	**roo**-seeah
Africa	Africa	**ahf**-ree-kah
United States	Stati Uniti	**stah**-tee oo-**nee**-tee
Canada	Canada	kah-nah-**dah**
world	mondo	**mohn**-doh

Places in Italy

Bologna	Bologna	boh-**lohn**-yah
Cinque Terre	Cinque Terre	**cheeng**-kway **tehr**-ray
Civita	Civita	chee-**vee**-tah
Florence	Firenze	fee-**rehn**-tsay
Italian	Riviera	reev-**yehr**-rah
Riviera	Ligure	lee-**goo**-ray
Lake Como	Lago di Como	**lah**-goh dee **koh**-moh
Milan	Milano	mee-**lah**-noh
Naples	Napoli	**nah**-poh-lee
Orvieto	Orvieto	or-vee**ay**-toh
Pisa	Pisa	**pee**-zah
Rome	Roma	**roh**-mah
San Gimignano	San Gimignano	sahn jee-meen-**yah**-noh
Sicily	Sicilia	see-**chee**-leeah
Siena	Siena	see-**ehn**-ah
Sorrento	Sorrento	sor-**rehn**-toh
Varenna	Varenna	vah-**rehn**-nah
Vatican City	Città del	cheet-**tah** dayl
	Vaticano	vah-tee-**kah**-noh
Venice	Venezia	vay-**nayt**-seeah
Vernazza	Vernazza	vehr-**naht**-tsah

Buses and Subways

At the Bus Station or Metro Stop

TRAVELING

ticket	*biglietto*	beel-**yay**-toh
city bus	*autobus*	**ow**-toh-boos
long-distance bus	*pullman,*	**pool**-mahn,
	corriera	koh-ree-**ehr**-ah
bus stop	*fermata*	fehr-**mah**-tah
bus station	*stazione*	staht-seeoh-nay
	degli autobus	**dayl**-yee ow-toh-boos
subway	*metropolitana*	may-troh-poh-lee-**tah**-nah
subway	*stazione della*	staht-seeoh-nay **day**-lah
station	*metropolitana*	may-troh-poh-lee-**tah**-nah
subway map	*cartina*	kar-**tee**-nah
subway entrance	*entrata*	ayn-**trah**-tah
subway stop	*fermata*	fehr-**mah**-tah
subway exit	*uscita*	oo-**shee**-tah
direct	*diretto*	dee-**reht**-toh
connection	*coincidenza*	koh-een-chee-**dehnt**-sah
pickpocket	*borsaiolo*	bor-sah-**yoh**-loh

Most big cities offer deals on transportation, such as one-day tickets (*biglietto giornaliero*) and cheaper fares for youths and seniors. On a map, *voi siete qui* means "you are here." Venice has boats instead of buses. Zip around on *traghetti* (gondola ferries) and *vaporetti* (motorized ferries).

KEY PHRASES: BUSES AND SUBWAYS

bus	*autobus*	**ow**-toh-boos
subway	*metropolitana*	may-troh-poh-lee-**tah**-nah
ticket	*biglietto*	beel-**yay**-toh
How do you get to ___?	*Come si va a ___?*	**koh**-may see vah ah
Which stop for ___?	*Qual'è la fermata per___?*	kwah-**leh** lah fehr-**mah**-tah pehr
Tell me when to get off?	*Mi dice quando devo scendere?*	mee **dee**-chay **kwahn**-doh **day**-voh **shehn**-day-ray

Taking Buses and Subways

How do you get to___?	*Come si va a ___?*	**koh**-may see vah ah ___
How much is a ticket?	*Quanto costa un biglietto?*	**kwahn**-toh **koh**-stah oon beel-**yay**-toh
Where can I buy a ticket?	*Dove posso comprare un biglietto?*	**doh**-vay **poh**-soh kohm-**prah**-ray oon beel-**yay**-toh
Where can we buy tickets?	*Dove possiamo comprare i biglietti?*	**doh**-vay poh-see**ah**-moh kohm-**prah**-ray ee beel-**yay**-tee
One ticket, please.	*Un biglietto, per favore*	oon beel-**yay**-toh pehr fah-**voh**-ray
Two tickets.	*Due biglietti.*	**doo**-ay beel-**yay**-tee
Is this ticket valid (for ___)?	*Questo biglietto è valido (per ___)?*	**kwehs**-toh beel-**yay**-toh eh **vah**-lee-doh (pehr ___)
Is there a one-day pass?	*C'è un biglietto giornaliero?*	cheh oon beel-**yay**-toh jor-nahl-**yay**-roh
Which bus to ___?	*Quale autobus per ___?*	**kwah**-lay **ow**-toh-boos pehr
Does it stop at ___?	*Si ferma a ___?*	see **fehr**-mah ah ___

TRAVELING

Which metro stop for ___?	Qual'è la fermata per___?	kwah-**leh** lah fehr-**mah**-tah pehr
Which direction for ___?	Da che parte è ___?	dah kay **par**-tay eh
Must I transfer?	Devo cambiare?	**day**-voh kahm-bee**ah**-ray
Must we transfer?	Dobbiamo cambiare?	doh-bee**ah**-moh kahm-bee**ah**-ray
When does... leave?	Quando parte...?	**kwahn**-doh **par**-tay
...the first	...il primo	eel **pree**-moh
...the next	...il prossimo	eel **proh**-see-moh
...the last	...l'ultimo	**lool**-tee-moh
...bus / subway	...autobus / metropolitana	**ow**-toh-boos / may-troh-poh-lee-**tah**-nah
What's the frequency per hour / day?	Quante volte passa all'ora / al giorno?	**kwahn**-tay **vohl**-tay **pah**-sah ah-**loh**-rah / ahl **jor**-noh
Where does it leave from?	Da dove parte?	dah **doh**-vay **par**-tay
What time does it leave?	A che ora parte?	ah kay **oh**-rah **par**-tay
I'm going to ___.	Vado a ___.	**vah**-doh ah
We're going to ___.	Andiamo a ___.	ahn-dee**ah**-moh ah
Tell me when to get off?	Mi dice quando devo scendere?	mee **dee**-chay **kwahn**-doh **day**-voh **shehn**-day-ray
Tell us when to get off?	Ci dice quando dobbiamo scendere?	chee **dee**-chay **kwahn**-doh doh-bee**ah**-moh **shehn**-day-ray

Taxis

Getting a Taxi

Taxi!	*Taxi!*	**tahk**-see
Can you call a taxi?	*Può chiamare un taxi?*	pwoh kee-ah-**mah**-ray oon **tahk**-see
Where is a taxi stand?	*Dov'è una fermata dei taxi?*	doh-**veh oo**-nah fehr-**mah**-tah **deh**ee **tahk**-see
Where can I get a taxi?	*Dov'è posso prendere un taxi?*	doh-**veh poh**-soh **prehn**-day-ray oon **tahk**-see
Where can we get a taxi?	*Dov'è possiamo prendere un taxi?*	doh-**veh** poh-see**ah**-moh **prehn**-day-ray oon **tahk**-see
Are you free?	*È libero?*	eh **lee**-bay-roh
Occupied.	*Occupato.*	oh-koo-**pah**-toh
To ___ , please.	*A ___, per favore.*	ah ___ pehr fah-**voh**-ray
To this address.	*A questo indirizzo.*	ah **kwehs**-toh een-dee-**reed**-zoh
Take me to ___.	*Mi porti a ___.*	mee **por**-tee ah ___
Take us to ___.	*Ci porti a ___.*	chee **por**-tee ah ___
Approximately how much will it cost to go...?	*Quanto costa più o meno fino...?*	**kwahn**-toh **koh**-stah pew oh **may**-noh **fee**-noh
...to ___	*...a ___*	ah ___
...to the airport	*...all'aeroporto*	ah-lah-ay-roh-**por**-toh
...to the train station	*...alla stazione ferroviaria*	**ah**-lah staht-see**oh**-nay fay-roh-vee-**ah**-reeah
...to this address	*...a questo indirizzo*	ah **kweh**-stoh een-dee-**reed**-zoh
Any extra supplement?	*C'è qualche supplemento?*	cheh **kwahl**-kay soo-play-**mehn**-toh
Too much.	*Troppo.*	**troh**-poh

Can you take ___ people?	Può portare ___ persone?	pwoh por-**tah**-reh ___ pehr-**soh**-nay
Any extra fee?	C'è un sovrapprezzo?	cheh oon soh-vrah-**prehd**-zoh
Do you have an hourly rate?	Ha una tariffa oraria?	ah **oo**-nah tah-**ree**-fah oh-**rah**-reeah
How much for a one-hour city tour?	Quant'è per un giro della città di un'ora?	kwahn-**teh** pehr oon **jee**-roh **day**-lah chee-**tah** dee oon-**oh**-rah

Cab fares are reasonable, and most drivers are honest. Expect a charge for luggage. Three or more tourists are usually better off hailing a cab than messing with city buses in Italy. If you're having a tough time hailing a taxi, ask for the nearest taxi stand (*fermata dei taxi*). The simplest way to tell a cabbie where you want to go is by stating your destination followed by "please" ("*Uffizi, per favore*"). Tipping isn't expected, but it's polite to round up.

In the Taxi

The meter, please.	Il tassametro, per favore.	eel tah-sah-**may**-troh pehr fah-**voh**-ray
Where is the meter?	Dov'è il tassametro?	doh-**veh** eel tah-sah-**may**-troh
I'm / We're in a hurry.	Sono / Siamo di fretta.	**soh**-noh / seeah-moh dee **fray**-tah
Slow down.	Rallenti.	rah-**lehn**-tee
If you don't slow down, I'll throw up.	Se non rallenta, vomito.	say nohn rah-**lehn**-tah, **voh**-mee-toh
Left / Right / Straight.	A sinistra / A destra / Diritto.	ah see-**nee**-strah / ah **dehs**-trah / dee-**ree**-toh
I'd like to stop here briefly.	Vorrei fermarmi un momento.	vor-**reh**ee fehr-**mar**-mee oon moh-**mehn**-toh
We'd like to stop here briefly.	Vorremmo fermarci un momento.	vor-**ray**-moh fehr-**mar**-chee oon moh-**mehn**-toh

TRAVELING

Please stop here for ___ minutes.	Si fermi qui per ___ minuti, per favore.	see **fehr**-mee kwee pehr ___ mee-**noo**-tee pehr fah-**voh**-ray
Can you wait?	Può aspettare?	pwoh ah-spay-**tah**-ray
Crazy traffic, isn't it?	Un traffico incredibile, vero?	oon **trah**-fee-koh een-kray-**dee**-bee-lay **vay**-roh
You drive like...	Guida come...	**gwee**-dah **koh**-may
...a madman!	...un pazzo!	oon **pahd**-zoh
...Michael Schumacher.	...Michael Schumacher.	"Michael Schumacher"
You drive very well.	Guida molto bene.	**gwee**-dah **mohl**-toh **behn**-ay
Where did you learn to drive?	Ma dove ha imparato a guidare?	mah **doh**-vay ah eem-pah-**rah**-toh ah gwee-**dah**-ray
Stop here.	Si fermi qui.	see **fehr**-mee kwee
Here is fine.	Va bene qui.	vah **behn**-ay kwee
At this corner.	A questo angolo.	ah **kwehs**-toh **ahn**-goh-loh
The next corner.	Al prossimo angolo.	ahl **proh**-see-moh **ahn**-goh-loh
My change, please.	Il resto, per favore.	eel **rehs**-toh pehr fah-**voh**-ray
Keep the change.	Tenga il resto.	**tayn**-gah eel **rehs**-toh
This ride...	Questo viaggio ...	**kwehs**-toh veeah-joh...
more fun than Disneyland.	più divertente di Disneyland.	pew dee-vehr-**tehn**-tay dee "Disneyland"
...is / was	...è / è stato	...eh / eh **stah**-toh

TRAVELING

KEY PHRASES: TAXIS

Taxi!	Taxi!	**tahk**-see
Are you free?	È libero?	eh **lee**-bay-roh
To ___, please.	A ___, per favore.	ah ___ pehr fah-**voh** ray
meter	tassametro	tah-sah-**may**-troh
Stop here.	Si fermi qui.	see **fehr**-mee kwee
Keep the change.	Tenga il resto.	**tayn**-gah eel **rehs**-toh

Driving

Rental Wheels

car rental agency	*agenzia di autonoleggio*	ah-**jehnt**-seeah dee ow-toh-noh-**leh**-joh
I'd like to rent...	*Vorrei noleggiare...*	vor-**reh**ee noh-leh-**jah**-ray
We'd like to rent...	*Vorremmo noleggiare...*	vor-**ray**-moh noh-leh-**jah**-ray
...a car.	*...una macchina.*	**oo**-nah **mah**-kee-nah
...a station wagon.	*...una station wagon.*	**oo**-nah **staht**-see-ohn **wah**-gohn
...a van.	*...un monovolume.*	oon moh-noh-voh-**loo**-may
...a motorcycle.	*...una motocicletta.*	**oo**-nah moh-toh-chee-**klay**-tah
...a motor scooter.	*...un motorino.*	oon moh-toh-**ree**-noh
How much...?	*Quanto...?*	**kwahn**-toh
...per hour	*...all'ora*	ah-**loh**-rah
...per half day	*...per mezza giornata*	pehr **mehd**-zah jor-**nah**-tah

TRAVELING

KEY PHRASES: DRIVING

car	*macchina*	**mah**-kee-nah
gas station	*benzinaio*	baynd-zee-**nah**-yoh
parking lot	*parcheggio*	par-**kay**-joh
accident	*incidente*	een-chee-**dehn**-tay
left / right	*sinistra / destra*	see-**nee**-strah / **dehs**-trah
straight ahead	*sempre diritto*	**sehm**-pray dee-**ree**-toh
downtown	*centro*	**chehn**-troh
How do you get to ___?	*Come si va a ___?*	**koh**-may see vah ah
Where can I park?	*Dove posso parcheggiare?*	**doh**-vay **poh**-soh par-kay-**jah**-ray

...per day	...al giorno	ahl **jor**-noh
...per week	...alla settimana	**ah**-lah say-tee-**mah**-nah
Unlimited mileage?	Chilometraggio illimitato?	kee-loh-may-**trah**-joh eel-lee-mee-**tah**-toh
When must I bring it back?	Quando devo riportarla?	**kwahn**-doh **day**-voh ree-por-**tar**-lah
Is there...?	C'è...?	cheh
...a helmet	...un casco	oon **kah**-skoh
...a discount	...uno sconto	**oo**-noh **skohn**-toh
...a deposit	...una caparra	**oo**-nah kah-**pah**-rah
...insurance	...l'assicurazione	lah-see-koo-raht-see**oh**-nay

At the Gas Station

gas station	benzinaio	baynd-zee-**nah**-yoh
The nearest gas station?	Il benzinaio più vicino?	eel baynd-zee-**nah**-yoh pew vee-**chee**-noh
Self-service?	Self-service?	"self service"
Fill the tank.	Il pieno.	eel pee**ay**-noh
Wash the windows.	Pulisce le finestrine.	poo-**lee**-shay lay fee-nay-**stree**-nay
I need...	Ho bisogno di...	oh bee-**zohn**-yoh dee
We need...	Abbiamo bisogno di...	ah-bee**ah**-moh bee-**zohn**-yoh dee
...gas.	...benzina.	baynd-**zee**-nah
...unleaded.	...benzina verde.	baynd-**zee**-nah **vehr**-day
...regular.	...normale.	nor-**mah**-lay
...super.	...super.	**soo**-pehr
...diesel.	...gasolio.	gah-**zoh**-leeoh
Check...	Controlli...	kohn-**troh**-lee
...the oil.	...l'olio.	**loh**-leeoh
...the air in the tires.	...l'aria nelle gomme.	**lah**-reeah **nay**-lay **goh**-may
...the radiator.	...il radiatore.	eel rah-deeah-**toh**-ray
...the battery.	...la batteria.	lah bah-tay-**ree**-ah

...the sparkplugs.	...le candele.	lay kahn-**day**-lay
...the headlights.	...gli anabbaglianti.	lyee ah-nah-bahl-yee**ahn**-tee
...the tail lights.	...le luci posteriori.	lay **loo**-chee pos-tay-ree**oh**-ree
...the directional signal.	...la freccia.	lah **freh**-chah
...the brakes.	...i freni.	ee **fray**-nee
...the transmission fluid.	...il liquido della trasmissione.	eel **lee**-kwee-doh **day**-lah trahs-mee-see**oh**-nay
...the windshield wipers.	...i tergicristalli.	ee tehr-gee-kree-**stah**-lee
...the fuses.	...i fusibili.	ee foo-**zee**-bee-lee
...the fan belt.	...la cinghia del ventilatore.	lah **cheen**-geeah dayl vehn-tee-lah-**toh**-ray
...my pulse.	...il mio battito cardiaco.	eel **mee**-oh bah-**tee**-toh kar-dee**ah**-koh
...my husband / wife.	...mio marito / mia moglie.	**mee**-oh mah-**ree**-toh / **mee**-ah **mohl**-yay

Getting gas in Italy is a breeze. Regular is *normale* and super is *super,* and euros and liters replace dollars and gallons. If a euro is equal to a dollar and there are about four liters in a gallon, gas costing €1 a liter = $4 a gallon. The freeway rest stops and city *automat* gas pumps are the only places that sell gas during the afternoon siesta hours. Gas is always more expensive on the super highways.

Car Trouble

accident	incidente	een-chee-**dehn**-tay
breakdown	guasto	goo**ah**-stoh
dead battery	batteria scarica	bah-tay-**ree**-ah skah-**ree**-kah
funny noise	rumore strano	roo-**moh**-ray **strah**-noh
electrical problem	problema elettrico	proh-**blay**-mah ay-**leht**-ree-koh
flat tire	gomma a terra	**goh**-mah ah **tay**-rah

shop with parts	*negozio di pezzi di ricambio*	nay-**goht**-seeoh dee **pehd**-zee dee ree-**kahm**-beeoh
My car won't start.	*La mia macchina non parte.*	lah **mee**-ah **mah**-kee-nah nohn **par**-tay
My car is broken.	*La mia macchina è rotta.*	lah **mee**-ah **mah**-kee-nah eh **roh**-tah
This doesn't work.	*Non funziona.*	nohn foont-see**oh**-nah
It's overheating.	*Si sta surriscaldando.*	see stah soo-ree-skahl-**dahn**-doh
It's a lemon (a swindle).	*È una fregatura.*	eh **oo**-nah fray-gah-**too**-rah
I need...	*Ho bisogno di...*	oh bee-**zohn**-yoh dee
We need...	*Abbiamo bisogno di...*	ah-bee**ah**-moh bee-**zohn**-yoh dee
...a tow truck.	*...un carro attrezzi.*	oon **kar**-roh ah-**trayd**-zee
...a mechanic.	*...un meccanico.*	oon may-**kah**-nee-koh
...a stiff drink.	*...un whiskey.*	oon "whiskey"

For help with repair, see "Repair" in the Services chapter on page 178.

Parking

parking lot	*parcheggio*	par-**kay**-joh
parking garage	*garage*	gah-**rahj**
Where can I park?	*Dove posso parcheggiare?*	**doh**-vay **poh**-soh par-kay-**jah**-ray
Is parking nearby?	*È vicino il parcheggio?*	eh vee-**chee**-noh eel par-**kay**-joh
Can I park here?	*Posso parcheggiare qui?*	**poh**-soh par-kay-**jah**-ray kwee
Is this a safe place to park?	*È sicuro parcheggiare qui?*	eh see-**koo**-roh par-kay-**jah**-ray kwee
How long can I park here?	*Per quanto tempo posso parcheggiare qui?*	pehr **kwahn**-toh **tehm**-poh **poh**-soh par-kay-**jah**-ray kwee

Must I pay to park here?	È a pagamento questo parcheggio?	eh ah pah-gah-**mayn**-toh **kweh**-stoh par-**kay**-joh
How much per hour / day?	Quanto costa all'ora / al giorno?	**kwahn**-toh **koh**-stah ahl-**loh**-rah / ahl **jor**-noh

Parking in Italian cities is expensive and hazardous. Plan to pay to use a parking garage in big cities. Leave nothing in your car at night. Always ask at your hotel about safe parking. Take parking restrictions seriously to avoid getting fines and having your car towed away (an interesting but costly experience).

Finding Your Way

TRAVELING

I'm going to ___.	Vado a ___.	**vah**-doh ah
We're going to ___.	Andiamo a ___.	ahn-dee**ah**-moh ah
How do you get to ___?	Come si va a ___?	**koh**-may see vah ah
Do you have a...?	Ha una...?	ah **oo**-nah
...city map	...cartina della città	kar-**tee**-nah **day**-lah chee-**tah**
...road map	...cartina stradale	kar-**tee**-nah strah-**dah**-lay
How many minutes...?	Quanti minuti...?	**kwahn**-tee mee-**noo**-tee
How many hours...?	Quante ore...?	**kwahn**-tay **oh**-ray
...on foot	...a piedi	ah pee**ay**-dee
...by bicycle	...in bicicletta	een bee-chee-**klay**-tah
...by car	...in macchina	een **mah**-kee-nah
How many kilometers to...?	Quanti chilometri per...?	**kwahn**-tee kee-**loh**-may-tree pehr
What is the... route to Rome?	Qual'è la strada... per andare a Roma?	kwah-**leh** lah **strah**-dah... pehr ahn-**dah**-ray ah **roh**-mah
...most scenic	...più panoramica	pew pah-noh-**rah**-mee-kah

...fastest	...più veloce	pew vay-**loh**-chay
...most interesting	...più interessante	pew een-tay-ray-**sahn**-tay
Point it out?	Me lo mostra?	may loh **mohs**-trah
I'm lost.	Mi sono perso[a].	mee **soh**-noh **pehr**-soh
Where am I?	Dove sono?	**doh**-vay **soh**-noh
Where is...?	Dov'è...?	doh-**veh**
The nearest...?	Il più vicino...?	eel pew vee-**chee**-noh
Where is this address?	Dov'è questo indirizzo?	doh-**veh kweh**-stoh een-dee-**reed**-zoh

Route-Finding Words

map	cartina	kar-**tee**-nah
road map	cartina stradale	kar-**tee**-nah strah-**dah**-lay
downtown	centro	**chehn**-troh
straight ahead	sempre diritto	**sehm**-pray dee-**ree**-toh
left	sinistra	see-**nee**-strah
right	destra	**dehs**-trah
first	prima	**pree**-mah
next	prossima	**proh**-see-mah
intersection	incrocio	een-**kroh**-choh
corner	angolo	**ahn**-goh-loh
block	isolato	ee-zoh-**lah**-toh
roundabout	rotonda	roh-**tohn**-dah
stoplight	semaforo	say-mah-**foh**-roh
(main) square	piazza (principale)	peeaht-sah (preen-chee-**pah**-lay)
street	strada, via	**strah**-dah, **vee**-ah
bridge	ponte	**pohn**-tay
tunnel	tunnel	**toon**-nehl
highway	autostrada	ow-toh-**strah**-dah
freeway	superstrada	soo-pehr-**strah**-dah
north	nord	nord
south	sud	sood
east	est	ayst
west	ovest	**oh**-vehst

TRAVELING

In Italy, the shortest distance between any two points is the *autostrada*. Tolls are not cheap (about a dollar for each ten minutes), and there aren't as many signs as we are used to, so stay alert or you may miss your exit. Italy's *autostrada* rest stops are among the best in Europe.

The Police

As in any country, the flashing lights of a patrol car are a sure sign that someone's in trouble. If it's you, try this handy phrase: "*Mi dispiace, sono un turista*" (Sorry, I'm a tourist). Or, for the adventurous: "*Se non le piace come guido, si tolga dal marciapiede*" (If you don't like how I drive, stay off the sidewalk).

I'm late for my tour.	Sono in ritardo per il tour.	**soh**-noh een ree-**tar**-doh pehr eel toor
Can I buy your hat?	Mi vende il suo cappello?	mee **vehn**-day eel **soo**-oh kah-**pehl**-loh
What seems to be the problem?	Quale sarebbe il problema?	**kwah**-lay sah-**reh**-bay eel proh-**blay**-mah

Reading Road Signs

alt / stop	stop
carabinieri	police
centro, centrocittà	to the center of town
circonvallazione	ring road
dare la precedenza	yield
deviazione	detour
entrata	entrance
lavori in corso	road work ahead
prossima uscita	next exit
rallentare	slow down
senso unico	one-way street
tutti le (altre) destinazioni	to all (other) destinations
uscita	exit
zona pedonale	pedestrian zone

Standard Road Signs

AND LEARN THESE ROAD SIGNS

Speed Limit (km/hr)

Yield

No Passing

End of No Passing Zone

One Way

Intersection

Main Road

Freeway

Danger

No Entry

No Entry for Cars

All Vehicles Prohibited

Parking

No Parking

Customs

Peace

Other Signs You May See

acqua non potabile	undrinkable water
affittasi, in affitto	for rent or for hire
aperto	open
aperto da... a...	open from... to...
attenzione	caution
bagno, gabinetto, toilette, toletta, WC	toilet
cagnaccio	mean dog
camere libere	vacancy
chiuso	closed
chiuso per ferie	closed for vacation
chiuso per restauro	closed for restoration
completo	no vacancy
donne	women
entrata libera	free admission
entrata vietata	no entry
fuori servizio / guasto	out of service
non toccare	do not touch
occupato	occupied
parcheggio vietato	no parking
pericolo	danger
proibito	prohibited
saldo	sale
sciopero	on strike
signore	women
signori	men
spingere / tirare	push / pull
torno subito	I'll return soon (sign on store)
uomini	men
uscita d'emergenza	emergency exit
vendesi, in vendita	for sale
vietato	forbidden
vietato fumare	no smoking
vietato l'accesso	keep out

SLEEPING

Places to Stay

hotel	*hotel, albergo*	**oh**-tehl, ahl-**behr**-goh
small hotel (often family-run)	*pensione, locanda*	payn-see**oh**-nay, loh-**kahn**-dah
rooms for rent	*affita camere*	ah-**fee**-tah **kah**-may-ray
youth hostel	*ostello della gioventù*	oh-**stehl**-loh **dehl**-lah joh-vehn-**too**
vacancy	*camere libere*	**kah**-may-ray **lee**-bay-ray
no vacancy	*completo*	kohm-**play**-toh

Reserving a Room

I like to reserve rooms a few days in advance as I travel. But if my itinerary is set, I reserve before I leave home. To reserve from the U.S. by e-mail or fax, use the handy form in the Appendix (online at www.ricksteves.com/reservation).

Hello.	*Buon giorno.*	bwohn **jor**-noh
Do you speak English?	*Parla inglese?*	**par**-lah een-**glay**-zay
Do you have a room for...?	*Avete una camera per...?*	ah-**vay**-tay **oo**-nah **kah**-may-rah pehr
...one person	*...una persona*	**oo**-nah pehr-**soh**-nah

KEY PHRASES: SLEEPING

I want to make / confirm a reservation.	Vorrei fare / confermare una prenotazione.	vor-**reh**ee **fah**-ray / kohn-fehr-**mah**-ray **oo**-nah pray-noh-taht-see**oh**-nay
I'd like a room (for two people), please.	Vorrei una camera (per due persone), per favore.	vor-**reh**ee **oo**-nah **kah**-may-rah (pehr **doo**-ay pehr-**soh**-nay) pehr fah-**voh**-ray
...with / without / and	...con / senza / e	kohn / **sehn**-sah / ay
...toilet	...toilette	twah-**leht**-tay
...shower	...doccia	**doh**-chah
Can I see the room?	Posso vedere la camera?	**poh**-soh vay-**day**-ray lah **kah**-may-rah
How much is it?	Quanto costa?	**kwahn**-toh **koh**-stah
Credit card O.K.?	Carta di credito è O.K.?	**kar**-tah dee **kray**-dee-toh eh "O.K."

...two people	...due persone	**doo**-ay pehr-**soh**-nay
...tonight	...stanotte	stah-**noh**-tay
...two nights	...due notti	**doo**-ay **noh**-tee
...Friday	...venerdì	vay-nehr-**dee**
...June 21	...il ventuno giugno	eel vayn-**too**-noh **joon**-yoh
Yes or no?	Si o no?	see oh noh
I'd like...	Vorrei...	vor-**reh**ee
We'd like...	Vorremmo...	vor-**ray**-moh
...a private bathroom.	...un bagno completo.	oon **bahn**-yoh kohm-**play**-toh
...your cheapest room.	...la camera più economica.	lah **kah**-may-rah pew ay-koh-**noh**-mee-kah
...___ bed (beds)	...___ letto (letti)	___ **leht**-toh (**leht**-tee)
for ___ people	per ___ persone	pehr ___ pehr-**soh**-nay
in ___ room (in ___rooms).	nella ___ camera (nelle ___ camere).	**nay**-lah ___ **kah**-may-rah (**nay**-lay ___ **kah**-may-ray)
How much is it?	Quanto costa?	**kwahn**-toh **koh**-stah
Anything cheaper?	Niente di più economico?	nee-**ehn**-tay dee pew ay-koh-**noh**-mee-koh
I'll take it.	La prendo.	lah **prehn**-doh

SLEEPING

My name is ___.	*Mi chiamo ___.*	mee kee**ah**-moh ___
I'll stay / We'll stay...	*Starò / Staremo...*	stah-**roh** / stah-**ray**-moh
...for ___ night (nights).	*...per ___ notte (notti).*	pehr ___ **noh**-tay (**noh**-tee)
I'll come / We'll come...	*Arriverò / Arriveremo...*	ah-ree-vay-**roh** / ah-ree-vay-**ray**-moh
...in the morning.	*...la mattina.*	lah mah-**tee**-nah
...in the afternoon.	*...il pomeriggio.*	eel poh-may-**ree**-joh
...in the evening.	*...la sera.*	lah **say**-rah
...in one hour.	*...tra un'ora.*	trah oon-**oh**-rah
...before 16:00.	*...prima delle sedici.*	**pree**-mah **dehl**-lay **say**-dee-chee
...Friday before 6 p.m.	*...venerdí entro le sei di sera.*	vay-nehr-**dee ehn**-troh lay **seh**ee dee **say**-rah
Thank you.	*Grazie.*	**graht**-seeay

Using a Credit Card

If you need to secure your reservation with a credit card, here's the lingo.

Is a deposit required?	*Bisogna lasciare una caparra?*	bee-**sohn**-yah lah-**shah**-ray **oo**-nah kah-**pah**-rah
Credit card O.K.?	*Carta di credito è O.K.?*	**kar**-tah dee **kray**-dee-toh eh "O.K."
credit card	*carta di credito*	**kar**-tah dee **kray**-dee-toh
debit card	*bancomat*	**bahnk**-oh-maht
The name on the card is___ .	*Il nome sulla carta*	il **noh**-may **soo**-lah **kar**-tah eh
The credit card number is...	*Il numero della carta di credito è...*	eel **noo**-may-roh **dehl**-lah **kar**-tah dee **kray**-dee-toh eh
0	*zero*	**zay**-roh
1	*uno*	**oo**-noh
2	*due*	**doo**-ay
3	*tre*	tray
4	*quattro*	**kwah**-troh
5	*cinque*	**cheeng**-kway

SLEEPING

6	*sei*	**seh**ee
7	*sette*	**seht**-tay
8	*otto*	**oh**-toh
9	*nove*	**noh**-vay
The expiration date is...	*La data di scadenza è...*	lah **dah**-tah dee shah-**dehnt**-sah eh
January	*gennaio*	jay-**nah**-yoh
February	*febbraio*	fay-**brah**-yoh
March	*marzo*	**mart**-soh
April	*aprile*	ah-**pree**-lay
May	*maggio*	**mah**-joh
June	*giugno*	**joon**-yoh
July	*luglio*	**lool**-yoh
August	*agosto*	ah-**goh**-stoh
September	*settembre*	say-**tehm**-bray
October	*ottobre*	oh-**toh**-bray
November	*novembre*	noh-**vehm**-bray
December	*dicembre*	dee-**chehm**-bray
2003	*duemilatre*	doo-ay-mee-lah-**tray**
2004	*duemila-quattro*	doo-ay-mee-lah-**kwah**-troh
2005	*duemila-cinque*	doo-ay-mee-lah-**cheeng**-kway
2006	*duemilasei*	doo-ay-mee-lah-**seh**ee
2007	*duemilasette*	doo-ay-mee-lah-**seht**-tay
2008	*duemilaotto*	doo-ay-mee-lah-**oh**-toh
2009	*duemilanove*	doo-ay-mee-lah-**noh**-vay
2010	*duemila-dieci*	doo-ay-mee-lah-dee**ay**-chee
Can I reserve with a credit card and pay in cash?	*Posso prenotare con la carta di credito e pagare in contanti?*	**poh**-soh pray-noh-**tah**-ray kohn lah **kar**-tah dee **kray**-dee-toh ay pah-**gah**-ray een kohn-**tahn**-tee
I have another card.	*Ho un'altra carta.*	oh oo-**nahl**-trah **kar**-tah

If your *carta di credito* (credit card) is not approved, you can say "*Ho un'altra carta*" (I have another card)—if you do.

L' Alfabeto

If phoning, you can use the code alphabet below to spell out your name if necessary. Unless you're giving the hotelier your name as it appears on your credit card, consider using a shorter version of your name to make things easier.

a	ah	*Ancona*	ahn-**koh**-nah
b	bee	*Bologna*	boh-**lohn**-yah
c	chee	*Como*	**koh**-moh
d	dee	*Domodossola*	doh-moh-**doh**-soh-lah
e	ay	*Empoli*	**ehm**-poh-lee
f	**ehf**-ay	*Firenze*	fee-**rehn**-tsay
g	jee	*Genova*	**jay**-noh-vah
h	ah-kah	*Hotel, "acca"*	**oh**-tehl, **ah**-kah
i	ee	*Imola*	**ee**-moh-lah
j	ee loon-goh	*i lunga*	ee **loon**-gah
k	**kahp**-ah	*"kappa"*	**kah**-pah
l	**ehl**-ay	*Livorno*	lee-**vor**-noh
m	**ehm**-ay	*Milano*	mee-**lah**-noh
n	**ehn**-ay	*Napoli*	**nah**-poh-lee
o	oh	*Otranto*	oh-**trahn**-toh
p	pee	*Palermo*	pah-**lehr**-moh
q	koo	*quaranta (40)*	kwah-**rahn**-tah
r	**ehr**-ay	*Rovigo*	roh-**vee**-goh
s	**ehs**-ay	*Savona*	sah-**voh**-nah
t	tee	*Treviso*	tray-**vee**-zoh
u	oo	*Urbino*	oor-**bee**-noh
v	vee	*Venezia*	vay-**nayt**-seeah
w	**dohp**-yah voo	*"doppia vu"*	**dohp**-yah voo
x	eeks	*"ics"*	eeks
y	**eep**-see-lohn	*"ispilon"*	**eep**-see-lohn
z	**zeht**-ah	*Zara*	**tsah**-rah

SLEEPING

Just the Fax, Ma'am

If you're booking a room by fax...

I want to send a fax.	*Vorrei mandare un fax.*	vor-**reh**ee mahn-**dah**-ray oon fahks
What is your fax number?	*Qual è il suo numero di fax?*	kwahl eh eel **soo**-oh **noo**-may-roh dee fahks
Your fax number is not working.	*Il suo numero di fax non funziona.*	eel **soo**-oh **noo**-may-roh dee fahks nohn foont-see**oh**-nah
Please turn on your fax machine.	*Per favore accendere il fax.*	pehr fah-**voh**-ray ah-**chehn**-day-ray eel fahks

Getting Specific

I'd like a room...	*Vorrei una camera...*	vor-**reh**ee **oo**-nah **kah**-may-rah
We'd like a room...	*Vorremmo una camera...*	vor-**ray**-moh **oo**-nah **kah**-may-rah
...with / without / and	*...con / senza / e*	kohn / **sehn**-sah / ay
...toilet	*...toilette*	twah-**leht**-tay
...shower	*...doccia*	**doh**-chah
...shower down the hall	*...doccia in fondo al corridoio*	**doh**-chah een **fohn**-doh ahl kor-ree-**doh**-yoh
...bathtub	*...vasca da bagno*	**vah**-skah dah **bahn**-yoh
...double bed	*...letto matrimoniale*	**leht**-toh mah-tree-moh-nee**ah**-lay
...twin beds	*...letti singoli*	**leht**-tee **seeng**-goh-lee
...balcony	*...balcone*	bahl-**koh**-nay
...view	*...vista*	**vee**-stah
...only a sink	*...solo un lavandino*	**soh**-loh oon lah-vahn-**dee**-noh
...on the ground floor	*...al piano terra*	ahl pee**ah**-noh **tay**-rah
...television	*...televisione*	tay-lay-vee-zee**oh**-nay

...telephone	...telefono	tay-**lay**-foh-noh
...air conditioning	...aria	**ah**-reeah
	condizionata	kohn-deet-see-oh-**nah**-tah
...kitchenette	...cucina	koo-**chee**-nah
Do you have...?	Avete...?	ah-**vay**-tay
...an elevator	...l'ascensore	lah-shehn-**soh**-ray
...a swimming pool	...la piscina	lah pee-**shee**-nah
I arrive Monday,	Arrivo lunedì,	ah-**ree**-voh loo-nay-**dee**
depart Wednesday.	parto mercoledì.	**par**-toh mehr-koh-lay-**dee**
We arrive Monday,	Arriviamo	ah-ree-veeah-moh
depart	lunedì,	loo-nay-**dee**,
Wednesday.	partiamo	par-teeah-moh
	mercoledì.	mehr-koh-lay-**dee**
I am desperate.	Sono disperato[a].	**soh**-noh dee-spay-**rah**-toh
We are	Siamo	seeah-moh
desperate.	disperati.	dee-spay-**rah**-tee
I will / We will	Posso / Possiamo	**poh**-soh / poh-seeah-moh
sleep anywhere.	dormire	dor-**mee**-ray
	ovunque.	oh-**voon**-kway
I have a sleeping	Ho un sacco	oh oon **sah**-koh
bag.	a pelo.	ah **pay**-loh
We have	Abbiamo i	ah-beeah-moh ee
sleeping bags.	sacchi a pelo.	**sah**-kee ah **pay**-loh
Will you call	Chiamerebbe	keeah-may-**reh**-bay
another hotel	un altro	oon **ahl**-troh
for me?	albergo per me?	ahl-**behr**-goh pehr may

Families

Do you have...?	Avete...?	ah-**vay**-tay
...a room for	...una camera	**oo**-nah **kah**-may-rah
families	grande per	**grahn**-day pehr
	una famiglia	**oo**-nah fah-**meel**-yah
...a family rate	...una tariffa	**oo**-nah tah-**ree**-fah
	per famiglie	pehr fah-**meel**-yay
...a discount	...uno sconto per	**oo**-noh **skohn**-toh pehr
for children	i bambini	ee bahm-**bee**-nee

I / We have...	Ho / Abbiamo...	oh / ah-beeah-moh
...one child, age	...un bambino di	oon bahm-bee-noh dee
___ months / years.	___ mesi / anni.	___ may-zee / ahn-nee
...two children,	...due bambini,	doo-ay bahm-bee-nee
ages ___ and	di ___ e ___ anni.	dee ___ ay ___ ahn-nee
___ years.		
I'd like...	Vorrei...	vor-rehee
We'd like...	Vorremmo...	vor-ray-moh
...a crib.	...una culla.	oo-nah koo-lah
...a small extra	...un letto	oon leht-toh
bed.	singolo in più.	seeng-goh-loh een pew
...bunk beds.	...letti a castello.	lay-tee ah kah-stehl-loh
babysitting service	servizio di	sehr-veet-seeoh dee
	baby sitter	bay-bee see-tehr
Is a... nearby?	C'è.... qui vicino?	cheh... kwee vee-chee-noh
...park	...un parco	oon par-koh
...playground	...un parco giochi	oon par-koh joh-kee
...swimming pool	...una piscina	oo-nah pee-shee-nah

For fun, the Italians call kids *marmocchi* (munchkins).

Mobility Issues

Stairs are... for	Le scale sono...	lay skah-lay soh-noh...
me / us /	per me / noi /	pehr may / nohee /
my husband /	mio marito /	mee-oh mah-ree-toh /
my wife.	mia moglie.	mee-ah mohl-yay
...impossible	...impossibili	eem-poh-see-bee-lee
...difficult	...difficili	dee-fee-chee-lee
Do you have...?	Avete...?	ah-vay-tay
...an elevator	...l'ascensore	lah-shehn-soh-ray
...a ground floor	...una camera al	oo-nah kah-may-rah ahl
room	piano terra	peeah-noh tay-rah
...a wheelchair-	...una camera	oo-nah kah-may-rah
accessible room	accessibile	ah-cheh-see-bee-lay
	con la sedia	kohn lah say-dee-ah
	a rotelle	ah roh-tehl-lay

Confirming, Changing, and Canceling Reservations

Use this template for your telephone call.

I have / We have a reservation.	Ho / Abbiamo una prenotazione.	oh /ah-bee**ah**-moh **oo**-nah pray-noh-taht-see**oh**-nay
My name is ___.	Mi chiamo ___.	mee kee**ah**-moh
I'd like to... my reservation.	Vorrei fare... una prenotazione.	vor-**reh**ee **fah**-ray...**oo**-nah pray-noh-taht-see**oh**-nay
...confirm	...confermare	kohn-fehr-**mah**-ray
...reconfirm	...riconfermare	ree-kohn-fehr-**mah**-ray
...cancel	...annullare	ah-noo-**lah**-ray
...change	...cambiare	kahm-bee**ah**-ray
The reservation is / was for...	La prenotazione è / era per...	lah pray-noh-taht-see**oh**-nay eh / **ehr**-ah pehr
...one person	...una persona	**oo**-nah pehr-**soh**-nah
...two people	...due persone	**doo**-ay pehr-**soh**-nay
...today / tomorrow	...oggi / domani	**oh**-jee / doh-**mah**-nee
...the day after tomorrow	...dopodomani	doh-poh-doh-**mah**-nee
...August 13	...il tredici agosto	eel **tray**-dee-chee ah-**goh**-stoh
...one night / two nights	...una notte / due notti	**oo**-nah **noh**-tay / **doo**-ay **noh**-tee
Can you find my / our reservation?	Può trovare la mia / nostra prenotazione?	pwoh troh-**vah**-ray lah **mee**-ah / **noh**-strah pray-noh-taht-see**oh**-nay
What is your cancellation policy?	Qual è il vostro regolamento riguardo alla cancellazione delle prenotazioni?	kwahl eh eel **voh**-stroh ray-goh-lah-**mehn**-toh ree-**gwar**-doh **ahl**-lah kahn-chehl-aht-see**oh**-nay **dehl**-lay pray-noh-taht-see**oh**-nee

Will I be billed for the first night if I can't make it?	Mi addebitate la prima notte se non ce la faccio?	mee ah-day-bee-**tah**-tay lah **pree**-mah **noh**-tay say nohn chay lah **fah**-choh
I'd like to arrive instead on...	Invece vorrei arrivare...	een-**vay**-chay voh-**reh**ee ah-ree-**vah**-ray
We'd like to arrive instead on...	Invece vorremmo arrivare...	een-**vay**-chay vor-**ray**-moh ah-ree-**vah**-ray
Is everything O.K.?	Va bene?	vah **behn**-ay
Thank you. I'll see you then.	Grazie. Ci vediamo al mio arrivo.	**graht**-seeay chee vay-dee**ah**-moh ahl **mee**-oh ah-**ree**-voh
We'll see you then.	Ci vediamo al nostro arrivo.	chee vay-dee**ah**-moh ahl **noh**-stroh ah-**ree**-voh
I'm sorry I need to cancel.	Mi dispiace ma devo annullare.	mee dee-spee**ah**-chay mah **day**-voh ah-noo-**lah**-ray

Nailing Down the Price

How much is...?	Quanto costa...?	**kwahn**-toh **koh**-stah
...a room	...una camera	**oo**-nah **kah**-may-rah
for ___ people	per ___ persone	pehr ___ pehr-**soh**-nay
...your cheapest room	...la camera più economica	lah **kah**-may-rah pew ay-koh-**noh**-mee-kah
Is breakfast included?	La colazione è inclusa?	lah koh-laht-see**oh**-nay eh een-**kloo**-zah
Is breakfast required?	È obbligatoria la colazione?	eh oh-blee-gah-**toh**-reeah lah koh-laht-see**oh**-nay
How much without breakfast?	Quant'è senza la colazione?	kwahn-**teh sehn**-sah lah koh-laht-see**oh**-nay
Is half-pension required?	E' obbligatoria la mezza pensione?	ay oh-blee-gah-**toh**-reeah lah **mehd**-zah pehn-see**oh**-nay
Complete price?	Prezzo completo?	**prehd**-zoh kohm-**play**-toh
Is it cheaper for three-night stays?	È più economico se mi fermo tre notti?	eh pew ay-koh-**noh**-mee-koh say mee **fehr**-moh tray **noh**-tee

I will stay	*Mi fermo*	mee **fehr**-moh
three nights.	*tre notti.*	tray **noh**-tee
We will stay	*Ci fermiamo*	chee fehr-mee**ah**-moh
three nights.	*tre notti.*	tray **noh**-tee
Is it cheaper if	*È più economico*	eh pew ay-koh-**noh**-mee-koh
I pay in cash?	*se pago in*	say **pah**-goh een
	contanti?	kohn-**tahn**-tee
What is the cost	*Quanto costa*	**kwahn**-toh **koh**-stah
per week?	*a settimana?*	ah say-tee-**mah**-nah

Italian hotels almost always have larger rooms to fit three to six people. Your price per person plummets as you pack more into a room. Breakfasts are usually basic (coffee, rolls and marmalade) and expensive ($6 to $8). They're often optional.

In resort towns, some hotels offer *mezza pensione* (half-pension), consisting of two meals per day served at the hotel: breakfast and your choice of lunch or dinner. The price for half-pension is often listed per person rather than per room. Hotels that offer half-pension often require it in summer. The meals are usually good, but if you want the freedom to forage for food, look for hotels that don't push half-pension.

Choosing a Room

Can I see	*Posso vedere*	**poh**-soh vay-**day**-ray
the room?	*la camera?*	lah **kah**-may-rah
Can we see	*Possiamo*	poh-see**ah**-moh
the room?	*vedere la*	vay-**day**-ray lah
	camera?	**kah**-may-rah
Show me another	*Mi mostra*	mee **moh**-strah
room?	*un'altra camera?*	oo-**nahl**-trah **kah**-may-rah
Show us another	*Ci mostra*	chee **moh**-strah
room?	*un'altra camera?*	oo-**nahl**-trah **kah**-may-rah
Do you have	*Avete*	ah-**vay**-tay
something...?	*qualcosa...?*	kwahl-**koh**-zah
...larger / smaller	*...più grande /*	pew **grahn**-day /
	più piccola	pew **pee**-koh-lah
...better / cheaper	*...più bella /*	pew **behl**-lah /
	più economica	pew ay-koh-**noh**-mee-kah

...brighter	...più luminosa	pew loo-mee-**noh**-zah
...in the back	...al di dietro	ahl dee dee**ay**-troh
...quieter	...più tranquilla	pew trahn-**kwee**-lah
Sorry, it's not right for me.	Mi dispiace, non mi va.	mee dee-spee**ah**-chay nohn mee vah
Sorry, it's not right for us.	Mi dispiace, non va per noi.	mee dee-spee**ah**-chay nohn vah pehr **noh**ee
I'll take it.	La prendo.	lah **prehn**-doh
We'll take it.	La prendiamo.	lah prehn-dee**ah**-moh
My key, please.	La mia chiave, per favore.	lah **mee**-ah kee**ah**-vay pehr fah-**voh**-ray
Sleep well.	Sogni d'oro.	**sohn**-yee **doh**-roh
Good night.	Buona notte.	**bwoh**-nah **noh**-tay

Breakfast

Is breakfast included?	La colazione è inclusa?	lah koh-laht-see**oh**-nay eh een-**kloo**-zah
How much is breakfast?	Quanto costa la colazione?	**kwahn**-toh **koh**-stah lah koh-laht-see**oh**-nay
When does breakfast start?	Quando comincia la colazione?	**kwahn**-doh koh-**meen**-chah lah koh-laht-see**oh**-nay
When does breakfast end?	Quando finisce la colazione?	**kwahn**-doh fee-**nee**-shay lah koh-laht-see**oh**-nay
Where is breakfast served?	Dove è servita la colazione?	**doh**-vay eh sehr-**vee**-tah lah koh-laht-see**oh**-nay

Hotel Help

I'd like...	Vorrei...	vor-**reh**ee
We'd like...	Vorremmo...	vor-**ray**-moh
...a / another	...un / un altro	oon / oon **ahl**-troh
...towel.	...asciugamano.	ah-shoo-gah-**mah**-noh
...a clean bath towel / clean bath towels.	...un asciugamano pulito / degli asciugamani puliti.	oon ah-shoo-gah-**mah**-noh poo-**lee**-toh / **day**-lee ah-shoo-gah-**mah**-nee poo-**lee**-tee

SLEEPING

...pillow.	...cuscino.	koo-**shee**-noh
...clean sheets.	...lenzuola pulite.	lehnt-soo**oh**-lah poo-**lee**-tay
...blanket.	...coperta.	koh-**pehr**-tah
...glass.	...bicchiere.	bee-keeay-ray
...sink stopper.	...tappo.	**tah**-poh
...soap.	...sapone.	sah-**poh**-nay
...toilet paper.	...carta igienica.	**kar**-tah ee-**jay**-nee-kah
...electrical adapter.	...adattatore elettrico.	ah-dah-tah-**toh**-ray ay-**leht**-ree-koh
...brighter light bulb.	...lampadina più potente.	lahm-pah-**dee**-nah pew poh-**tehn**-tay
...lamp.	...lampada.	lahm-**pah**-dah
...chair.	...sedia.	say-**dee**-ah
...table.	...tavolo.	**tah**-voh-loh
...modem.	...modem.	**moh**-dehm
...Internet access.	...l'accesso a Internet.	lah-**chay**-soh ah **een**-tehr-neht
...different room.	...altra camera.	**ahl**-trah **kah**-may-rah
...silence.	...silenzio.	see-**lehnt**-seeoh
...to speak to the manager.	...parlare con il direttore.	par-**lah**-ray kohn eel dee-reht-**toh**-ray
I've fallen and I can't get up.	Sono caduto[a] e non riesco ad alzarmi.	**soh**-noh kah-**doo**-toh ay nohn reeay-skoh ahd ahlt-**sahr**-mee
How can I make the room cooler / warmer?	Come faccio a rinfrescare / riscaldare la camera?	**koh**-may **fah**-choh ah reen-frehs-**kah**-ray / rees-kahl-**dah**-ray lah **kah**-may-rah
Where can I...?	Dove posso...?	**doh**-vay **poh**-soh
...wash my laundry	...fare del bucato	**fah**-ray dayl boo-**kah**-toh
...hang my laundry	...stendere il bucato	**stehn**-day-ray eel boo-**kah**-toh
Is a full-service laundry nearby?	C'è una lavanderia qui vicino?	cheh **oo**-nah lah-vahn-deh-**ree**ah kwee vee-**chee**-noh

Is a self-service laundry nearby?	C'è una lavanderia automatica qui vicino?	cheh **oo**-nah lah-vahn-deh-**ree**ah ow-toh-**mah**-tee-kah kwee vee-**chee**-noh
I'd like to stay another night.	Vorrei fermarmi un'altra notte.	vor-**reh**ee fehr-**mar**-mee oo-**nahl**-trah **noh**-tay
We'd like to stay another night.	Vorremmo fermarci un'altra notte.	vor-**ray**-moh fehr-**mar**-chee oo-**nahl**-trah **noh**-tay
Where can I park?	Dove posso parcheggiare?	**doh**-vay **poh**-soh par-kay-**jah**-ray
When do you lock up?	A che ora chiude?	ah kay **oh**-rah kee**oo**-day
Please wake me at 7:00.	Mi svegli alle sette, per favore.	mee **zvayl**-yee **ah**-lay **seht**-tay pehr fah-**voh**-ray
Where do you go for lunch / dinner / coffee?	Dove si va per il pranzo / la cena / il caffè?	**doh**-vay see vah pehr eel **prahnt**-soh / lah **chay**-nah / eel kah-**fay**

Chill Out

Many hotel rooms in the Mediterranean part of Europe come with air-conditioning that you control—often with a stick (like a TV remote). Various sticks have basically the same features:

- fan icon (click to toggle through the wind power from light to gale).
- louver icon (click to choose: steady air flow or waves)
- snowflakes and sunshine icons (heat or cold, generally just one or the other is possible: cool in summer, heat in winter).
- two clock settings (to determine how many hours the air-conditioning will stay on before turning off, or stay off before turning on).
- temperature control (20 or 21 is a comfortable temperature in Celsius); see the thermometer on pg. 208.

SLEEPING

Hotel Hassles

Come with me.	*Venga con me.*	**vayn**-gah kohn may
I have / We have	*Ho / Abbiamo*	oh / ah-bee**ah**-moh
a problem in	*un problema*	oon proh-**blay**-mah
the room.	*con la camera.*	kohn lah **kah**-may-rah
bad odor	*cattivo odore*	kah-**tee**-voh oh-**doh**-ray
bugs	*insetti*	een-**seht**-tee
mice	*topi*	**toh**-pee
cockroaches	*scarafaggi*	skah-rah-**fah**-jee
prostitutes	*prostitute*	proh-stee-**too**-tay
I'm covered	*Sono pieno[a]*	**soh**-noh peeay-noh
with bug bites.	*di punture di*	dee poon-**too**-ray dee
	insetti.	een-**seht**-tee
The bed is too	*Il letto è troppo*	eel **leht**-toh eh **troh**-poh
soft / hard.	*morbido / duro.*	**mor**-bee-doh / **doo**-roh
I can't sleep.	*Non riesco a*	nohn ree**ay**-skoh ah
	dormire.	dor-**mee**-ray
The room is too...	*La camera è*	lah **kah**-may-rah eh
	troppo...	**troh**-poh
...hot / cold.	*...calda / fredda.*	**kahl**-dah / **fray**-dah
...noisy / dirty.	*...rumorosa /*	roo-moh-**roh**-zah /
	sporca.	**spor**-kah
I can't open...	*Non riesco*	nohn ree**ay**-skoh
	ad aprire...	ahd ah-**pree**-ray
I can't shut...	*Non riesco a*	nohn ree**ay**-skoh ah
	chiudere...	keeoo-**day**-ray
...the door /	*...la porta /*	lah **por**-tah /
the window.	*la finestra.*	lah fee-**nay**-strah
Air conditioner...	*Condiziona-*	kohn-deet-see-oh-nah-
	tore...	**toh**-ray
Lamp...	*Lampada...*	lahm-**pah**-dah
Lightbulb...	*Lampadina...*	lahm-pah-**dee**-nah
Electrical outlet...	*Presa...*	**pray**-zah
Key...	*Chiave...*	kee**ah**-vay
Lock...	*Serratura...*	say-rah-**too**-rah

Window...	*Finestra...*	fee-**nay**-strah
Faucet...	*Rubinetto...*	roo-bee-**nay**-toh
Sink...	*Lavabo...*	**lah**-vah-boh
Toilet...	*Toilette...*	twah-**leht**-tay
Shower...	*Doccia...*	**doh**-chah
...doesn't work.	*...non funziona.*	nohn foont-seeoh-nah
There is no hot water.	*Non c'è acqua calda.*	nohn cheh **ah**-kwah **kahl**-dah
When is the water hot?	*A che ora è calda l'acqua?*	ah kay **oh**-rah eh **kahl**-dah **lah**-kwah

Checking Out

When is check-out time?	*A che ora devo lasciare la camera?*	ah kay **oh**-rah **day**-voh lah-**shah**-ray lah **kah**-may-rah
I'll leave...	*Parto...*	**par**-toh
We'll leave...	*Partiamo...*	par-teeah-moh
...today / tomorrow.	*...oggi / domani.*	**oh**-jee / doh-**mah**-nee
...very early.	*...molto presto.*	**mohl**-toh **prehs**-toh
Can I pay now?	*Posso pagare subito?*	**poh**-soh pah-**gah**-ray **soo**-bee-toh
Can we pay now?	*Possiamo pagare subito?*	poh-seeah-moh pah-**gah**-ray **soo**-bee-toh
The bill, please.	*Il conto, per favore.*	eel **kohn**-toh pehr fah-**voh**-ray
Credit card O.K.?	*Carta di credito è O.K.?*	**kar**-tah dee **kray**-dee-toh eh "O.K."
Everything was great.	*Tutto magnifico.*	**too**-toh mahn-**yee**-fee-koh
I slept like a rock.	*Ho dormito come un sasso.*	oh dor-**mee**-toh **koh**-may oon **sah**-soh
Will you call my next hotel...?	*Può chiamare il mio prossimo hotel...?*	pwoh kee-**mah**-ray eel **mee**-oh **proh**-see-moh **oh**-tehl
...for tonight	*...per stasera*	pehr stah-**say**-rah

SLEEPING

...to make a reservation	...per fare una prenotazione	pehr **fah**-ray **oo**-nah pray-noh-taht-see**oh**-nay
...to confirm a reservation	...per confermare una prenotazione	pehr kohn-fehr-**mah**-ray **oo**-nah pray-noh-taht-see**oh**-nay
I will pay for the call.	Pago la chiamata.	**pah**-goh lah keeah-**mah**-tah
Can I...?	Posso...?	**poh**-soh
Can we...?	Possiamo...?	poh-see**ah**-moh
...leave baggage here until ___	...lasciare il bagaglio qui fino a ___	lah-**shah**-ray eel bah-**gahl**-yoh kwee **fee**-noh ah ___

I never tip beyond the included service charges in hotels or for hotel services.

Camping

camping	campeggio	kahm-**pay**-joh
campsite	piazzuola	pee-ahd-**zwoh**-lah
tent	tenda	**tayn**-dah
The nearest campground?	Il campeggio più vicino?	eel kahm-**pay**-joh pew vee-**chee**-noh
Can I...?	Posso...?	**poh**-soh
Can we...?	Possiamo...?	poh-see**ah**-moh
...camp here for one night	...campeggiare qui per una notte	kahm-pay-**jah**-ray kwee pehr **oo**-nah **noh**-tay
Do showers cost extra?	Costano extra le docce?	koh-**stah**-noh **ehk**-strah lay **doh**-chay
shower token	gettone per la doccia	jeht-**toh**-nay pehr lah **doh**-chah

In some Italian campgrounds and youth hostels, you must buy a *gettone* (token) to activate a coin-operated hot shower. It has a timer inside, like a parking meter. To avoid a sudden cold rinse, buy at least two *gettoni* before getting undressed.

EATING

Restaurants

Types of Restaurants

Italian food is one of life's pleasures. The Italians have an expression: "*A tavola non si invecchia*" (At the table, one does not age). Below is a guideline for restaurant types. Note that the first few names are sometimes interchangeable, and a *trattoria* can occasionally be more expensive than a *ristorante*. Always check the menu posted outside a restaurant to be sure.

Ristorante—A fine-dining establishment

Trattoria—Typically a family-owned place that serves home-cooked meals at moderate prices

Osteria—More informal, with large shared tables, good food, and wine

Pizzeria—A casual pizza joint that also offers pasta and more

Pizza Rustica—A cheap pizza shop that sells pizza by the weight or slice (often take-out only)

Rosticceria—A take-out or sit-down shop specializing in roasted meats

Tavola calda—Inexpensive hot/cold buffet-style restaurant

Bar—The neighborhood hangout that serves coffee, soft drinks, beer, liquor, snacks, and ready-made sandwiches.
Enoteca—Wine shop or wine bar that also serves snacks
Freeflow—A self-serve cafeteria
Autogrill—Cafeteria and snack bar, found at freeway rest stops and often in city centers (Ciao is a popular chain)
Locanda—A countryside restaurant serving simple local specialties

Finding a Restaurant

Where's a good...	*Dov'è un buon*	doh-**veh** oon bwohn
restaurant nearby?	*ristorante...*	ree-stoh-**rahn**-tay...
	qui vicino?	kwee vee-**chee**-noh
...cheap	*...economico*	ay-koh-**noh**-mee-koh
...local-style	*...con cucina*	kohn koo-**chee**-nah
	casereccia	kah-zay-**ray**-chah

KEY PHRASES: RESTAURANTS

Where's a good	*Dov'è un buon*	doh-**veh** oon bwohn
restaurant nearby?	*ristorante*	ree-stoh-**rahn**-tay
	qui vicino?	kwee vee-**chee**-noh
I'd like...	*Vorrei...*	vor-**reh**ee
We'd like...	*Vorremmo...*	vor-**ray**-moh
...a table for	*...una tavola*	**oo**-nah **tah**-voh-lah
one / two.	*per uno / due.*	pehr **oo**-noh / **doo**-ay
Non-smoking,	*Non fumare,*	nohn foo-**mah**-ray
if possible.	*se possibile.*	say poh-**see**-bee-lay
Is this seat free?	*È libero*	eh **lee**-bay-roh
	questo posto?	**kwehs**-toh **poh**-stoh
The menu	*Il menù*	eel may-**noo**
(in English),	*(in inglese),*	(een een-**glay**-zay),
please.	*per favore.*	pehr fah-**voh**-ray
Bill, please.	*Conto,*	**kohn**-toh
	per favore.	pehr fah-**voh**-ray
Credit card O.K.?	*Carta di*	**kar**-tah dee
	credito è O.K.?	**kray**-dee-toh eh "O.K."

EATING

...untouristy	...non per turisti	nohn pehr too-**ree**-stee
...vegetarian	...vegetariano	vay-jay-tah-ree**ah**-noh
...fast food (Italian-style)	...tavola calda	**tah**-voh-lah **kahl**-dah
...self-service buffet	...self-service	sehlf-**sehr**-vees
...Chinese	...cinese	chee-**nay**-zay
with terrace	con terrazza	kohn tay-**rahd**-zah
with a salad bar	con un banco delle insalate	kohn oon **bahn**-koh **dehl**-lay een-sah-**lah**-tay
with candles	con candele	kohn kahn-**day**-lay
romantic	romantico	roh-**mahn**-tee-koh
moderate price	a buon mercato	ah bwohn mer-**kah**-toh
to splurge	fare sfoggio	**fah**-ray **sfoh**-joh
Is it better than McDonald's?	È migliore di McDonald's?	eh meel-**yoh**-ray dee "McDonald's"

Getting a Table

What time does this open / close?	A che ora apre / chiude?	ah kay **oh**-rah **ah**-pray / kee**oo**-day
Are you open...?	È aperto...?	eh ah-**pehr**-toh
...today / tomorrow	...oggi / domani	**oh**-jee / doh-**mah**-nee
...for lunch / dinner	...per pranzo / cena	pehr **prahnt**-soh / **chay**-nah
Should I / we make reservations?	Mi / Ci consiglia prenotare una tavolo?	mee / chee kohn-**seel**-yah pray-noh-**tah**-ray **oo**-nah **tah**-voh-lah
I'd like...	Vorrei...	vor-**reh**ee
We'd like...	Vorremmo...	vor-**ray**-moh
...a table for one / two.	...una tavola per uno / due.	**oo**-nah **tah**-voh-lah pehr **oo**-noh / **doo**-ay
...to reserve a table for two people...	...prenotare un tavola per due persone...	pray-noh-**tah**-ray oon **tah**-voh-lah pehr **doo**-ay pehr-**soh**-nay
...for today / tomorrow	...per oggi / domani	pehr **oh**-jee / doh-**mah**-nee
...at 8:00 p.m.	...alle venti	**ah**-lay **vayn**-tee
My name is ___.	Mi chiamo ___.	mee kee**ah**-moh

I have a reservation for ___ people.	Ho una prenotazione per ___ persone.	oh **oo**-nah pray-noh-taht-see**oh**-nay pehr ___ pehr-**soh**-nay
I'd like to sit...	Vorrei sedermi...	vor-**reh**ee say-**dehr**-mee
We'd like to sit...	Vorremmo sederci...	vor-**ray**-moh say-**dehr**-chee
...inside / outside.	...dentro/ fuori.	**dehn**-troh / **fwoh**-ree
...by the window.	...vicino alla finestra.	vee-**chee**-noh **ah**-lah fee-**nay**-strah
...with a view.	...con la vista.	kohn lah **vee**-stah
...where it's quiet.	...a una tavola tranquilla.	ah **oo**-nah **tah**-voh-lah trahn-**kee**-loh
Non-smoking, if possible.	Non fumare, se possibile.	nohn foo-**mah**-ray say poh-**see**-bee-lay
Is this table free?	È libero questa tavolo?	eh **lee**-behr-oh **kwehs**-tah **tah**-voh-lah
Can I sit here?	Posso sedermi qui?	**poh**-soh say-**dehr**-mee kwee
Can we sit here?	Possiamo sederci qui?	poh-see**ah**-moh say-**dehr**-chee kwee

Better restaurants routinely take telephone reservations. Guidebooks include phone numbers, and the process is simple. If you want to eat at a normal European dinnertime (later than 7:30 p.m.), it's smart to call and reserve a table. Many of my favorite restaurants are filled with Americans at 7:30 p.m. and can feel like tourist traps. But if you drop in at (or reserve ahead for) 8:30 or 9:00 p.m., when the Italians are eating, they feel completely local.

The Menu

menu	menù	may-**noo**
tourist menu	menù turistico	may-**noo** too-**ree**-stee-koh
menu of the day	menù del giorno	may-**noo** dayl **jor**-noh
specialty of the house	specialità della casa	spay-chah-lee-**tah** **dehl**-lah **kah**-zah
breakfast	colazione	koh-laht-see**oh**-nay

lunch	*pranzo*	**prahnt**-soh
dinner	*cena*	**chay**-nah
appetizers	*antipasti*	ahn-tee-**pah**-stee
sandwiches	*panini*	pah-**nee**-nee
bread	*pane*	**pah**-nay
salad	*insalata*	een-sah-**lah**-tah
soup	*minestra, zuppa*	mee-**nehs**-trah, **tsoo**-pah
first course (pasta, soup)	*primo piatto*	**pree**-moh peeah-toh
main course (meat, fish)	*secondo piatto*	say-**kohn**-doh peeah-toh
side dishes	*contorni*	kohn-**tor**-nee
meat	*carni*	**kar**-nee
poultry	*pollame*	poh-**lah**-may
fish	*pesce*	**peh**-shay
seafood	*frutti di mare*	**froo**-tee dee **mah**-ray
vegetables	*legumi*	lay-**goo**-mee
cheeses	*formaggi*	for-**mah**-jee
desserts	*dolci*	**dohl**-chee
munchies (tapas)	*spuntini*	spoon-**tee**-nee
beverages	*bevande, bibite*	bay-**vahn**-day, **bee**-bee-tay
beer	*birra*	**beer**-rah
wines	*vini*	**vee**-nee
cover charge	*coperto*	koh-**pehr**-toh
service included	*servizio incluso*	sehr-**veet**-seeoh een-**kloo**-zoh
service not included	*servizio non incluso*	sehr-**veet**-seeoh nohn een-**kloo**-zoh
hot / cold	*caldo / freddo*	**kahl**-doh / **fray**-doh
with / and / or / without	*con / e / o / senza*	kohn / ay / oh / **sehn**-sah

Pay attention to the money-saving words in this chapter. Without them, Italy is a very expensive place to eat. Budget eaters do best in places with no or minimal service and cover charges, and by sticking to the *primo piatto* (first course dishes). A hearty minestrone and/or pasta fills the average American. Pricier restaurants are wise to this, and some don't allow you to eat without ordering the more expensive *secondo* course (note that secondo courses often consist of just the entrée listed, without any vegetables). Usually a good deal, a *menù del giorno* (menu of the day) offers you a choice of appetizer, entrée, and dessert (plus sometimes wine or mineral water) at a fixed price.

Ordering

waiter	*cameriere*	kah-may-ree**ay**-ray
waitress	*cameriera*	kah-may-ree**ay**-rah
I'm ready / We're ready to order.	*Sono pronto / Siamo pronti per ordinare.*	**soh**-noh **prohn**-toh / see**ah**-moh **prohn**-tee pehr or-dee-**nah**-ray
I'd like / We'd like...	*Vorrei / Vorremmo...*	vor-**reh**ee / vor-**ray**-moh
...just a drink.	*...soltanto qualcosa da bere.*	sohl-**tahn**-toh kwahl-**koh**-zah dah **bay**-ray
...a snack.	*...uno spuntino.*	**oon**-oh spoon-**tee**-noh
...just a salad.	*...solo un'insalata.*	**soh**-loh oon-een-sah-**lah**-tah
...a half portion.	*...una mezza porzione.*	**oo**-nah **mehd**-zah port-see**oh**-nay
...only a pasta dish.	*...solo un primo piatto.*	**soh**-loh oon **pree**-moh pee**ah**-toh
...a tourist menu.	*...un menù turistico.*	oon may-**noo** too-**ree**-stee-koh
...to see the menu.	*...vedere il menù.*	vay-**day**-ray eel may-**noo**
...to order.	*...ordinare.*	or-dee-**nah**-ray
...to pay.	*...pagare.*	pah-**gah**-ray
...to throw up.	*...vomitare.*	voh-mee-**tah**-ray
Do you have...?	*Avete...?*	ah-**vay**-tay
...a menu in English	*...un menù in inglese*	oon may-**noo** een een-**glay**-zay

EATING

...a lunch special	...un piatto speciale per il pranzo	oon pee**ah**-toh spay-chee**ah**-lay pehr eel **prahnt**-soh
What do you recommend?	Che cosa raccomanda?	kay **koh**-zah rah-koh-**mahn**-dah
What's your favorite dish?	Qual'è il suo piatto preferito?	kwah-**leh** eel **soo**-oh pee**ah**-toh preh-feh-**ree**-toh
Is it...?	È...?	eh
...good	...buono	**bwoh**-noh
...expensive	...caro	**kah**-roh
...light	...leggero	lay-**jay**-roh
...filling	...sostanzioso	soh-stahnt-see**oh**-zoh
What is that?	Che cosa è quello?	kay **koh**-zah eh **kway**-loh
What is...?	Che cosa c'è...?	kay **koh**-zah cheh
...local	...di locale	dee loh-**kah**-lay
...fresh	...di fresco	dee **fray**-skoh
...cheap and filling	...di economico e sostanzioso	dee ay-koh-**noh**-mee-koh ay soh-stahnt-see**oh**-zoh
...fast	...di veloce	dee vay-**loh**-chay
Can we split this and have an extra plate?	Possiamo dividerlo e avere un altro piatto?	poh-see**ah**-moh dee-vee-**dehr**-loh ay ah-**vay**-ray oon **ahl**-troh pee**ah**-toh
I've changed my mind.	Ho cambiato idea.	oh kahm-bee**ah**-toh ee-**day**-ah
Nothing with eyeballs.	Niente con gli occhi.	nee**ehn**-tay kohn lyee **oh**-kee
Can I substitute (something) for the ___?	Posso sostituire (qualcosa d'altro) per il ___?	**poh**-soh soh-stee-**twee**-ray (kwahl-**koh**-zah **dahl**-troh) pehr eel
Can I / Can we get it "to go"?	Posso / Possiamo averlo da portar via?	**poh**-soh / poh-see**ah**-moh ah-**vehr**-loh dah **por**-tar **vee**-ah
"To go"? (for the road)	Da portar via?	dah **por**-tar **vee**-ah

To summon a waiter, ask *"Per favore?"* (Please?). The waiter brings a menu (*menù*) and asks what you'd like to drink (*Da bere?*). When ready to take your order, the waiter will ask, *"Prego?"* He'll often expect you to order multiple courses (he'll ask *"E dopo?"*—"And then?"), but it's O.K. to just get one course—just say *"È tutto."* (That's all). When you're finished, place your utensils on your plate with the handles pointing to your right as the Italians do. This tells the waiter you're done. He'll confirm by asking if you're finished (*Finito?*). He'll usually ask if you'd like dessert (*Qualcosa di dolce?*) and coffee (*Un caffè?*), and if you want anything else (*Altro?*). You ask for the bill: *"Il conto, per favore."*

Tableware and Condiments

plate	piatto	pee**ah**-toh
extra plate	un altro piatto	oon **ahl**-troh pee**ah**-toh
napkin	tovagliolo	toh-vahl-**yoh**-loh
silverware	posate	poh-**zah**-tay
knife	coltello	kohl-**tehl**-loh
fork	forchetta	for-**kay**-tah
spoon	cucchiaio	koo-kee**ah**-yoh
cup	tazza	**tahd**-zah
glass	bicchiere	bee-kee**ay**-ray
carafe	caraffa	kah-**rah**-fah
water	acqua	**ah**-kwah
bread	pane	**pah**-nay
breadsticks	grissini	gree-**see**-nee
butter	burro	**boo**-roh
margarine	margarina	mar-gah-**ree**-nah
salt / pepper	sale / pepe	**sah**-lay / **pay**-pay
sugar	zucchero	**tsoo**-kay-roh
artificial sweetener	dolcificante	dohl-chee-fee-**kahn**-tay
honey	miele	mee**ay**-lay
mustard	senape	**say**-nah-pay
ketchup	ketchup	"ketchup"
mayonnaise	maionese	mah-yoh-**nay**-zay
toothpick	stuzzicadente	stood-see-kah-**dehn**-tay

EATING

The Food Arrives

Is this included with the meal?	*È incluso nel pasto questo?*	eh een-**kloo**-zoh nayl **pah**-stoh **kweh**-stoh
I did not order this.	*Io questo non l'ho ordinato.*	**ee**oh **kweh**-stoh nohn loh or-dee-**nah**-toh
We did not order this.	*Noi questo non l'abbiamo ordinato.*	**noh**ee **kweh**-stoh nohn lah-bee**ah**-moh or-dee-**nah**-toh
Heat it up?	*Lo può scaldare?*	loh pwoh skahl-**dah**-ray
A little.	*Un po.'*	oon poh
More. / Another.	*Un altro po.' / Un altro.*	oon **ahl**-troh poh / oon **ahl**-troh
The same.	*Lo stesso.*	loh **stehs**-soh
Enough.	*Basta.*	**bah**-stah
Finished.	*Finito.*	fee-**nee**-toh
I'm full.	*Sono sazio.*	soh-noh **saht**-seeoh

After bringing your meal, your server might wish you a cheery *"Buon appetito!"* (pronounced *bwohn ah-pay-tee-toh*).

Complaints

This is...	*Questo è...*	**kweh**-stoh eh
...dirty.	*...sporco.*	**spor**-koh
...greasy.	*...grasso.*	**grah**-soh
...too salty.	*...troppo salato.*	**troh**-poh sah-**lah**-toh
...undercooked.	*...troppo crudo.*	**troh**-poh **kroo**-doh
...overcooked.	*...troppo cotto.*	**troh**-poh **koh**-toh
...inedible.	*...immangiabile.*	eem-mahn-**jah**-bee-lay
...cold.	*...freddo.*	**fray**-doh
Do any of your customers return?	*Ritornano i vostri clienti?*	ree-**tor**-nah-noh ee **voh**-stree klee-**ehn**-tee
Yuck!	*Che schifo!*	kay **skee**-foh

EATING

Compliments to the Chef

Yummy!	*Buono!*	**bwoh**-noh
Delicious!	*Delizioso!*	day-leet-see**oh**-zoh
Divinely good!	*Una vera bontà!*	**oo**-nah **vay**-rah bohn-**tah**
My compliments to the chef!	*Complimenti al cuoco!*	kohm-plee-**mayn**-tee ahl koo**oh**-koh
I love Italian food / this food.	*Adoro la cucina italiana / questo piatto.*	ah-**doh**-roh lah koo-**chee**-nah ee-tah-lee**ah**-nah / **kwehs**-toh pee**ah**-toh
Better than mom's cooking.	*Meglio della cucina di mia mamma.*	**mehl**-yoh **dehl**-lah koo-**chee**-nah dee **mee**-ah **mah**-mah

Paying for Your Meal

The bill, please.	*Il conto, per favore.*	eel **kohn**-toh pehr fah-**voh**-ray
Together.	*Conto unico.*	**kohn**-toh **oo**-nee-koh
Separate.	*Conto separato.*	**kohn**-toh say-pah-**rah**-toh
Credit card O.K.?	*Carta di credito è O.K.?*	**kar**-tah dee **kray**-dee-toh eh "O.K."
Is there a cover charge?	*Si paga per il coperto?*	see **pah**-gah pehr eel koh-**pehr**-toh
Is service included?	*È incluso il servizio?*	eh een-**kloo**-zoh eel sehr-**veet**-seeoh
This is not correct.	*Questo non è giusto.*	**kweh**-stoh nohn eh **joo**-stoh
Explain it?	*Lo può spiegare?*	loh pwoh speeay-**gah**-ray
Can you explain / itemize the bill?	*Può spiegare / dettagliare il conto?*	pwoh speeay-**gah**-ray / day-tahl-**yah**-ray eel **kohn**-toh
What if I wash the dishes?	*E se lavassi i piatti?*	ay say lah-**vah**-see ee pee**ah**-tee

Is tipping expected?	*Bisogna lasciare una mancia?*	bee-**sohn**-yah lah-**shah**-ray **oo**-nah **mahn**-chah
What percent?	*Che percentuale?*	kay pehr-chehn-too**ah**-lay
tip	*mancia*	**mahn**-chah
Keep the change.	*Tenga il resto.*	**tayn**-gah eel **rehs**-toh
This is for you.	*Questo è per lei.*	**kweh**-stoh eh pehr **leh**ee
Could I have a receipt, please?	*Posso avere una ricevuta, per favore?*	**poh**-soh ah-**vay**-ray **oo**-nah ree-chay-**voo**-tah pehr fah-**voh**-ray

Most menus list the *coperto* (cover charge) and *servizio* (service) charge. There's no need to tip beyond that, but if you're happy with the service, toss in a euro or two per person. If there's no service charge, tip around 10 percent.

If you're uncertain whether to tip, ask another customer if tipping is expected (*Bisogna lasciare una mancia?*).

In Italian bars and freeway rest stops, pay first at the *cassa* (cash register), then take your receipt to the counter to get your food. There's no need to tip.

Special Concerns

In a Hurry

I'm / We're in a hurry.	*Sono / Siamo di fretta.*	**soh**-noh / see**ah**-moh dee **fray**-tah
I need to be served quickly. Is that a problem?	*Ho bisogno di essere servito[a] rapidamente. È un problema?*	oh bee-**zohn**-yoh dee eh-**say**-ray sehr-**vee**-toh rah-pee-dah-**mehn**-tay eh oon proh-**blay**-mah
We need to be served quickly. Is that a problem?	*Avremmo bisogno di essere serviti rapidamente. È un problema?*	ah-**vray**-moh bee-**zohn**-yoh dee eh-**say**-ray sehr-**vee**-tee rah-pee-dah-**mehn**-tay eh oon proh-**blay**-mah

EATING

| I must / We must leave in a half hour / one hour. | Devo / Dobbiamo andarcene tra mezz'ora / un'ora. | **day**-voh / doh-bee**ah**-moh ahn-dar-**chay**-nay trah med-**zoh**-rah / oo-**noh**-rah |
| When will the food be ready? | Tra quanto è pronto il cibo? | trah **kwahn**-toh eh **prohn**-toh eel **chee**-boh |

Dietary Restrictions

I'm allergic to...	Sono allergico[a] al...	**soh**-noh ahl-**lehr**-jee-koh ahl
I cannot / He cannot / She cannot eat...	Non posso / Lui non può / lei non può mangiare...	nohn **poh**-soh / lwee nohn pwoh / **leh**ee nohn pwoh mahn-**jah**-ray
...dairy products.	...latticini.	lah-tee-**chee**-nee
...wheat.	...frumento.	froo-**mehn**-toh
...meat / pork.	...carne / maiale.	**kar**-nay / mah-**yah**-lay
...salt / sugar.	...sale / zucchero.	**sah**-lay / **tsoo**-kay-roh
...shellfish.	...molluschi e crostacei.	moh-**loos**-kee ay kroh-**stah**-chayee
...spicy foods.	...cibo piccante.	**chee**-boh pee-**kahn**-tay
...nuts.	...noci e altra frutta secca.	**noh**-chee ay **ahl**-trah **froo**-tah **say**-kah
I am diabetic.	Ho il diabete.	oh eel deeah-**bay**-tay
I'd like / We'd like a...	Vorrei / Vorremmo un...	vor-**reh**ee / vor-**ray**-moh oon
...low-fat meal.	...pasto a basso contenuto calorico.	**pah**-stoh ah **bah**-soh kohn-tay-**noo**-toh kah-**loh**-ree-koh
...kosher meal.	...pasto kasher.	**pah**-stoh **kah**-shehr
No salt / sugar.	Senza sale / zucchero.	**sehn**-sah **sah**-lay / **tsoo**-kay-roh
I eat only insects.	Mangio solo insetti.	**mahn**-joh **soh**-loh een-**seht**-tee
No fat.	Senza grassi.	**sehn**-sah **grah**-see
Minimal fat.	Pochi grassi.	**poh**-kee **grah**-see
Low cholesterol.	Basso colesterolo.	**bah**-soh koh-lay-stay-**roh**-loh
No caffeine.	Senza caffeina.	**sehn**-sah kah-fay**ee**-nah

No alcohol.	Niente alcool.	neee**ehn**-tay **ahl**-kohl
Organic.	Biologico.	bee-oh-**loo**-jee-koh
I'm a...	Sono un...	**soh**-noh oon
...vegetarian.	...vegetariano[a].	vay-jay-tah-ree**ah**-noh
...strict vegetarian.	...strettamente vegetariano[a].	stray-tah-**mayn**-tay vay-jay-tah-ree**ah**-noh
...carnivore.	...carnivoro[a].	kar-**nee**-voh-roh
...big eater.	...mangione.	mahn-jee**oh**-nay
Is any meat or animal fat used in this?	Contiene carne o grassi animali?	kohn-teee**ay**-nay **kar**-nay oh **grah**-see ah-nee-**mah**-lee

Children

Do you have...?	Avete...?	ah-**vay**-tay
...a children's portions	...un platto per i bambini	oon peeah-toh pehr ee bahm-**bee**-nee
...a half portion	...una mezza porzione	**oo**-nah **mehd**-zah port-seee**oh**-nay
...a high chair / booster seat	...un seggiolone / seggiolino	oon seh-joh-**loh**-nay / seh-joh-**lee**-noh
plain noodles	della pasta in bianco	**dehl**-lah **pah**-stah een beee**ahn**-koh
plain rice	del riso in bianco	dehl **ree**-zoh een beee**ahn**-koh
with butter	con il burro	kohn eel **boo**-roh
no sauce	senza sugo	**sehn**-sah **soo**-goh
with sauce / dressing on the side	con il sugo / il condimento a parte	kohn eel **soo**-goh / eel kohn-dee-**mehn**-toh ah **par**-tay
pizza	pizza	**peed**-zah
...cheese only	...Margherita	mar-gehr-**ee**-tah
...pepperoni and cheese	...diavolo	deee**ah**-voh-loh
cheese sandwich...	un panino... al formaggio	oon pah-**nee**-noh... ahl for-**mah**-joh
...toasted	...scaldato	skahl-**dah**-toh

hot dog	*wurstel*	**woor**-stehl
hamburger	*hamburger*	**ahm**-boor-ger
cheeseburger	*hamburger con formaggi*	**ahm**-boor-ger kohn for-**mah**-jee
French fries	*patate fritte*	pah-**tah**-tay **free**-tay
ketchup	*ketchup*	"ketchup"
crackers	*crackers*	"crackers"
Nothing spicy.	*Niente di piccante.*	neee**ehn**-tay dee pee-**kahn**-tay
Not too hot.	*Non troppo caldo.*	nohn **troh**-poh **kahl**-doh
Please keep the food separate	*Per favore tenete separato*	pehr fah-**voh**-ray tay-**nay**-tay say-pah-**rah**-toh
on the plate.	*il cibo nel piatto.*	eel **chee**-boh nehl peeah-toh
He / She will share our meal.	*Lui / Lei mangia parte del nostro pasto.*	lwee / **leh**ee **mahn**-jah **par**-tay dehl **noh**-stroh **pah**-stoh
They will share our meal.	*Loro mangiano parte del nostro pasto.*	**loh**-roh mahn-**jah**-noh **par**-tay dehl **noh**-stroh **pah**-stoh
Please bring the food quickly.	*Per favore ci porti da mangiare velocemente.*	pehr fah-**voh**-ray chee **por**-tee dah mahn-**jah**-ray vay-loh-chay-**mehn**-tay
Can I / Can we have an extra...?	*Potrei / Potremmo avere un altro...*	poh-**tray**ee / poh-**tray**-moh ah-**vay**-ray oon **ahl**-troh
...plate	*...piatto*	peeah-toh
...cup	*...tazza*	**tahd**-zah
...spoon / fork	*...cucchiaio / forchetta*	koo-keeah-yoh / for-**kay**-tah
Can I / Can we have two extra...?	*Potrei / Potremmo avere altri due...?*	poh-**tray**ee / poh-**tray**-moh ah-**vay**-ray **ahl**-tree **doo**-ay
...plates	*...piatti*	peeah-tee
...cups	*...tazze*	**tahd**-zay
...spoons / forks	*...cucchiai / forchette*	koo-keeah-ee / for-**kay**-tay
Small milk (in a plastic cup).	*Un po di latte (in una tazza di plastica).*	oon poh dee **lah**-tay (een **oo**-nah **tahd**-zah dee **plah**-stee-kah

EATING

straw / straws	*cannuccia / cannucce*	kah-**noo**-chah / kah-**noo**-chay
More napkins, please.	*Degli altri tovaglioli, per favore.*	**day**-lee **ahl**-tree toh-vahl-**yoh**-lee pehr fah-**voh**-ray
Sorry for the mess.	*Scusi per il pasticcio.*	**skoo**-zee pehr eel pah-**stee**-choh

Don't expect to find peanut butter sandwiches in Italy. Italian kids would rather have a sandwich with Nutella (*un panino con la Nutella*), the popular chocolate-hazelnut spread.

What's Cooking?

Breakfast?

breakfast	*colazione*	koh-laht-see**oh**-nay
bread	*pane*	**pah**-nay
roll	*brioche*	bree-**ohsh**
croissant	*cornetto*	kor-**nay**-toh
toast	*toast*	tohst
butter	*burro*	**boo**-roh
jam	*marmellata*	mar-mehl-**lah**-tah
jelly	*gelatina*	jay-lah-**tee**-nah
milk	*latte*	**lah**-tay
coffee / tea (see Drinking)	*caffè / tè*	kah-**feh** / teh
Is breakfast included?	*La colazione è inclusa?*	lah koh-laht-see**oh**-nay eh een-**kloo**-zah

What's Probably Not For Breakfast

omelet	omelette, frittata	oh-may-**leht**-tay, free-**tah**-tah
eggs...	uova...	**woh**-vah
...fried	...fritte	**free**-tay
...scrambled	...strapazzate	strah-pahd-**zah**-tay
boiled egg...	uovo alla coque...	**who**-voh **ah**-lah kohk
...soft / hard	...molle / sodo	**moh**-lay / **soh**-doh
ham	prosciutto cotto	proh-**shoo**-toh **koh**-toh
cheese	formaggio	for-**mah**-joh
yogurt	yogurt	**yoh**-goort
cereal	cereali	chay-ray-**ah**-lee
pastry	pasticcini	pah-stee-**chee**-nee
fruit juice	succo di frutta	**soo**-koh dee **froo**-tah
fresh orange juice	spremuta di arancia	spray-**moo**-tah dee ah-**rahn**-chah
hot chocolate	cioccolata calda	choh-koh-**lah**-tah **kahl**-dah

Italian breakfasts, like Italian bath towels, are small: coffee and a roll with butter and marmalade. The strong coffee is often mixed about half-and-half with milk. At your hotel, refills are usually free. The delicious red orange juice is made from Sicilian blood oranges (*arancia tarocco*). Local open-air markets thrive in the morning, and a picnic breakfast followed by a *cappuccino* in a bar is a good option.

Appetizers

antipasto misto	ahn-tee-**pah**-stoh **mee**-stoh	salami and marinated vegetables
bruschetta	broo-**skay**-tah	toast brushed w/ olive oil and garlic or chopped tomatoes

KEY PHRASES: WHAT'S COOKING

food	*cibo*	**chee**-boh
breakfast	*colazione*	koh-laht-see**oh**-nay
lunch	*pranzo*	**prahnt**-soh
dinner	*cena*	**chay**-nah
bread	*pane*	**pah**-nay
cheese	*formaggio*	for-**mah**-joh
soup	*minestra,*	mee-**nehs**-trah,
	zuppa	**tsoo**-pah
salad	*insalata*	een-sah-**lah**-tah
meat	*carni*	**kar**-nee
chicken	*pollo*	**poh**-loh
fish	*pesce*	**peh**-shay
fruit	*frutta*	**froo**-tah
vegetables	*legumi*	lay-**goo**-mee
dessert	*dolci*	**dohl**-chee
Delicious!	*Delizioso!*	day-leet-see**oh**-zoh

carciofi alla Giudia / Romana	kar-**choh**-fee **ah**-lah **joo**-dah / roh-**mah**-nah	artichokes—deep-fried (Jewish style) or stuffed with garlic, mint, and parsley (Roman style)
carpaccio	kar-**pah**-choh	thinly sliced air-cured beef served with olive oil, lemon, and parmesan
crostini	kroh-**stee**-nee	toast topped with liver pates and other pastes
frittata con le erbe	free-**tah**-tah kohn lay **ehr**-bay	egg scrambled with fresh herbs, then pan-fried
prosciutto e melone / fichi	proh-**shoo**-toh ay may-**loh**-nay / **fee**-kee	air-cured ham wrapped around melon / fresh figs
sarde in saor	**sar**-day een **sah**or	sardines marinated with onions
salumi misti	sah-**loo**-mee **mee**-stee	assortment of sliced, cured meats
spizziccare	speed-zee-**kah**-ray	snack
vitello tonato	vee-**tehl**-loh toh-**nah**-toh	thin-sliced roasted veal w/ tuna-caper mayonnaise

Pizza and Quick Meals

For fresh, fast, and frugal pizza, *Pizza Rustica* shops offer the cheapest hot meal in any Italian town, selling pizza by the slice (*pezzo*) or weight (*etto* = 100 grams, around a quarter pound). *Due etti* (200 grams) makes a good light lunch. You can always get it to go (*"Da portar via"*—for the road), or, if there are seats, you can eat it on the spot. For handier pizza, nearly any bar has lousy, microwavable pizza snacks. To get cold pizza warmed up, say, *"Calda, per favore"* (Hot, please). To get an extra plate, ask for a *"Un altro piatto."* Here are some pizza words:

acciughe	ah-**choo**-gay	anchovies
alla diavola	**ah**-lah dee**ah**-voh-lah	spicy
bianca, ciaccina	bee**ahn**-kah, chah-**chee**-nah	"white" pizza (no tomato sauce)
calzone	kahlt-**soh**-nay	folded pizza with various fillings
capricciosa	kah-pree-**choh**-zah	means "chef's choice"— usually ham, mushrooms, olives, and artichokes
carciofi	kar-**choh**-fee	artichokes
funghi	**foong**-gee	mushrooms
Margherita	mar-gehr-**ee**-tah	cheese and tomato sauce
melanzane	may-lahnt-**sah**-nay	eggplant
Napoletana	nah-poh-lay-**tah**-nah	cheese, anchovies, and tomato sauce
peperoni	pay-pehr-**oh**-nee	green or red peppers (not sausage!)
porcini	pohr-**chee**-nee	porcini mushrooms
prosciutto	proh-**shoo**-toh	ham
quattro stagioni	**kwah**-troh stah-jee**oh**-nee	four toppings on separate quarters of a pizza
ripieno	ree-pee**ay**-noh	stuffed
salame piccante	sah-**lah**-may pee-**kahn**-tay	pepperoni

salsiccia	sahl-**see**-chah	sausage
Siciliana	see-chee-leea**ah**-nah	capers and olives
vegetariana,	vay-jay-tah-reea**ah**-nah	veggie
ortolana	or-toh-**lah**-nah	

For other quick, tasty meals, drop by a *Rosticceria* deli, where you'll find a cafeteria-style display of reasonably priced food. Get it "to go" or grab a seat and eat.

Say Cheese

cheese	*formaggio*	for-**mah**-joh
fresh, mild, and soft	*fresco*	**fray**-skoh
aged, sharp, and hard	*stagionato*	stah-joh-**nah**-toh
cheese plate	*piatto di formaggi misti*	peea**ah**-toh dee for-**mah**-jee **mee**-stee
Can I try a taste?	*Posso avere un'assagio?*	**poh**-soh ah-**vay**-ray oo-nah-**sah**-joh

Italian Cheeses

asiago	ah-zee**ah**-goh	hard, sharp, aged cow's milk cheese
di capra	dee **kah**-prah	goat cheese
fontina	fohn-**tee**-nah	creamy, nutty, gruyere-style cheese
gorgonzola	gor-gohnt-**sohl**-lah	blue-veined cheese, either creamy (*dolce*) or aged and hard
mascarpone	mahs-kar-**poh**-nay	sweet, buttery dessert cheese
mozzarella	mohd-zah-**rehl**-lah	handmade cheese from water buffalo
bocconcini	boh-kohn-**chee**-nee	small balls of mozzarella
parmigiano	par-mee-**jah**-noh	hard cheese with a nutty flavor

EATING

pecorino	pay-koh-**ree**-noh	sheep's milk cheese, soft and mild or aged and sharp
provolone	proh-voh-**loh**-nay	rich, firm, aged cow's milk cheese
ricotta	ree-**koht**-tah	soft, airy cheese made from whey
stracchino	strah-**kee**-noh	spreadable, soft cow's milk cheese
taleggio	tah-**lay**-joh	rich, creamy cheese

If ordering *gorgonzola* or *pecorino* cheese, specify if you'd like it *fresco* (soft and mild) or *stagionato* (hard and sharp).

Sandwiches

I'd like a sandwich.	*Vorrei un panino.*	vor-**reh**ee oon pah-**nee**-noh
We'd like two sandwiches.	*Vorremmo due panini.*	vor-**ray**-moh doo-ay pah-**nee**-nee
small sandwiches	*tramezzini*	trah-mehd-**zee**-nee
toasted ham and cheese	*toast*	"toast"
toasted	*tostato*	toh-**stah**-toh
cheese	*formaggio*	for-**mah**-joh
chicken	*pollo*	**poh**-loh
egg salad	*insalata con uova*	een-sah-**lah**-tah kohn **woh**-vah
fish	*pesce*	**peh**-shay
ham	*prosciutto*	proh-**shoo**-toh
pork	*porchetta*	por-**kay**-tah
salami	*salame*	sah-**lah**-may
tuna	*tonno*	**toh**-noh
turkey	*tacchino*	tah-**kee**-noh
lettuce	*lattuga*	lah-**too**-gah
mayonnaise	*maionese*	mah-yoh-**nay**-zay
tomatoes	*pomodori*	poh-moh-**doh**-ree
mustard	*senape*	**say**-nah-pay

ketchup	*ketchup*	"ketchup"
onions	*cipolle*	chee-**poh**-lay
Does this come	*Si mangia*	see **mahn**-jah
cold or warm?	*freddo o caldo?*	**fray**-doh oh **kahl**-doh
Heated, please.	*Caldo, per*	**kahl**-doh pehr
	favore.	fah-**voh**-ray

Many bars sell small, ready-made sandwiches called
tramezzini. These crustless white bread sandwiches,
displayed behind glass, come with a variety of fillings (such
as shrimp) mixed with a mayonnaise dressing. Two or three
make a fast, easy meal. *Panini,* made from heartier bread
with meat, cheese, and veggie combinations, can be delicious toasted. Say, "*Calda, per favore*" (Heated, please).
Prices are usually posted. Pay the cashier for the sandwich
and your beverage, then give your receipt to the person
behind the bar to get your food.

   In central Italy, *porchetta* stands serve tasty rolls
stuffed with slices of roasted suckling pig.

If You Knead Bread

bread	*pane*	**pah**-nay
whole-grain bread	*pane*	**pah**-nay
	integrale	een-tay-**grah**-lay
olive bread	*pane di olive*	**pah**-nay dee oh-**lee**-vay
rye bread	*pane di segale*	**pah**-nay dee say-**gah**-lay
brown bread	*pane scuro*	**pah**-nay **skoo**-roh
Tuscan bread	*pane Toscano*	**pah**-nay toh-**skah**-noh
(unsalted)		
breadsticks	*grissini*	gree-**see**-nee

Every region of Italy has its own bread, highly prized by
the locals. We say "good as gold," but the Italians say,
"good as bread."

Bread Specialties

focaccia	foh-**kah**-chah	thick Ligurian flatbread, baked plain or with rosemary, onion, or cheese
piadina	peeah-**dee**-nah	soft, flat bread stuffed with various vegetables, meat, and cheese
schiacciata	skah-**chah**-tah	pizza-like flatbread sprinkled w/ oil and salt

Soups and Salads

soup	minestra, zuppa	mee-**nehs**-trah, **tsoo**-pah
soup of the day	zuppa del giorno	**tsoo**-pah dayl **jor**-noh
broth...	brodo...	**broh**-doh
...chicken	...di pollo	dee **poh**-loh
...beef	...di carne	dee **kar**-nay
...vegetable	...di verdura	dee vehr-**doo**-rah
...with noodles	...con pastina	kohn pah-**stee**-nah
...with rice	...con riso	kohn **ree**-zoh
vegetable soup	minestrone	mee-nay-**stroh**-nay
salad...	insalata...	een-sah-**lah**-tah
...green	...verde	**vehr**-day
...mixed	...mista	**mee**-stah
...with ham and cheese	...con prosciutto e formaggio	kohn proh-**shoo**-toh ay for-**mah**-joh
...with egg	...con uova	kohn **woh**-vah
lettuce	lattuga	lah-**too**-gah
tomatoes	pomodori	poh-moh-**doh**-ree
onion	cipolla	chee-**poh**-lah
cucumbers	cetrioli	chay-treeoh-lee
oil / vinegar	olio / aceto	**oh**-leeoh / ah-**chay**-toh
tray with oil and vinegar	oliera	oh-leeay-ah

EATING

| What is in this salad? | *Che cosa c'è in questa insalata?* | kay **koh**-zah cheh een **kweh**-stah een-sah-**lah**-tah |
| dressing on the side | *condimento a parte* | kohn-dee-**mehn**-toh ah **par**-tay |

Created in Tuscany, *ribollita* is a stew of white beans, veggies, and olive oil, layered with day-old bread.

In Italian restaurants, salad dressing is normally just the oil and vinegar at the table (if it's missing, ask for the *oliera*). Salad bars at fast food restaurants and *autostrada* rest stops can be a good budget bet.

Salad Specialties

insalata caprese	een-sah-**lah**-tah kah-**pray**-say	sliced tomato topped with fresh mozzarella, basil leaves, and olive oil
insalata di mare	een-sah-**lah**-tah dee **mah**-ray	chilled, cooked seafood tossed with parsley, lemon, and olive oil
insalata russa (Russian salad)	een-sah-**lah**-tah **roo**-sah	vegetable salad with mayonnaise
panzanella	pahnt-sah-**nehl**-lah	chunks of day-old bread, chopped tomatoes, onions, and basil tossed in a light vinaigrette

Pasta

Italy is the land of *pasta,* with more than 500 varieties. While there are a few differences in ingredients, the big deal is basically the shape. Watch for *rigatoni* (little tubes), *cannelloni* (big tubes), *fettuccine* (long, flat egg noodles), *farfalle* (butterfly-shaped pasta), *gnocchi* (shell-shaped, hand-rolled noodles made from potatoes), *linguine* (thin, flat noodles), *penne* (angle-cut tubes), *rotelli* (wheel-

EATING

shaped), *tagliatelle* (long, flat noodles), *tortellini* (small, C-shaped pasta filled with meat or cheese), *pici* (rough-cut thick twists), *bucatini* (hollow, thicker spaghetti), *orecchiette* (ear-shaped), *radiatore* (radiator-shaped), and surprise... *spaghetti*. Once you've decided on the pasta type, you'll need to top it with something. Here are your options:

Pasta Sauces

ai funghi	**ah**ee **foong**-gee	with porcini mushrooms
alfredo	ahl-**fray**-doh	butter, cream, and parmesan
amatriciana	ah-mah-tree-chee**ah**-nah	Roman-style with bacon, tomato, chili peppers, and onion
arrabbiata (literally "angry style")	ah-rah-bee**ah**-tah	spicy tomato sauce with chili peppers
Bolognese	boh-lohn-**yay**-zay	meat and tomato sauce
burro e salvia	**boo**-roh ay **sahl**-veeah	butter and sage
carbonara	kar-boh-**nah**-rah	bacon, egg, cheese, and pepper
in brodo	een **broh**-doh	in broth
marinara	mah-ree-**nah**-rah	tomato and garlic
panna	**pah**-nah	cream
seafood	pehs-kah-**toh**-rah	pescatora
pesto, Genovese	**pehs**-toh, jay-noh-**vay**-zay	olive oil, garlic, pine nuts, and basil
pomodoro	poh-moh-**doh**-roh	tomato only
puttanesca (literally "harlot")	poo-tah-**nays**-kah	zesty, spicy tomato sauce
quattro formaggi	**kwah**-troh for-**mah**-jee	four cheeses
ragù	rah-**goo**	meaty tomato sauce
sugo	**soo**-goh	sauce, usually tomato
vongole	**vohn**-goh-lay	with clams and spices

EATING

Seafood

seafood	*frutti di mare*	**froo**-tee dee **mah**-ray
assorted seafood	*misto di frutti di mare*	**mee**-stoh dee **froo**-tee dee **mah**-ray
fish	*pesce*	**peh**-shay
anchovies	*acciughe*	ah-**choo**-gay
barnacles	*balani*	bah-**lah**-nee
bream (fish)	*orata*	oh-**rah**-tah
clams	*vongole*	**vohn**-goh-lay
cod	*merluzzo*	mehr-**lood**-zoh
crab	*granchio*	**grahn**-keeoh
crayfish	*gambero, aragosta*	gahm-**bay**-roh, ah-rah-**goh**-stah
cuttlefish	*seppie*	**sehp**-eeay
herring	*aringa*	ah-**reeng**-gah
lobster	*aragosta*	ah-rah-**goh**-stah
mussels	*cozze*	**kohd**-zay
octopus	*polipo, polpo*	**poh**-lee-poh, **pohl**-poh
oysters	*ostriche*	**ohs**-tree-kay
prawns	*scampi, gamberi*	**skahm**-pee, gahm-**bay**-ree
salmon	*salmone*	sahl-**moh**-nay
sardines	*sardine*	sar-**dee**-nay
scad (like mackerel)	*sgombro*	**sgohm**-broh
scallops	*capesante*	kah-pay-**zahn**-tay
sea bass	*branzino*	brahnt-**see**-noh
shrimp	*gamberetti*	gahm-bay-**ray**-tee
sole	*sogliola*	sohl-**yoh**-lah
squid	*calamari*	kah-lah-**mah**-ree
swordfish	*pesce spada*	**peh**-shay **spah**-dah
tiger shrimp	*gamberoni*	gahm-bay-**roh**-nee
trout	*trota*	**troh**-tah
tuna	*tonno*	**toh**-noh
How much for a portion?	*Quanto per una porzione?*	**kwahn**-toh pehr **oo**-nah port-see**oh**-nay

EATING

What's fresh today?	*Cosa c'è di fresco oggi?*	**koh**-zah cheh dee **fray**-skoh **oh**-jee
Do you eat this part?	*Si mangia anche questa parte?*	see **mahn**-jah **ahn**-kay **kweh**-stah **par**-tay
Just the head, please.	*Solo la testa, per favore.*	**soh**-loh lah **tehs**-tah pehr fah-**voh**-ray

Italians like to stuff seafood with delicious herbs, breadcrumbs, and cheese, be it mussels, sardines, or anchovies. Most fish are served grilled and whole. Seafood is sometimes sold by the weight; if you see *100 g* or *l'etto* by the price on the menu, that's the price you'll pay per 100 grams, about a quarter pound. To find out how much a typical portion costs, ask, *"Quanto per una porzione?"*

Seafood Specialties

branzino al cartoccio	brahnt-**see**-noh ahl kar-**toh**-choh	sea bass steamed in parchment
cozze ripiene	**kohd**-zay ree-peeay-nay	mussels stuffed with herbs, cheese, and bread crumbs
fritto misto	**free**-toh **mee**-stoh	deep-fried calamari, prawns, and assorted small fish
nero di seppie e polenta	**nay**-roh dee **sehp**-eeay ay poh-**lehn**-tah	cuttlefish (large squid-like creature) cooked in its own ink and served on cornmeal squares
spiedini alla griglia	speeay-**dee**-nee **ah**-lah **greel**-yah	grilled fish or shellfish on a skewer, often with vegetables
zuppa di pesce	**tsoo**-pah dee **peh**-shay	fish soup or stew

EATING

Poultry

poultry	*pollame*	poh-**lah**-may
chicken	*pollo*	**poh**-loh
duck	*anatra*	**ah**-nah-trah
turkey	*tacchino*	tah-**kee**-noh
How long has this been dead?	*Da quanto tempo è morto questo?*	dah **kwahn**-toh **tehm**-poh eh **mor**-toh **kweh**-stoh

Meat

meat	*carne*	**kar**-nay
beef	*manzo*	**mahnt**-soh
beef steak	*bistecca di manzo*	bee-**stay**-kah dee **mahnt**-soh
sirloin steak	*entrecote*	ayn-tray-**koh**-tay
ribsteak	*costata*	koh-**stah**-tah
roast beef	*roast beef*	"roast beef"
brains	*cervella*	chehr-**vehl**-lah
bunny	*coniglio*	koh-**neel**-yoh
cutlet (veal)	*cotoletta*	koh-toh-**lay**-tah
goat, baby	*capretto*	kah-**pray**-toh
ham	*prosciutto*	proh-**shoo**-toh
cooked ham	*prosciutto cotto*	proh-**shoo**-toh **koh**-toh

AVOIDING MIS-STEAKS

alive	*vivo*	**vee**-voh
raw	*crudo*	**kroo**-doh
very rare	*molto al sangue*	**mohl**-toh ahl **sahn**-gway
rare	*al sangue*	ahl **sahn**-gway
medium	*cotto*	**koh**-toh
well-done	*ben cotto*	bayn **koh**-toh
very well-done	*completamente cotto*	kohm-play-tah-**mehn**-tay **koh**-toh
almost burnt	*quasi bruciato*	**kwah**-zee broo-**chah**-toh

EATING

dried, air-cured ham	prosciutto crudo	proh-**shoo**-toh **kroo**-doh
lamb	agnello	ahn-**yehl**-loh
liver	fegato	**fay**-gah-toh
meat stew	stufato di carne	stoo-**fah**-toh dee **kar**-nay
pork	maiale	mah-**yah**-lay
salt-cured bacon	pancetta	pahn-**chay**-tah
sausage	salsiccia	sahl-**see**-chah
snails	lumache	loo-**mah**-chay
suckling pig	porchetta	por-**kay**-tah
sweetbreads (calf pancreas)	animelle di vitello	ah-nee-**mehl**-lay dee vee-**tehl**-loh
tongue	lingua	**leeng**-gwah
tripe	trippa	**tree**-pah
veal	vitello	vee-**tehl**-loh
thin-sliced veal	scaloppine	skah-loh-**pee**-nay
wild boar	cinghiale	cheeng-**gah**-lay

On a menu, the price of steak is often listed per *etto* (100 grams, about a quarter of a pound). When ordering *bistecca* (beef steak) in a restaurant, it is most common to order four or five *ettos* and share it.

Main Course Specialties

abbacchio alla Romana	ah-**bah**-keeoh **ah**-lah roh-**mah**-nah	spring lamb roasted with potatoes, rosemary, and garlic (Easter)
assortito di carne arrosto	ah-sor-**tee**-toh dee **kar**-nay ah-**rohs**-toh	assortment of roasted meats, usually veal, pork, and lamb
bistecca alle Fiorentina	bee-**stay**-kah **ah**-lay feeoh-rehn-**tee**-nah	thick T-bone steak, grilled and lightly seasoned
bollito misto	boh-**lee**-toh **mee**-stoh	various meats boiled and served with a selection of sauces
fegato alla Veneziana	**fay**-gah-toh **ah**-lah vay-nayt-see**ah**-nah	liver and onions

involtini	een-vohl-**tee**-nee	meat or fish filets rolled around vegetables and other fillings
ossobuca alla Genovese	oh-soh-**boo**-kah **ah**-lah jay-noh-**vay**-zay	veal shank braised in broth with carrots, onions, and tomatoes
pollo alla cacciatora (literally "hunter's style")	**poh**-loh **ah**-lah kah-chah-**toh**-rah	chicken with olive oil, rosemary, garlic, and tomato
saltimbocca alla Romana	sahl-teem-**boh**-kah **ah**-lah roh-**mah**-nah	veal cutlet sautéed with sage, *prosciutto*, and white wine

Bollito misto can sometimes be quite elaborate: a cart is wheeled to your table for you to choose your meat. The side dishes and sauces often include *mostarda* (pickled vegetables), bone marrow sauce, and an herb-caper sauce.

How Food is Prepared

assorted	*assortiti*	ah-sor-**tee**-tee
baked	*al forno*	ahl **for**-noh
boiled	*bollito, lesso*	boh-**lee**-toh, **lay**-soh
braised	*brasato*	brah-**zah**-toh
broiled	*alla graticola*	**ah**-lah grah-tee-**koh**-lah
cold	*freddo*	**fray**-doh
cooked	*cotto*	**koh**-toh
deep-fried	*fritto*	**free**-toh
fillet	*filetto*	fee-**lay**-toh
fresh	*fresco*	**fray**-skoh
fried	*fritto*	**free**-toh
fried with breadcrumbs	*alla Milanese*	**ah**-lah mee-lah-**nay**-zay
grilled	*alla griglia*	**ah**-lah **greel**-yah
homemade	*casalingo*	kah-zah-**leen**-goh
hot	*caldo*	**kahl**-doh
in cream sauce	*con panna*	kohn **pah**-nah

medium	medio	**may**-deeoh
microwave	forno a microonde	**for**-noh ah mee-kroh-**ohn**-day
mild	non piccante	nohn pee-**kahn**-tay
mixed	misto	**mee**-stoh
poached	affogato	ah-foh-**gah**-toh
rare	al sangue	ahl **sahn**-gway
raw	crudo	**kroo**-doh
roasted	arrosto	ah-**roh**-stoh
sautéed	saltato in padella	sahl-**tah**-toh een pah-**dehl**-lah
smoked	affumicato	ah-foo-mee-**kah**-toh
sour	agro	**ah**-groh
spicy hot	piccante	pee-**kahn**-tay
steamed	al vapore	ahl vah-**poh**-ray
steamed in parchment	al cartoccio	ahl kar-**toh**-choh
stuffed	ripieno	ree-peeay-noh
sweet	dolce	**dohl**-chay
well-done	ben cotto	bayn **koh**-toh
with cheese and breadcrumbs	alla Parmigiana	**ah**-lah par-mee-**jah**-nah
with rice	con il riso	kohn eel **ree**-zoh

Veggies

vegetables	legumi, verdure	lay-**goo**-mee, vehr-**doo**-ray
mixed vegetables	misto di verdure	**mee**-stoh dee vehr-**doo**-ray
asparagus	asparagi	ah-spah-**rah**-jee
artichoke	carciofo	kar-**choh**-foh
giant artichoke	mame	**mah**-may
beans	fagioli	fah-**joh**-lee
beets	barbabietole	bar-bah-beeay-**toh**-lay
broccoli	broccoli	**broh**-koh-lee
cabbage	verza	**vehrt**-sah

carrots	*carote*	kah-**roh**-tay
cauliflower	*cavolfiore*	kah-vohl-fee**oh**-ray
corn	*granturco*	grahn-**toor**-koh
cucumber	*cetrioli*	chay-tree**oh**-lee
eggplant	*melanzana*	may-lahnt-**sah**-nah
fennel	*finocchio*	fee-**noh**-keeoh
French fries	*patate fritte*	pah-**tah**-tay **free**-tay
garlic	*aglio*	**ahl**-yoh
green beans	*fagiolini*	fah-joh-**lee**-nee
lentils	*lenticchie*	lehn-**tee**-keeay
mushrooms	*funghi*	**foong**-gee
olives	*olive*	oh-**lee**-vay
onions	*cipolle*	chee-**poh**-lay
peas	*piselli*	pee-**zehl**-lee
peppers...	*peperoni*	pay-pay-**roh**-nee
...green / red	*...verdi / rossi*	**vehr**-dee / **roh**-see
pickles	*cetriolini*	chay-treeoh-**lee**-nee
potatoes	*patate*	pah-**tah**-tay
rice	*riso*	**ree**-zoh
spinach	*spinaci*	spee-**nah**-chee
tomatoes	*pomodori*	poh-moh-**doh**-ree
truffles	*tartufi*	tar-**too**-fee
zucchini	*zucchine*	tsoo-**kee**-nay

Vegetables are often ordered as a *contorno* (side dish) with a *secondo* course. Common side dishes include *patate fritte* or *patate arrosto* (potatoes fried or roasted), *spinaci* (spinach), *fagioli* (green beans), *asparagi* (asparagus) and *insalate verde* or *insalate mista* (green salad or mixed with carrots and tomato). Sometimes more elaborate choices are available, such as *fiore di zucca* (fried zucchini blossoms stuffed with mozzarella). Although the Italians are experts at cooking pasta, they overcook vegetables.

Fruits

apple	mela	**may**-lah
apricot	albicocca	ahl-bee-**koh**-kah
banana	banana	bah-**nah**-nah
berries	frutti di bosco	**froo**-tee dee **bohs**-koh
cantaloupe	melone	may-**loh**-nay
cherry	ciliegia	chee-lee**ay**-jah
dates	datteri	**dah**-tay-ree
fig	fico	**fee**-koh
fruit	frutta	**froo**-tah
grapefruit	pompelmo	pohm-**pehl**-moh
grapes	uva	**oo**-vah
honeydew melon	melone verde	may-**loh**-nay **vehr**-day
lemon	limone	lee-**moh**-nay
orange	arancia	ah-**rahn**-chah
peach	pesca	**pehs**-kah
pear	pera	**pay**-rah
pineapple	ananas	**ah**-nah-nahs
plum	susina	soo-**zee**-nah
prune	prugna	**proon**-yah
raspberry	lampone	lahm-**poh**-nay
strawberry	fragola	**frah**-goh-lah
tangerine	mandarino	mahn-dah-**ree**-noh
watermelon	cocomero	koh-koh-**may**-roh

On a menu, you might see *frutta fresca di stagione* (fresh fruit of the season). Mixed berries are called *frutti di bosco* (forest fruits). If you ask for *sottobosco* (under the forest), you'll get a bowl of mixed berries with lemon and sugar.

EATING

Nuts to You

almond	*mandorle*	mahn-**dor**-lay
chestnut	*castagne*	kah-**stahn**-yay
coconut	*noce di cocco*	**noh**-chay dee **koh**-koh
hazelnut	*nocciola*	noh-**choh**-lah
peanuts	*noccioline*	noh-choh-**lee**-nay
pine nuts	*pinoli*	pee-**noh**-lee
pistachio	*pistacchio*	pee-**stah**-keeoh
walnut	*noce*	**noh**-chay

Just Desserts

dessert	*dolci*	**dohl**-chee
cake	*torta*	**tor**-tah
ice cream	*gelato*	jay-**lah**-toh
sherbet	*sorbetto*	sor-**bay**-toh
fruit cup	*macedonia senza zucchero*	mah-chay-**doh**-neeah **sehn**-sah **tsoo**-kay-roh
fruit salad	*macedonia*	mah-chay-**doh**-neeah
fruit with ice cream	*coppa di frutta*	**koh**-pah dee **froo**-tah
tart	*tartina*	tar-**tee**-nah
pie	*crostata*	kroh-**stah**-tah
whipped cream	*panna*	**pah**-nah
chocolate mousse	*mousse*	moos
pudding	*budino*	boo-**dee**-noh
pastry	*pasta*	**pah**-stah
strudel	*strudel*	**stroo**-dehl
cookies	*biscotti*	bee-**skoh**-tee
candies	*caramelle*	kah-rah-**mehl**-lay
low calorie	*poche calorie*	**poh**-kay kah-loh-**ree**-ay
homemade	*casalingo*	kah-zah-**leen**-goh
We'll split one.	*Ne dividiamo uno.*	nay dee-vee-deea**ah**-moh **oo**-noh
Two forks / spoons, please.	*Due forchette / cucchiai, per favore.*	**doo**-ay for-**kay**-tay / koo-kee**ah**-yee pehr fah-**voh**-ray

EATING

I shouldn't, but...	Non dovrei, ma...	nohn doh-**vreh**ee mah
Exquisite!	Squisito!	skwee-**zee**-toh
It's heavenly!	Da sogno!	dah **sohn**-yoh
I'm a glutton	Sono golosa	**soh**-noh goh-**loh**-zah
for chocolate.	per cioccolato.	pehr choh-koh-**lah**-toh
Better than sex.	Meglio del sesso.	**mehl**-yoh dehl **say**-soh
Just looking at	Fa ingrassare	fah een-grah-**sah**-ray
it fattens you.	solo a guardarlo.	**soh**-loh ah gwar-**dar**-loh
Sinfully good.	Un peccato	oon pay-**kah**-toh
(a sin of the throat)	di gola.	dee **goh**-lah
So good I even	Così buono che	koh-**zee bwoh**-noh kay
licked my	mi sono leccato	mee **soh**-noh lay-**kah**-toh
moustache.	anche i baffi.	**ahn**-kay ee **bah**-fee

Gelati Talk

cone / cup	cono / coppa	**koh**-noh / **koh**-pah
one scoop	una pallina	**oo**-nah pah-**lee**-nah
two scoops	due palline	**doo**-ay pah-**lee**-nay
with whipped cream	con panna	kohn **pah**-nah
A little taste?	Un assaggio?	oon ah-**sah**-joh
How many	Quanti gusti	**kwahn**-tee **goo**-stee
flavors can I get	posso avere	**poh**-soh ah-**vay**-ray
per scoop?	per pallina?	pehr pah-**lee**-nah
apricot	albicocca	ahl-bee-**koh**-kah
berries	frutti di bosco	**froo**-tee dee **bohs**-koh
blueberry	mirtillo	meer-**tee**-loh
cantaloupe	melone	may-**loh**-nay
coconut	cocco	**koh**-koh
chocolate	cioccolato	choh-koh-**lah**-toh
super chocolate	tartufo	tar-**too**-foh
vanilla and	stracciatella	strah-chah-**tehl**-lah
chocolate chips		
chocolate hazelnut	bacio	**bah**-choh
chocolate and mint	After Eight	"After Eight"
coffee	caffè	kah-**feh**
hazelnut	nocciola	noh-**choh**-lah

EATING

lemon	*limone*	lee-**moh**-nay
milk	*fior di latte*	**fee**or dee **lah**-tay
mint	*menta*	**mayn**-tah
orange	*arancia*	ah-**rahn**-chah
peach	*pesca*	**pehs**-kah
pear	*pera*	**pay**-rah
pineapple	*ananas*	**ah**-nah-nahs
raspberry	*lampone*	lahm-**poh**-nay
rice	*riso*	**ree**-zoh
strawberry	*fragola*	**frah**-goh-lah
vanilla	*crema*	**kray**-mah
yogurt	*yogurt*	**yoh**-goort

Bacio (chocolate hazelnut) also means "kiss." *Baci* (kisses) are Italy's version of Chinese fortune cookies. The poetic fortunes, wrapped around chocolate balls, are written by people whose love of romance exceeds their grasp of English.

Dessert Specialties

bignole	been-**yoh**-lay	cream puffs (Florence)
cannoli	kah-**noh**-lee	fried pastry tubes filled w/ whipped ricotta, candied fruit, and chocolate
cassata	kah-**sah**-tah	ice cream, sponge cake, ricotta cheese, fruit, and pistachios (Sicily)
granita	grah-**nee**-tah	snow cone
millefoglie (literally "a thousand leaves")	mee-lay-**fohl**-yay	layers of sweet, buttery pastry
panettone	pah-nay-**toh**-nay	Milanese yeast cake with raisins and candied fruit
panforte	pahn-**for**-tay	dense fruit and nut cake (Siena)
panna cotta	**pah**-nah koh-tah	rich, cooked cream served with berries

profiterole	proh-fee-tay-**roh**-lay	cream-filled pastry with warm chocolate sauce
sfogliatella	sfohl-yah-**tehl**-lah	crispy scallop shell shaped pastry filled w/ sweetened ricotta cheese (Naples)
tartufo	tar-**too**-foh	super-chocolate ice cream (Rome)
tiramisú	tee-rah-mee-**zoo**	espresso-soaked cake with chocolate, cream, and marsala
torta di mele	**tor**-tah dee **may**-lay	apple cake
zabaglione	tsah-bahl-yee**oh**-nay	delicious egg and liquor cream
zuppa inglese	**tsoo**-pah een-**glay**-zay	trifle—rum-soaked cake layered with whipped cream and fruit

There are also hundreds of different cookies made in Italy, especially in the Veneto region. Every holiday is an excuse to celebrate with a new tasty treat. *Bussoli* are for Easter. *Frittole* (small doughnuts) are eaten during *Carnevale.* Even Romeo and Juliet have their own special sweets named for them: *baci di Giulietta* (vanilla meringues, literally "Juliet's kisses") and *sospiri di Romeo* (hazelnut and chocolate cookies, literally "Romeo's sighs").

EATING

Drinking

Water, Milk, and Juice

mineral water...	acqua minerale...	**ah**-kwah mee-nay-**rah**-lay
...with / without gas	...gassata / non gassata	gah-**sah**-tah / nohn gah-**sah**-tah
tap water	acqua del rubinetto	**ah**-kwah dayl roo-bee-**nay**-toh
whole milk	latte intero	**lah**-tay een-**tay**-roh
skim milk	latte magro	**lah**-tay **mah**-groh
fresh milk	latte fresco	**lah**-tay **fray**-skoh
milk shake	frappè	frah-**peh**
hot chocolate...	cioccolata calda...	choh-koh-**lah**-tah **kahl**-dah
...with whipped cream	...con panna	kohn **pah**-nah
orange soda	aranciata	ah-rahn-**chah**-tah
lemon soda	limonata	lee-moh-**nah**-tah
juice...	succo di...	**soo**-koh dee
...fruit	...frutta	**froo**-tah
...apple	...mela	**may**-lah
...apricot	...albicocca	ahl-bee-**koh**-kah
...grapefruit	...pompelmo	pohm-**pehl**-moh
...orange	...arancia	ah-**rahn**-chah
...peach	...pesca	**pehs**-kah
...pear	...pera	**pay**-rah
freshly-squeezed orange juice	spremuta d'arancia	spray-**moo**-tah dah-**rahn**-chah
100% juice	succo al cento per cento	**soo**-koh ahl **chehn**-toh pehr **chehn**-toh
with / without...	con / senza...	kohn / **sehn**-sah
...sugar	...zucchero	**tsoo**-kay-roh
...ice	...ghiaccio	gee**ah**-choh
glass / cup	bicchiere / tazza	bee-kee**ay**-ray / **tahd**-zah

KEY PHRASES: DRINKING		
drink	*bibite*	bee-**bee**-tay
(mineral) water	*acqua (minerale)*	**ah**-kwah (mee-nay-**rah**-lay)
tap water	*acqua del rubinetto*	**ah**-kwah dayl roo-bee-**nay**-toh
milk	*latte*	**lah**-tay
juice	*succo*	**soo**-koh
coffee	*caffè*	kah-**feh**
tea	*tè*	teh
wine	*vino*	**vee**-noh
beer	*birra*	**bee**-rah
Cheers!	*Cin cin!*	cheen cheen

bottle...	*bottiglia...*	boh-**teel**-yah
...small / large	*...piccola / grande*	**pee**-koh-lah / **grahn**-day
Is this water safe to drink?	*È potabile quest'acqua?*	eh poh-**tah**-bee-lay kweh-**stah**-kwah

I drink the tap water in Italy (Venice's is piped in from a mountain spring, and Florence's is very chlorinated), but it's good style and never expensive to order a *litro* (liter) or *mezzo litro* (half liter) of bottled water with your meal.

Coffee and Tea

coffee...	*caffè...*	kah-**feh**
...with milk	*...latte*	**lah**-tay
...with a little milk	*...macchiato*	mah-keeah-toh
...with whipped cream	*...con panna*	kohn **pah**-nah
...with water	*...lungo*	**loon**-goh
...iced	*...freddo*	**fray**-doh
...instant	*...solubile*	soo-**loo**-bee-lay
...American-style	*...Americano*	ah-may-ree-**kah**-noh
coffee with foamy milk	*cappuccino*	kah-poo-**chee**-noh

EATING

decaffeinated	decaffeinato, Haag	day-kah-fay-**nah**-toh, hahg
black	nero	**nay**-roh
milk...	latte...	**lah**-tay
...with a little coffee	...macchiato	mah-kee**ah**-toh
sugar	zucchero	**tsoo**-kay-roh
hot water	acqua calda	**ah**-kwah **kahl**-dah
tea / lemon	tè / limone	teh / lee-**moh**-nay
herbal tea	tisana	tee-**zah**-nah
tea bag	bustina di tè	boo-**stee**-nah dee teh
fruit tea	tè alla frutta	teh **ah**-lah **froo**-tah
mint tea	tè alla menta	teh **ah**-lah **mehn**-tah
iced tea	tè freddo	teh **fray**-doh
small / large	piccola / grande	**pee**-koh-lah / **grahn**-day
Another cup.	Un'altra tazza.	oo-**nahl**-trah **tahd**-zah
Same price if I sit	Costa uguale	**koh**-stah oo-**gwah**-lay
or stand?	al tavolo o al	ahl **tah**-voh-loh oh ahl
	banco?	**bahn**-koh

Caffè is espresso served in a teeny tiny cup. Foamy *cappuccino* was named after the monks with their brown robes and frothy cowls. A *corretto* is coffee and firewater (literally "coffee corrected"). In a bar, you'll pay at the *cassa,* then take your receipt to the person who makes the coffee. Refills are never free, except at hotel breakfasts.

When you're ordering coffee in bars in bigger cities, you'll notice that the price board (*Lista dei prezzi*) clearly lists two price levels: the cheaper level for the stand-up *bar* and the more expensive for the *tavolo* (table) or *terrazza* (out on the terrace or sidewalk).

Wine

I would like...	Vorrei....	vor-**reh**ee
We would like...	Vorremo...	vor-**ray**-moh
...a glass	...un bicchiere	oon bee-kee**ay**-ray
...a quarter liter	...un quarto litro	oon **kwar**-toh **lee**-troh
...a half liter	...un mezzo litro	oon **mehd**-zoh **lee**-troh
...a carafe	...una caraffa	**oo**-nah kah-**rah**-fah

...a half bottle	...una mezza bottiglia	**oo**-nah **mehd**-zah boh-**teel**-yah
...a bottle	...una bottiglia	**oo**-nah boh-**teel**-yah
...a 5-liter jug	...una damigiana da cinque litri	**oo**-nah dah-mee-**jah**-nah dah **cheeng**-kway **lee**-tree
...a barrel	...un barile	oon bah-**ree**-lay
...a vat	...un tino	oon **tee**-noh
...of red wine	...di rosso	dee **roh**-soh
...of white wine	...di bianco	dee beeahn-koh
...of rosé wine	...di rosato	dee roh-**zah**-toh
...the wine list	...la lista dei vini	lah **lee**-stah **deh**ee **vee**-nee

Galileo once wrote, "Wine is light held together by water." It is certainly a part of the Italian culinary trinity—the vine, olive, and wheat. Visit an *enoteca* (wine shop or bar) to sample a variety of regional wines.

Wine Words

Italian wines are named by grape, place, descriptive term, or a combination of these. Below is a list of vocabulary to help you identify what you're looking for in a wine and where to find it.

wine / wines	vino / vini	**vee**-noh / **vee**-nee
select wine (good year)	vino selezionato	**vee**-noh say-layt-seeoh-**nah**-toh
table wine	vino da tavola	**vee**-noh dah **tah**-voh-lah
house wine	vino della casa	**vee**-noh **dehl**-lah **kah**-zah
local	locale	loh-**kah**-lay
of the region	della regione	**dehl**-lah ray-**joh**-nay
red	rosso	**roh**-soh
white	bianco	bee**ahn**-koh
rosé	rosato	roh-**zah**-toh
sparkling	frizzante	freed-**zahn**-tay

EATING

fruity	amabile	ah-**mah**-bee-lay
light / heavy	leggero / pesante	lay-**jay**-roh / pay-**zahn**-tay
sweet	dolce, abboccato	**dohl**-chay, ah-boh-**kah**-toh
medium	medio	**may**-deeoh
semi-dry	semi-secco	say-mee-**say**-koh
dry	secco	**say**-koh
very dry	molto secco	**mohl**-toh **say**-koh
full-bodied	pieno, corposo	pee**ay**-noh, kor-**poh**-zoh
mature	maturo	mah-**too**-roh
cork	tappo	**tah**-poh
corkscrew	cavitappi	kah-vee-**tah**-pee
grapes	uva	**oo**-vah
vintage	annata	ah-**nah**-tah
vineyard	vigneto	veen-**yay**-toh
wine-tasting	degustazione	day-goo-staht-see**oh**-nay
What is a good year?	Qual'è una buon'annata?	kwah-**leh oo**-nah bwoh-nah-**nah**-tah
What do you recommend?	Cosa raccomanda?	**koh**-zah rah-koh-**mahn**-dah

Wine Labels

DOCG	meets nationwide regulations for the highest quality wine (e.g., permitted grape varieties and minimum alcohol content)
DOC	meets national standards for high quality wine
IGT	meets regional standards
riserva	DOCG or DOC wine matured for a longer, specified time
classico	from a defined, select area
annata	year of harvest
vendemmia	harvest
imbottigliato dal produttore all' origin	bottled by producers

To save money, order "*Una caraffa di vino della casa*" (a carafe of the house wine). Red wine dominates in Italy.

Many small-town Italians in the hotel business have a cellar or cantina that they are proud to show off. They'll often jump at any excuse to descend and drink. For a memorable and affordable adventure in Venice, have a "pub crawl" dinner. While *cicchetti* (bar munchies) aren't as common as they used to be, many bars (called *ciccheteria*) are still popular for their wide selection of often ugly, always tasty hors d'oeuvres on toothpicks. Ask for *un'ombra* (a small glass of wine) to wash them down.

Some wines to look for by region:

- The big, bold, dry reds of Piedmont: **Barbaresco, Barolo,** and **Barbera**
- From Tuscany, **Brunello di Montalcino** (smooth, dry red), **Chianti Classico** (not just Chianti in the basket bottle), **Montepulciano d'Abruzzo** (dry, medium-bodied red), **Vernaccia** (light white from the San Gimignano region), and the holy (dessert) wine, **Vin Santo**
- From the Veneto, **Bardolino** and **Amarone** (both full-bodied reds), **Valpolicella** (light red), **Soave** (dry white), and the bubbly white **Prosecco**
- From Umbria, **Orvieto Classico**, a golden, dry white
- From the Cinque Terre, **Bianca della Cinque Terre**, a light white wine, and **Sciacchetrà**, a sweet, potent after-dinner wine

Beer

beer	birra	**bee**-rah
bar	bar	bar
from the tap	alla spina	**ah**-lah **spee**-nah
glass of draft beer	una birra alla spina	**oo**-nah **bee**-rah **ah**-lah **spee**-nah
20 cl draft beer	una birra piccola	**oo**-nah **bee**-rah **pee**-koh-lah
33 cl draft beer	una birra media	**oo**-nah **bee**-rah **may**-deeah

EATING

50 cl draft beer	*una birra grande*	**oo**-nah **bee**-rah **grahn**-day
1 liter draft beer	*un litro di birra alla spina*	oon **lee**-troh dee **bee**-rah **ah**-lah **spee**-nah
bottle	*bottiglia*	boh-**teel**-yah
light / dark	*chiara / scura*	kee**ah**-rah / **skoo**-rah
local / imported	*locale / importata*	loh-**kah**-lay / eem-por-**tah**-tah
Italian beer	*birra nazionale*	**bee**-rah naht-seeoh-**nah**-lay
German beer	*birra tedesca*	**bee**-rah tay-**dehs**-kah
Irish beer	*birra irlandese*	**bee**-rah eer-lahn-**day**-zay
small / large	*piccola / grande*	**pee**-koh-lah / **grahn**-day
low calorie	*leggera*	lay-**jay**-rah
cold	*fredda*	**fray**-dah
colder	*più fredda*	pew **fray**-dah

Bar Talk

Shall we go for a drink?	*Andiamo a prendere qualcosa da bere?*	ahn-dee**ah**-moh ah **prehn**-day-ray kwahl-**koh**-zah dah **bay**-ray
I'll buy you a drink	*Ti offro una bevanda.*	tee **oh**-froh **oo**-nah bay-**vahn**-dah
It's on me.	*Pago io.*	**pah**-goh **ee**oh
The next one's on me.	*Offro io la prossima.*	**oh**-froh **ee**oh lah **proh**-see-mah
What would you like?	*Che cosa prende?*	kay **koh**-zah **prehn**-day
I'll have...	*Prendo...*	**prehn**-doh
I don't drink.	*Non bevo.*	nohn **bay**-voh
alcohol-free	*analcolica*	ahn-ahl-**koh**-lee-kah
What is the local specialty?	*Qual'è la specialità locale?*	kwah-**leh** lah spay-chah-lee-**tah** loh-**kah**-lay

EATING

What is a good drink for a man / for a woman?	Qual'è una buona bevanda per un uomo / per una donna?	kwah-**leh oo**-nah **bwoh**-nah bay-**vahn**-dah pehr oon **woh**-moh / pehr **oo**-nah **doh**-nah
Straight.	Liscio.	**lee**-sho
With / Without...	Con / Senza...	kohn / **sehn**-sah
...alcohol.	...alcool.	**ahl**-kohl
...ice.	...ghiaccio.	gee**ah**-choh
One more.	Un altro.	oon **ahl**-troh
Cheers!	Cin cin!	cheen cheen
To your health!	Salute!	sah-**loo**-tay
Long life!	Lunga vita!	**loong**-gah **vee**-tah
Long live Italy!	Viva l'Italia!	**vee**-vah lee-**tahl**-yah
I'm feeling...	Mi sento...	mee **sehn**-toh
...tipsy.	...brillo[a].	**bree**-loh
...a little drunk.	...un po' ubriaco[a].	oon poh oo-bree**ah**-koh
...blitzed. (colloq.)	...ubriaco[a] fradicio[a].	oo-bree**ah**-koh **frah**-dee-choh
I'm hung over.	Ho la sbornia.	oh lah **sbor**-neeah

Before dinner, try an *aperitivo* to stimulate your palate. There are many specialties, including the popular brands of vermouth, *Cinzano* and *Martini*, that come in red or white. Look for sweet or dry *Campari* (a dark-colored bitters with herbs and orange peel), *Cynar* (flavored with artichoke), *Americano* (vermouth with bitters, brandy, and lemon peel), *Bellini* (prosecco and white peach juice, a Venetian speciality), *Punt e Mes* (created from sweet red vermouth and red wine), and *spremuta di frutta* (freshly-squeezed fruit juice).

After dinner, try a *digestivo*, a liqueur thought to aid in digestion: *Amaro* (sweet, strong bitters; well-known brands are *Montenegro* and *Fernet Branca*); *Grappa* (fire-water distilled from grape skins and stems), *Sambuca* (syrupy anise-flavored liqueur), *Nocino* (walnut liqueur), *Amaretto* (almond-flavored liqueur), and *Frangelico* (hazelnut liqueur).

EATING

Picnicking

At the Grocery

Is it self-service?	*È self-service?*	eh sehlf-**sehr**-vees
Ripe for today?	*Da mangiare oggi?*	dah mahn-**jah**-ray **oh**-jee
Does it need to be cooked?	*Bisogna cucinarlo prima di mangiarlo?*	bee-**zohn**-yah koo-chee-**nar**-loh **pree**-mah dee mahn-**jar**-loh
A little taste?	*Un assaggio?*	oon ah-**sah**-joh
Fifty grams.	*Cinquanta grammi.*	cheeng-**kwahn**-tah **grah**-mee
One hundred grams.	*Un etto.*	oon **eht**-toh
More. / Less.	*Più. / Meno.*	pew / **may**-noh
A piece.	*Un pezzo.*	oon **pehd**-zoh
A slice.	*Una fetta.*	**oo**-nah **fay**-tah
Four slices.	*Quattro fette.*	**kwah**-troh **fay**-tay
Sliced (fine).	*Tagliato (a fette sottili).*	tahl-**yah**-toh (ah **fay**-tay soh-**tee**-lee)
Half.	*Metà.*	may-**tah**
A small bag.	*Un sacchettino.*	oon sah-keht-**tee**-noh
A bag, please.	*Un sacchetto, per favore.*	oon sah-**keht**-toh pehr fah-**voh**-ray
Will you make... for me / us?	*Mi / Ci può fare...?*	mee / chee pwoh **fah**-ray
...a sandwich	*...un panino*	oon pah-**nee**-noh
...two sandwiches	*...due panini*	**doo**-ay pah-**nee**-nee
To take out.	*Da portar via.*	dah **por**-tar **vee**-ah
Can I / Can we use...?	*Posso / Possiamo usare...?*	**poh**-soh / poh-seeah-moh oo-**zah**-ray
...the microwave	*...il forno a microonde*	eel **for**-noh ah mee-kroh-**ohn**-day
May I borrow a...?	*Posso prendere in prestito...?*	**poh**-soh **prehn**-day-ray een preh-**stee**-toh
Do you have a...?	*Ha per caso...?*	ah pehr **kah**-zoh

EATING

Where can I buy / find a...?	Dove posso comprare / trovare un...?	**doh**-vay **poh**-soh kohm-**prah**-ray / troh-**vah**-ray oon
...corkscrew	...cavatappi	kah-vah-**tah**-pee
...can opener	...apriscatole	ah-pree-shah-**toh**-lay
Is there a park nearby?	C'è un parco qui vicino?	cheh oon **par**-koh kwee vee-**chee**-noh
Where is a good place to picnic?	Dov'è un bel posto per fare un picnic?	doh-**veh** oon behl **poh**-stoh pehr **fah**-ray oon **peek**-neek
Is picnicking allowed here?	Va bene fare un picnic qui?	vah **behn**-nay **fah**-ray oon **peek**-neek kwee
Enjoy your meal!	Buon appetito!	bwohn ah-pay-**tee**-toh

Tasty Picnic Words

picnic	picnic	**peek**-neek
open air market	mercato	mehr-**kah**-toh
grocery store	alimentari	ah-lee-mayn-**tah**-ree
supermarket	supermercato	soo-pehr-mehr-**kah**-toh
delicatessen	salumeria	sah-loo-may-**ree**-ah
bakery	panetteria, forno	pah-nay-tay-**ree**-ah, **for**-noh
sandwich shop	paninoteca	pah-nee-noh-**tay**-kah
pastry shop	pasticceria	pah-stee-chay-**ree**-ah
sandwich or roll	panino	pah-**nee**-noh
bread	pane	**pah**-nay
cured ham (pricey)	prosciutto crudo	proh-**shoo**-toh **kroo**-doh
cooked ham	prosciutto cotto	proh-**shoo**-toh **koh**-toh
sausage	salsiccia	sahl-**see**-chah
cheese	formaggio	for-**mah**-joh
mustard...	senape...	**say**-nah-pay
mayonnaise...	maionese...	mah-yoh-**nay**-zay
...in a tube	...in tubetto	een too-**bay**-toh
yogurt	yogurt	**yoh**-goort
fruit	frutta	**froo**-tah

EATING

box of juice	*cartone di succo di frutta*	kar-**toh**-nay dee **soo**-koh dee **froo**-tah
spoon / fork...	*cucchiaio / forchetta...*	koo-kee**ah**-yoh / for-**kay**-tah
...made of plastic	*...di plastica*	dee **plah**-stee-kah
cup / plate...	*bicchiere / piatto...*	bee-kee**ay**-ray / pee**ah**-toh
...made of paper	*...di carta*	dee **kar**-tah

Make your own sandwiches by getting the ingredients at a market. Order meat and cheese by the gram. One hundred grams (what the Italians call an *etto*) is about a quarter pound, enough for two sandwiches.

MENU DECODER

Italian/English

This handy decoder won't list every word on the menu, but it will help you get *trota* (trout) instead of *tripa* (tripe).

abbacchio	lamb (Rome)
abbacchio alla Romana	roasted spring lamb
abbocato	sweet (wine)
acciughe	anchovies
aceto	vinegar
acqua	water
acqua del rubinetto	tap water
acqua minerale	mineral water
affogato	poached
affumicato	smoked
After Eight	chocolate and mint (gelato)
aglio	garlic
agnello	lamb
agro	sour
ai funghi	with mushrooms
al cartoccio	steamed in parchment
al dente	not overcooked (pasta)
al forno	baked

al sangue	rare (meat)
al vapore	steamed
albicocca	apricot
alcool	alcohol
alfredo	butter, cream, cheese sauce
all'arrabbiata	with bacon, tomato—spicy hot
alla cacciatora	"hunter's style," with olive oil, rosemary, garlic, tomato
alla diavola	spicy
alla graticola	broiled
alla Parmigiana	with cheese and breadcrumbs
alla spina	from the tap (beer)
amabile	fruity (wine)
amatriciana	with bacon, tomato, and spices
analcolica	alcohol-free
ananas	pineapple
anatra	duck
animelle di vitello	sweetbreads
annata	vintage (wine)
antipasti	appetizers
antipasto misto	salami and marinated vegetables
aragosta	lobster
arancia	orange
aranciata	orange soda
aringa	herring
arrabiata	spicy tomato-chili sauce
arrosto	roasted
asiago	hard and spicy cheese
asparagi	asparagus
assortiti	assorted
assortito di carne arrosto	roasted assortment of meats
astice	male lobster
bacio	chocolate hazelnut candy
balani	barnacles
barbabietole	beets
basilico	basil
ben cotto	well-done (meat)
bevande	beverages

bianca	"white" pizza (no tomato sauce)
bianco	white
bibite	beverages
bicchiere	glass
bignole	cream puffs (Florence)
biologico	organic
birra	beer
biscotti	cookies
bistecca	beef steak
bistecca alle Fiorentina	T-bone steak
bocconcini	small balls of mozzarella
bollente	boiling hot
bollito	boiled
bollito misto	various boiled meats with sauces
Bolognese	meat and tomato sauce
bottiglia	bottle
branzino	bass
brasato	braised
brioche	roll
brodo	broth
bruschetta	toast with tomatoes and basil
bucatini	hollow, thick spaghetti
budino	pudding
burro	butter
burro d'arachidi	peanut butter
bustina di tè	tea bag
caciucco	Tuscan fish soup
caffè	coffee
caffè Americano	American-style coffee
caffè con panna	coffee with whipped cream
caffè freddo	iced coffee
caffè latte	coffee with milk
caffè lungo	coffee with water
caffè macchiato	coffee with a little milk
caffè solubile	instant coffee
caffeina	caffeine
calamari	squid
caldo	hot

calzone	folded pizza
cannelloni	large tube-shaped noodles
cannoli	fried pastry tubes filled with ricotta, fruit, and chocolate
cantucci	Tuscan almond cookies
capesante	scallops
cappuccino	coffee with foam
capra	goat
caprese	mozzarella and tomato salad
capretto	baby goat
capricciosa	chef's choice
caprino	goat cheese
capriolo	venison
caraffa	carafe
caramelle	candy
carbonara	with meat sauce
carciofo	artichoke
carne	meat
carote	carrots
carpaccio	thinly sliced air-cured meat
casa	house
casalingo	homemade
cassa	cash register
cassata siciliana	Sicilian sponge cake
castagne	chestnut
cavatappi	corkscrew
cavolfiore	cauliflower
cavolini de Bruxelles	Brussels sprouts
cavolo	cabbage
ceci	chickpeas
cena	dinner
cereali	cereal
cervella	brains
cervo	venison
cetrioli	cucumber
cetriolini	pickles
ciabatta	crusty, flat, rustic bread
ciaccina	"white" pizza (no tomato sauce)

cibo	food
ciccheti	small appetizers
ciliegia	cherry
cinese	Chinese
cinghiale	wild boar
cioccolata	chocolate
cipolle	onions
cocomero	watermelon
colazione	breakfast
con	with
con panna	with whipped cream
coniglio	rabbit
cono	cone
contorni	side dishes
coperto	cover charge
coppa	small bowl
coretto	coffee and firewater
cornetto	croissant
corposo	full-bodied (wine)
costata	rib steak
cotoletta	cutlet
cotto	cooked; medium (meat)
cozze	mussels
crema	vanilla
crème caramel	caramelized topped custard
crescenza	mild cheese
crostata	pie with jam
crostini	toast with paté
crudo	raw
cucina	cuisine
cuoco	chef
da portar via	"to go"
datteri	dates
decaffeinato	decaffeinated
del giorno	of the day
della casa	of the house
di	of
digestivo	after-dinner drink

dolce	sweet
dolci	desserts
dragoncello	tarragon
e	and
emmenthal	Swiss cheese
entrecote	sirloin steak
erbe	herb
etto	one hundred grams
fagiano	pheasant
fagioli	beans
fagiolini	green beans
farcito	stuffed
farfalle	butterfly-shaped pasta
farinata	porridge
fatto in casa	homemade
fegato	liver
fegato alla Veneziana	liver and onions
fettina	slice
fettucine	long, flat noodles
fico	fig
filetto	fillet
filone	large unsalted bread
finocchio	fennel
fior di latte	milk (gelato flavor)
focaccia	flat bread
fontina	creamy, nutty, gruyere-style cheese
formaggio	cheese
fragola	strawberry
frangelico	hazelnut liqueur
frappè	milkshake
freddo	cold
fresco	fresh
frittata	omelet
fritto	fried
fritto misto	fried seafood
frizzante	sparkling
frumento	wheat
frutta	fruit

frutti di bosco	berries
frutti di mare	seafood
funghi	mushrooms
gamberetti	small shrimp
gamberi	shrimp
gamberoni	big shrimp
gassata	carbonated
gelatina	jelly
gelato	Italian ice cream
Genovese	with pesto sauce
ghiaccio	ice
giorno	day
gnocchi	potato noodles
gorgonzola	bleu cheese
granchione	crab
grande	large
granita	snow cone
granturco	corn
grappa	firewater
griglia	grilled
grissini	breadsticks
groviera	Swiss cheese
gusti	flavors
Haag	decaffeinated coffee
importata	imported
incluso	included
insalata	salad
insalata con uova	egg salad
insalata di mare	seafood salad
involtini	meat or fish filets with fillings
kasher	kosher
lampone	raspberry
latte	milk
latte fresco	fresh milk
latte intero	whole milk
latte macchiato	milk with a little coffee
latte magro	skim milk
latticini	small mozzarella balls

lattuga	lettuce
leggero	light
legumi	vegetables
lenticchie	lentils
lepre	hare
limonata	lemon soda
limone	lemon
lingua	tongue
linguine	thin, flat noodles
locale	local
lumache	snails
maccheroni	tube-shaped pasta
macedonia	fresh fruit salad
maiale	pork
maionese	mayonnaise
mame	giant artichokes
mandarino	tangerine
mandorle	almond
manzo	beef
margarina	margarine
Margherita	pizza with cheese and tomato sauce
marinara	tomato and garlic sauce
marmellata	jam
mascarpone	sweet, buttery dessert cheese
maturo	mature (wine)
mela	apple
melanzana	eggplant
melone	cantaloupe
melone verde	honeydew melon
menta	mint
menù del giorno	menu of the day
menù turistico	fixed-price menu
mercato	open-air market
merluzzo	cod
mezzo	half
miele	honey
Milanese	fried in breadcrumbs

millefoglie	layers of sweet, buttery pastry
minerale-acqua	mineral water
minestra	soup
minestrone	vegetable soup
mirtillo	blueberry
misto	mixed
molto	very
molto al sangue	very rare (meat)
mozzarella	handmade water buffalo cheese
Napoletana	pizza with cheese, anchovies, and tomato sauce
nero	black
nero di seppie e polenta	cuttlefish cooked in its own ink
nocciola	hazelnut
noccioline	peanut
noce	walnut
noce di cocco	coconut
nocino	walnut liqueur
non	not
non fumare	non-smoking
non fumatori	non-smoking
o	or
olio	oil
olive	olives
omelette	omelet
orata	bream (fish)
orecchiette	small, ear-shaped pasta
organico	organic
ortolana	vegetarian pizza
ossobuca alla Genovese	veal shank braised in broth
ossobuco	bone marrow
ostriche	oysters
pallina	scoop
pancetta	salt-cured bacon
pane	bread
pane aromatico	herb or vegetable bread
pane casereccia	home-style bread
pane di olive	olive bread

pane di segale	rye bread
pane integrale	whole grain bread
pane scuro	brown bread
pane Toscano	rustic bread made without salt
paneficio	bakery
panettone	Milanese yeast fruitcake
panforte	fruitcake
panino	roll, sandwich
panna	cream, whipped cream
panna cotta	cooked cream with berries
pansotti	pasta stuffed with veggies
panzanella	bread and vegetable salad
parmigiano	parmesan cheese
pasticceria	pastry shop
pasticcini	pastry
pastina	noodles
patate	potatoes
patate fritte	French fries
pecorino	sheep's cheese
penne	tube-shaped noodles
pepato	with pepper
pepe	pepper
peperonata	peppers with tomato sauce
peperoncino	paprika
peperoni	bell peppers
pera	pear
percorino	sheep cheese
pesante	heavy (wine)
pesca	peach
pescatora	seafood sauce
pesce	fish
pesce spada	swordfish
pesto	basil, pine nut, olive oil paste
petto di...	breast of...
pezzo	piece
piadina	stuffed, soft, flat bread
piatto	plate
piatto di formaggi misti	cheese plate

piccante	spicy hot
piccolo	small
pici	rough-cut thick twisted pasta
pieno	full-bodied (wine)
pinioli	pine nuts
piselli	peas
pistacchio	pistachio
poche calorie	low calorie
polenta	moist cornmeal
polipo	octopus
pollame	poultry
pollo	chicken
pollo alla cacciatora	chicken with olive oil, rosemary, garlic, and tomato
polpo	octopus
pomodoro	tomato
pompelmo	grapefruit
porchetta	roast suckling pig
porcini	porcini mushrooms
pranzo	lunch
prezzemolo	parsley
prima colazione	breakfast
primo piatto	first course
profiterole	cream-filled pastry with chocolate sauce
prosciutto	cured ham
prosciutto cotto	cooked ham
prosciutto crudo	dried, air-cured ham
prosciutto e melone / fichi	air-cured ham wrapped around melon / fresh figs
provolone	rich, firm aged cow's cheese
prugna	prune
puttanesca	zesty sauce
quattro	four
quattro formaggi	four cheeses
quattro stagioni	pizza with four separate toppings
radiattore	radiator-shaped pasta
ragù	meat and tomato sauce

ribollita	hearty bread and vegetable soup
ricivuta	receipt
ricotta	soft, airy cheese
rigatoni	tube-shaped noodles
ripieno	stuffed
riso	rice
risotto	saffron-flavored rice
rosato	rosé (wine)
rosmarino	rosemary
rosso	red
rotelli	wheel-shaped pasta
salame	pork sausage
salamino piccante	pepperoni
salato	salty
sale	salt
salmone	salmon
salsiccia	sausage
saltimbocca alla Romana	veal cutlet sautéed with sage, *prosciutto*, and white wine
salumi misti	assortment of sliced, cured meats
salvia	sage
sambuca	anise (licorice) liqueur
saporito	mild
sarde	sardines
scaloppine	thin-sliced veal
scampi	prawns
schiacciata	pizza-like flatbread
sciacchetra	sweet desert wine
secco	dry (wine)
secondo piatto	second course
selvaggina	game
senape	mustard
senza	without
seppie	cuttlefish, sometimes squid
servizio	service charge
servizio incluso	service included
servizio non incluso	service not included
sfogliatella	pastry filled with sweetened ricotta

sgombro	scad (like mackerel)
Siciliana	pizza with capers and olives
sogliola	sole
sono pieno	I'm stuffed
sorbetto	sherbet
specialità	specialty
spezzatino	meat, potato, tomato stew
spiedini alla griglia	grilled seafood on a skewer
spinaci	spinach
spizziccare	snack
spremuta	freshly squeezed juice
spuntino	snack
stagionato	aged, sharp, and hard (cheese)
stagioni	seasons (and pizza toppings)
stracchino	spreadable cheese
stracciatella	chocolate chips w/vanilla (gelato)
strangolapreti	twisted pasta
strapazzate	scrambled
stufato	stew
stuzzicadente	toothpick
succo	juice
sugo	sauce, usually tomato
susina	plum
tacchino	turkey
tagliatelle	flat noodles
taleggio	rich, creamy cheese
tartina	tart
tartufi	truffles
tartufo	super-chocolate ice cream
tavola calda	buffet-style
tavola	table
tazza	cup
tè	tea
tè alla frutta	fruit tea
tè alla menta	mint tea
tè freddo	iced tea
tiramisú	espresso-soaked cake with chocolate, cream, and marsala

tisana	herbal tea
tonno	tuna
torta	cake
torte	pie
tortellini	stuffed noodles
tovagliolo	napkin
tramezzini	small, crustless sandwiches
trippa	tripe
trota	trout
uova	eggs
uova fritte	fried eggs
uova strapazzate	scrambled eggs
uovo alla coque	boiled egg
(molle / sodo)	(soft / hard)
uva	grapes
vegetariano	vegetarian
veloce	fast
vendemmia	harvest (wine)
verde	green
verdure	vegetables
verza	cabbage
vigneto	vineyard
vino	wine
vino da tavola	table wine
vino della casa	house wine
vino selezionato	select wine (good year)
vino sfuso	house wine in a jug
vitello	veal
vitello tonato	thinly sliced veal with tuna-caper mayonnaise
vongole	clams
wurstel	hot dogs
yogurt	yogurt
zabaglione	egg and liquor cream
zucchero	sugar
zuppa	soup
zuppa di pesce	fish soup or stew
zuppa inglese	trifle

English/Italian

alcohol	alcool
alcohol-free	analcolica
almond	mandorle
anchovies	acciughe
and	e
appetizers	antipasti
appetizers, small	ciccheti
apple	mela
apricot	albicocca
artichoke	carciofo
artichokes, giant	mame
asparagus	asparagi
assorted	assortiti
bacon, salt-cured	pancetta
baked	al forno
bakery	paneficio
barnacles	balani
basil	basilico
bass	branzino
beans	fagioli
beef	manzo
beef steak	bistecca
beer	birra
beer from the tap	birra alla spina
beets	barbabietole
bell peppers	peperoni
berries	frutti di bosco
beverages	bevande, bibite
black	nero
bleu cheese	gorgonzola
blueberry	mirtillo
boar	cinghiale
boiled	bollito
boiled egg	uovo alla coque
(soft / hard)	(molle / sodo)

boiling hot	bollente
bone marrow	ossobuco
bottle	bottiglia
bowl, small (gelato)	coppa
brains	cervella
braised	brasato
bread	pane
bread, brown	pane scuro
bread, crusty, flat, rustic	ciabatta
bread, flat	focaccia
bread, herb or vegetable	pane aromatico
bread, home-style	pane casereccia
bread, olive	pane di olive
bread, rustic, without salt	pane Toscano
bread, rye	pane di segale
bread, stuffed, soft, flat	piadina
bread, unsalted	filone
bread, whole grain	pane integrale
breadsticks	grissini
breakfast	colazione, prima colazione
bream (fish)	orata
breast (of...)	petto (di...)
broiled	alla graticola
broth	brodo
Brussels sprouts	cavolini de Bruxelles
buffet-style	tavola calda
butter	burro
cabbage	cavolo, verza
caffeine	caffeina
cake	torta
candy	caramelle
cantaloupe	melone
carafe	caraffa
carbonated	gassata
carrots	carote
cash register	cassa
cauliflower	cavolfiore
cereal	cereali

cheese	formaggio
cheese plate	piatto di formaggi misti
chef	cuoco
cherry	ciliegia
chestnut	castagne
chicken	pollo
chickpeas	ceci
Chinese	cinese
chocolate	cioccolata
chocolate and mint (gelato)	After Eight
chocolate chips with vanilla (gelato)	stracciatella
chocolate hazelnut candy (also gelato)	bacio
chocolate, super- (gelato)	tartufo
clams	vongole
coconut	noce di cocco
cod	merluzzo
coffee	caffè
coffee and firewater	coretto
coffee with a little milk	caffè macchiato
coffee with foam	cappuccino
coffee with milk	caffè latte
coffee with water	caffè lungo
coffee with whipped cream	caffè con panna
coffee, American-style	caffè Americano
coffee, iced	caffè freddo
coffee, instant	caffè solubile
cold	freddo
cone	cono
cooked	cotto
cookies	biscotti
corkscrew	cavatappi
corn	granturco
course, first	primo piatto
course, second	secondo piatto
cover charge	coperto
crab	granchione

cream	panna
cream puffs	bignole
croissant	cornetto
cucumber	cetrioli
cuisine	cucina
cup	tazza
cup (gelato)	coppa
cutlet	cotoletta
cuttlefish	seppie
cuttlefish cooked in its own ink	nero di seppie e polenta
dates	datteri
day	giorno
day, of the	del giorno
decaffeinated	decaffeinato
decaffeinated coffee	Haag
desserts	dolci
dinner	cena
dry (wine)	secco
duck	anatra
egg	uovo
egg salad	insalata con uova
egg, boiled (soft / hard)	uovo alla coque (molle / sodo)
eggplant	melanzana
eggs, fried	uova fritte
eggs, scrambled	uova strapazzate
fast	veloce
fennel	finocchio
fig	fico
fillet	filetto
firewater	grappa
first course	primo piatto
fish	pesce
fish soup	zuppa di pesce
fixed-price menu	menù turistico
flavors	gusti
food	cibo
French fries	patate fritte
fresh	fresco

fried	fritto
fruit	frutta
fruit salad	macedonia
fruit tea	tè alla frutta
fruitcake	panforte
fruity (wine)	amabile
full, I'm	sono pieno
full-bodied (wine)	corposo, pieno
game	selvaggina
garlic	aglio
glass	bicchiere
goat	capra
goat cheese	caprino
goat, baby	capretto
grapefruit	pompelmo
grapes	uva
green	verde
green beans	fagiolini
grilled	griglia
half	mezzo
ham, cooked	prosciutto cotto
ham, cured	prosciutto
ham, dried, air-cured	prosciutto crudo
hare	lepre
harvest (wine)	vendemmia
hazelnut	nocciola
heavy (wine)	pesante
herb	erbe
herbal tea	tisana
herring	aringa
homemade	casalingo, fatto in casa
honey	miele
honeydew melon	melone verde
hot	caldo
hot dog	wurstel, salsiccia
house	casa
house wine	vino della casa, vino sfuso
house, of the	della casa

ice	ghiaccio
ice cream	gelato
iced coffee	caffè freddo
iced tea	tè freddo
imported	importata
included	incluso
instant coffee	caffè solubile
jam	marmellata
jelly	gelatina
juice	succo
juice, freshly squeezed	spremuta
kosher	kasher
lamb	agnello, abbacchio
large	grande
lemon	limone
lemon soda	limonata
lentils	lenticchie
lettuce	lattuga
light	leggero
liver	fegato
liver and onions	fegato alla Veneziana
lobster	aragosta
lobster (male)	astice
local	locale
low calorie	poche calorie
lunch	pranzo
margarine	margarina
mature (wine)	maturo
mayonnaise	maionese
meat	carne
meat and tomato sauce	Bolognese, ragù
meat, medium	cotto
meat, rare	al sangue
meat, very rare	molto al sangue
meat, very well-done	completamente cotto
meat, well-done	ben cotto
medium (meat)	cotto
melon, honeydew	melone verde

menu of the day	menù del giorno
menu, fixed-price	menù turistico
mild	saporito
milk	latte
milk (gelato flavor)	fior di latte
milk with a little coffee	latte macchiato
milk, fresh	latte fresco
milk, skim	latte magro
milk, whole	latte intero
milkshake	frappè
mineral water	acqua minerale, minerale-acqua
mint	menta
mint tea	tè alla menta
mixed	misto
mushrooms	funghi
mushrooms (porcini)	porcini
mussels	cozze
mustard	senape
napkin	tovagliolo
non-smoking	non fumatori, non fumare
noodles	pastina
not	non
octopus	polpo, polipo
of	di
of the day	del giorno
of the house	della casa
oil	olio
olives	olive
omelet	frittata, omelette
onions	cipolle
or	o
orange	arancia
orange soda	aranciata
organic	organico, biologico
oysters	ostriche
paprika	peperoncino
parchment, steamed in	al cartoccio
parsley	prezzemolo

pastry	pasticcini
pastry shop	pasticceria
peach	pesca
peanut	noccioline
peanut butter	burro d'arachidi
pear	pera
peas	piselli
pepper	pepe
pepperoni	salamino piccante
peppers with tomato sauce	peperonata
pheasant	fagiano
pickles	cetriolini
pie	torte
pie with jam	crostata
piece	pezzo
pig, roast suckling	porchetta
pine nuts	pinioli
pineapple	ananas
pistachio	pistacchio
pizza with capers and olives	Siciliana
pizza with cheese and tomato sauce	Margherita
pizza with cheese, anchovies, and tomato sauce	Napoletana
pizza with four toppings	quattro stagioni
pizza, "white" (no tomato sauce)	bianca, ciaccina
pizza, folded	calzone
pizza, vegetarian	ortolana
pizza-like flatbread	schiacciata
plate	piatto
plum	susina
poached	affogato
pork	maiale
pork sausage	salame
porridge	farinata
potato noodles	gnocchi
potatoes	patate

poultry	pollame
prawns	scampi
prune	prugna
pudding	budino
rabbit	coniglio
rare (meat)	al sangue
raspberry	lampone
raw	crudo
receipt	ricivuta
red	rosso
rib steak	costata
rice	riso
rice, saffron-flavored	risotto
roasted	arrosto
roll	brioche, panino
rosé (wine)	rosato
rosemary	rosmarino
sage	salvia
salad	insalata
salad, bread and vegetable	panzanella
salad, egg	insalata con uova
salad, fruit	macedonia
salad, mozzarella and tomato	caprese
salad, seafood	insalata di mare
salmon	salmone
salt	sale
salty	salato
sandwich	panino
sandwiches, small, crustless	tramezzini
sardines	sarde
sauce of butter, cream, cheese	alfredo
sauce, seafood	pescatora
sauce, spicy tomato-chili	arrabiata
sauce, usually tomato	sugo
sauce, zesty	puttanesca
sausage	salsiccia
scad (like mackerel)	sgombro

scallops	capesante
scoop	pallina
scrambled	strapazzate
scrambled eggs	uova strapazzate
seafood	frutti di mare
seafood salad	insalata di mare
seafood sauce	pescatora
second course	secondo piatto
service charge	servizio
service included	servizio incluso
service not included	servizio non incluso
sheep cheese	pecorino
sherbet	sorbetto
shrimp	gamberi
shrimp, big	gamberoni
shrimp, small	gamberetti
side dishes	contorni
sirloin steak	entrecote
slice	fettina
small	piccolo
smoked	affumicato
snack	spuntino, spizziccare
snails	lumache
snow cone	granita
sole	sogliola
soup	zuppa, minestra
soup, fish	zuppa di pesce
soup, hearty bread and vegetable	ribollita
soup, vegetable	minestrone
sour	agro
sparkling (wine)	frizzante
specialty	specialità
spicy hot	piccante, alla diavola
spinach	spinaci
squid	calamari
steak, rib	costata
steak, sirloin	entrecote

steak, T-bone	bistecca alle Fiorentina
steamed	al vapore
stew	stufato
stew of meat, potato, tomato	spezzatino
strawberry	fragola
stuffed	ripieno, farcito
sugar	zucchero
sweet	dolce
sweet (wine)	abbocato
sweetbreads (calf pancreas)	animelle di vitello
Swiss cheese	emmenthal, groviera
swordfish	pesce spada
table	tavola
table wine	vino da tavola
tangerine	mandarino
tap water	acqua del rubinetto
tap, from the (beer)	alla spina
tarragon	dragoncello
tart	tartina
T-bone steak	bistecca alle Fiorentina
tea	tè
tea bag	bustina di tè
tea, herbal	tisana
tea, iced	tè freddo
tea, mint	tè alla menta
"to go"	da portar via
tomato	pomodoro
tomato and garlic sauce	marinara
tomato and meat sauce	Bolognese, ragù
tongue	lingua
toothpick	stuzzicadente
trifle	zuppa inglese
tripe	trippa
trout	trota
truffles	tartufi
tuna	tonno
turkey	tacchino
vanilla	crema

veal	vitello
vegetable soup	minestrone
vegetables	verdure, legumi
vegetarian	vegetariano
venison	cervo, capriolo
very	molto
very rare (meat)	molto al sangue
very well-done (meat)	completamente cotto
vinegar	aceto
vineyard	vigneto
vintage (wine)	annata
walnut	noce
water	acqua
water, mineral	acqua minerale, minerale-acqua
water, tap	acqua del rubinetto
watermelon	cocomero
well-done (meat)	ben cotto
wheat	frumento
whipped cream	panna
white	bianco
wine	vino
wine, dry	secco
wine, fruity	amabile
wine, full-bodied	corposo, pieno
wine, harvest	vendemmia
wine, heavy	pesante
wine, house	vino della casa, vino sfuso
wine, mature	maturo
wine, red	rosso
wine, rosé	rosato
wine, select (good year)	vino selezionato
wine, sparkling	frizzante
wine, sweet	abboccato
wine, table	vino da tavola
wine, vintage	annata
wine, white	bianco
with	con
without	senza
yogurt	yogurt

ACTIVITIES

Sightseeing

Where?

Where is...?	Dov'è...?	doh-**veh**
...the best view	...la vista più bella	lah **vee**-stah pew **behl**-lah
...the main square	...la piazza principale	lah peeaht-sah preen-chee-**pah**-lay
...the old town center	...il centro storico	eel **chehn**-troh **stoh**-ree-koh
...the museum	...il museo	eel moo-**zay**-oh
...the castle	...il castello	eel kah-**stehl**-loh
...the palace	...il palazzo	eel pah-**lahd**-zoh
...the ruins	...le rovine	lay roh-**vee**-nay
...an amusement park	...un parco dei divertimenti	oon **par**-koh **deh**ee dee-vehr-tee-**mehn**-tee
...tourist information	...l'ufficio informazioni	loo-**fee**-choh een-for-maht-see**oh**-nee
...the toilet	...la toilette	lah twah-**leht**-tay
...the entrance / exit	...l'entrata / l'uscita	lehn-**trah**-tah / loo-**shee**-tah
Is there a festival nearby?	C'è un festival qui vicino?	cheh oon fehs-tee-**vahl** kwee vee-**chee**-noh

145

KEY PHRASES: SIGHTSEEING

Where is...?	*Dov'è...?*	doh-**veh**
How much is it?	*Quanto costa?*	**kwahn**-toh **koh**-stah
What time does	*A che ora*	ah kay **oh**-rah
this open / close?	*apre / chiude?*	**ah**-pray / keeoo-day
Do you have	*Avete un tour*	ah-**vay**-tay oon toor
a guided tour?	*guidato?*	gwee-**dah**-toh
When is the next	*Quando è il*	**kwahn**-doh eh eel
tour in English?	*prossimo tour*	**proh**-see-moh toor
	in inglese?	een een-**glay**-zay

At the Sight

Do you have...?	*Avete...?*	ah-**vay**-tay
...information	*...informazioni*	een-for-maht-see**oh**-nee
...a guidebook	*...una guida*	**oo**-nah **gwee**-dah
...in English	*...in inglese*	een een-**glay**-zay
Is it free?	*È gratis?*	eh **grah**-tees
How much is it?	*Quanto costa?*	**kwahn**-toh **koh**-stah
Is (the ticket)	*È valido per*	eh **vah**-lee-doh pehr
valid all day?	*tutto il giorno?*	**too**-toh eel **jor**-noh
Can I get back in?	*Posso rientrare?*	**poh**-soh ree-ehn-**trah**-ray
What time does	*A che ora*	ah kay **oh**-rah
this open / close?	*apre / chiude?*	**ah**-pray / keeoo-day
What time is the	*Quand'è l'ultima*	kwahn-**deh lool**-tee-mah
last entry?	*entrata?*	ayn-**trah**-tah

Please

PLEASE let	*PER FAVORE,*	pehr fah-**voh**-ray
me / us in.	*mi / ci faccia*	mee / chee **fah**-chah
	entrare.	ayn-**trah**-ray
I've traveled all	*Sono venuto[a]*	**soh**-noh vay-**noo**-toh
the way from ___.	*qui da ___.*	kwee dah
We've traveled all	*Siamo venuti[e]*	see**ah**-moh vay-**noo**-tee
the way from ___.	*qui da ___.*	kwee dah

I must leave tomorrow.	Devo partire domani.	**day**-voh par-**tee**-ray doh-**mah**-nee
We must leave tomorrow.	Dobbiamo partire domani.	doh-beeah-moh par-**tee**-ray doh-**mah**-nee
I promise I'll be fast.	Prometto che sarò veloce.	proh-**meht**-toh kay sah-**roh** vay-**loh**-chay
We promise we'll be fast.	Promettiamo che saremo veloci.	proh-meht-teeah-moh kay sah-**ray**-moh vay-**loh**-chee
It was my mother's dying wish that I see this.	Ho promesso a mia madre sul letto di morte che avrei visto questo.	oh proh-**mehs**-soh ah **mee**-ah **mah**-dray sool **leht**-toh dee **mor**-tay kay ah-**vray**ee vee-**stoh kweh**-stoh
I've / We've always wanted to see this.	Ho / Abbiamo sempre desiderato vedere questo.	oh / ah-beeah-moh **sehm**-pray day-zee-day-**rah**-toh vay-**dehr**-ay **kweh**-stoh

Tours

Do you have...?	Avete...?	ah-**vay**-tay
...an audioguide	...un'audioguida	oo-now-deeoh-**gwee**-dah
...a guided tour	...un tour guidato	oon toor gwee-**dah**-toh
...a city walking tour	...una visita guidata della città	**oo**-nah vee-**zee**-tah gwee-**dah**-tah **dehl**-lah chee-**tah**
...in English	...in inglese	een een-**glay**-zay
When is the next tour in English?	Quando è il prossimo tour in inglese?	**kwahn**-doh eh eel **proh**-see-moh toor een een-**glay**-zay
Is it free?	È gratis?	eh **grah**-tees
How much is it?	Quanto costa?	**kwahn**-toh **koh**-stah
How long does it last?	Quanto dura?	**kwahn**-toh **doo**-rah
Can I / Can we join a tour in progress?	Posso / Possiamo unirci ad un tour già iniziato?	**poh**-soh / poh-seeah-moh oon-**eer**-chee ahd oon toor jah ee-neet-seeah-toh

Entrance Signs

adulti	adults
giro guidato, tour	guided tour
mostra	special exhibit
siete qui	you are here (on map)

Discounts

You may be eligible for discounts at tourist sights, hotels, or on buses and trains—ask.

Is there a discount for...?	Fate sconti per...?	fah-tay skohn-tee pehr
...youth	...giovani	joh-vah-nee
...students	...studenti	stoo-dehn-tee
...families	...famiglie	fah-meel-yay
...seniors	...anziani	ahnt-seeah-nee
...groups	...comitive	koh-mee-tee-vay
I am...	Sono...	soh-noh
He / She is...	Lui / Lei ha...	lwee / lehee ah
... ___ years old.	... ___ anni.	___ ahn-nee
...extremely old.	...vecchissimo[a].	vehk-ee-see-moh

In the Museum

Where is...?	Dov'è...?	doh-veh
I'd / We'd like to see...	Mi / Ci piacerebbe vedere...	mee / chee peeah-chay-ray-bay vay-dehr-ay
Photo / video O.K.?	Foto / video è O.K.?	foh-toh / vee-day-oh eh "O.K."
No flash / tripod.	Vietato usare flash / trepiede.	veeay-tah-toh oo-zah-ray flahsh / tray-peeay-day
I like it.	Mi piace.	mee peeah-chay
It's so...	È così...	eh koh-zee
...beautiful.	...bello.	behl-loh

...ugly.	...brutto.	**broo**-toh
...strange.	...strano.	**strah**-noh
...boring.	...noioso.	noh-**yoh**-zoh
...interesting.	...interessante.	een-tay-ray-**sahn**-tay
...pretentious.	...presuntuoso.	pray-zoon-**twoh**-zoh
It's thought-provoking.	Fa pensare.	fah pehn-**sah**-ray
It's B.S.	È una stronzata.	eh **oo**-nah strohnt-**sah**-tah
I don't get it.	Non capisco.	nohn kah-**pees**-koh
Is it upside down?	È rovesciato?	eh roh-vay-**shah**-toh
Who did this?	Chi l'ha fatto?	kee lah **fah**-toh
How old is this?	Quanti anni ha?	**kwahn**-tee **ah**-nee ah
Wow!	Wow!	"wow"
My feet hurt!	Mi fanno male i piedi!	mee **fah**-noh **mah**-lay ee peeay-dee
I'm exhausted!	Sono stanco[a] morto[a]!	**soh**-noh **stahn**-koh **mor**-toh
We're exhausted!	Siamo stanchi[e] morti[e].	seeah-moh **stahn**-kee **mor**-tee

Be careful when planning your sightseeing. Many museums close in the afternoon from 1:00 p.m. until 3:00 or 4:00 p.m., and are closed all day on a weekday, usually Monday. Museums often stop selling tickets 45 minutes before closing. Historic churches usually open much earlier than museums.

Art and Architecture

art	arte	**ar**-tay
artist	artista	ar-**tee**-stah
painting	quadro	**kwah**-droh
self portrait	autoritratto	ow-toh-ree-**trah**-toh
sculptor	scultore	skool-**toh**-ray
sculpture	scultura	skool-**too**-rah
architect	architetto	ar-kee-**teht**-toh
architecture	architettura	ar-kee-teht-**too**-rah
original	originale	oh-ree-jee-**nah**-lay

restored	*restaurato*	ray-stow-**rah**-toh
B.C.	*A.C.*	ah chee
A.D.	*D.C.*	dee chee
century	*secolo*	**say**-koh-loh
style	*stile*	**stee**-lay
copy by ___	*copia di ___*	**koh**-peeah dee
after the style of ___	*nello stile di ___*	**nehl**-loh **stee**-lay dee
from the school of ___	*della scuola di ___*	**dehl**-lah **skwoh**-lah dee
abstract	*Astratto*	ah-**strah**-toh
ancient	*Antico*	ahn-**tee**-koh
Art Nouveau	*Arte Nouveau*	**ar**-tay **noo**-voh
Baroque	*Barocco*	bah-**roh**-koh
classical	*Classico*	**klah**-see-koh
Gothic	*Gotico*	**goh**-tee-koh
impressionist	*Impressionista*	eem-pray-seeoh-**nee**-stah
medieval	*Medievale*	may-deeay-**vah**-lay
modern	*Moderno*	moh-**dehr**-noh
neoclassical	*Neoclassico*	nee-oh-**klah**-see-koh
Renaissance	*Rinascimento*	ree-nah-shee-**mayn**-toh
Romanesque	*Romanico*	roh-**mahn**-ee-koh
Romantic	*Romantico*	roh-**mahn**-tee-koh

The Italians refer to their three greatest centuries of art in an unusual way. The 1300s are called *tre cento* (300s). The 1400s (early Renaissance) are called *quattro cento* (400s), and the 1500s (High Renaissance) are *cinque cento* (500s).

Castles and Palaces

castle	*castello*	kah-**stehl**-loh
palace	*palazzo*	pah-**lahd**-zoh
hall	*sala*	**sah**-lah
kitchen	*cucina*	koo-**chee**-nah
cellar	*cantina*	kahn-**tee**-nah
dungeon	*segrete*	say-**gray**-tay
moat	*fossato*	foh-**sah**-toh

fortified walls	muri fortificati	**moo**-ree for-tee-fee-**kah**-tee
tower	torre	**tor**-ray
fountain	fontana	fohn-**tah**-nah
garden	giardino	jar-**dee**-noh
king	re	ray
queen	regina	ray-**jee**-nah
knights	cavalieri	kah-vah-lee**ay**-ree

Religious Words

cathedral	duomo	**dwoh**-moh
church	chiesa	kee**ay**-zah
monastery	monastero	moh-nah-**stay**-roh
synagogue	sinagoga	see-nah-**goh**-gah
chapel	cappella	kah-**pehl**-lah
altar	altare	ahl-**tah**-ray
bells	campane	kahm-**pah**-nay
choir	coro	**kor**-oh
cloister	chiostro	kee**oh**-stroh
cross	croce	**kroh**-chay
crypt	cripta	**kreep**-tah
dome	cupola	**koo**-poh-lah
organ	organo	**or**-gah-noh
pulpit	pulpito	pool-**pee**-toh
relics	reliquie	ray-**lee**-kweeay
treasury	tesoro	tay-**zoh**-roh
baptistery	battistero	bah-tee-**stay**-roh
saint	santo[a]	**sahn**-toh
pope	Papa	**pah**-pah
God	Dio	**dee**-oh
Christian	cristiano[a]	kree-stee**ah**-noh
Protestant	protestante	proh-tay-**stahn**-tay
Catholic	cattolico[a]	kah-**toh**-lee-koh
Jewish	ebreo	ay-**bray**-oh
Muslim	mussulmano[a]	moo-sool-**mah**-noh
agnostic	agnostico[a]	ahn-**yoh**-stee-koh

atheist	*ateo[a]*	ah-**tay**-oh
When is the	*A che ora*	ah kay **oh**-rah
mass (service)?	*è la messa?*	eh lah **may**-sah
Are there church	*Ci sono*	chee **soh**-noh
concerts?	*concerti*	kohn-**chehr**-tee
	in chiesa?	een keeay-zah

The piano was invented in Italy. Unlike a harpsichord, it could be played soft and loud, so it was called just that: *piano-forte* (soft-loud). Here are other Italian musical words you might know: *subito* (suddenly), *crescendo* (growing louder), *sopra* (over), *sotto* (under), *ritardando* (slowing down), and *fine* (finish).

Shopping

Italian Shops

Where is a...?	*Dov'è un...?*	doh-**veh** oon
antique shop	*negozio di*	nay-**goht**-seeoh dee
	antiquariato	ahn-tee-kwah-reeah-toh
art gallery	*galleria d'arte*	gah-lay-**ree**-ah dar-tay
bakery	*panificio*	pah-nee-**fee**-choh
barber shop	*barbiere*	bar-beeay-ray
beauty salon	*parrucchiere*	pah-roo-keeay-ray
book shop	*libreria*	lee-bray-**ree**-ah
camera shop	*foto-ottica*	foh-toh-**oh**-tee-kah
cell phone shop	*negozio di*	nay-**goht**-seeoh dee
	cellulari	chehl-loo-**lah**-ree
clothing boutique	*boutique di*	boo-**teek** dee
	abbigliamento	ah-beel-yah-**mehn**-toh
coffee shop	*bar*	bar
department store	*grande*	**grahn**-day
	magazzino	mah-gahd-**zee**-noh
delicatessen	*salumeria*	sah-loo-may-**ree**-ah
flea market	*mercato delle*	mehr-**kah**-toh **dehl**-lay
	pulci	**pool**-chee

flower market	mercato dei fiori	mehr-**kah**-toh **deh**ee fee-**oh**-ree
grocery store	alimentari	ah-lee-mayn-**tah**-ree
hardware store	ferramenta	fehr-rah-**mehn**-tah
Internet café	Internet café	**een**-tehr-neht kah-**fay**
jewelry shop	gioielliera	joh-yay-lee**ay**-rah
launderette	lavanderia	lah-vahn-day-**ree**-ah
leather shop	pelletteria	pehl-leht-teh-**ree**-ah
newsstand	giornalaio	jor-nah-**lah**-yoh
office supplies	cartoleria	kar-toh-lay-**ree**-ah
open air market	mercato	mehr-**kah**-toh
optician	ottico	**oh**-tee-koh
pastry shop	pasticceria	pah-stee-chay-**ree**-ah
pharmacy	farmacia	far-mah-**chee**-ah
photocopy shop	copisteria	koh-pee-stay-**ree**-ah
pottery shop	negozio di ceramica	nay-**goht**-seeoh dee chay-**rah**-mee-kah
shopping mall	centro commerciale	**chehn**-troh koh-mehr-**chah**-lay
souvenir shop	negozio di souvenir	nay-**goht**-seeoh dee **soo**-vay-neer
supermarket	supermercato	soo-pehr-mehr-**kah**-toh
sweets shop	negozio di dolciumi, pasticceria	nay-**goht**-seeoh dee dohl-chee**oo**-mee, pah-stee-chay-**ree**-ah
toy store	negozio di giocattoli	nay-**goht**-seeoh dee joh-**kah**-toh-lee
travel agency	agenzia di viaggi	ah-jehnt-**see**-ah dee vee**ah**-jee
used bookstore	negozio di libri usati	nay-**goht**-seeoh dee **lee**-bree oo-**zah**-tee
...with books in English	...che vende libri in inglese	kay **vehn**-dray **lee**-bree een een-**glay**-zay
wine shop	negozio di vini	nay-**goht**-seeoh dee **vee**-nee

Most businesses are closed daily from 1:00 p.m. until 3:00 or 4:00 p.m. Many stores in the larger cities close for all or part of August—not a good time to plan a shopping spree.

KEY PHRASES: SHOPPING

Where can I buy...?	Dove posso comprare...?	**doh**-vay **poh**-soh kohm-**prah**-ray
Where is a...?	Dov'è un...?	doh-**veh** oon
grocery store	alimentari	ah-lee-mayn-**tah**-ree
department store	grande magazzino	**grahn**-day mah-gahd-**zee**-noh
Internet café	Internet café	**een**-tehr-neht kah-**fay**
launderette	lavanderia	lah-vahn-day-**ree**-ah
pharmacy	farmacia	far-mah-**chee**-ah
How much is it?	Quanto costa?	**kwahn**-toh **koh**-stah
I'm just browsing.	Sto solo guardando.	stoh **soh**-loh gwar-**dahn**-doh

Shop Till You Drop

opening hours	*orario d'apertura*	oh-**rah**-reeoh dah-pehr-**too**-rah
sale	*saldo*	**sahl**-doh
I'd like / We'd like...	*Vorrei / Vorremmo...*	vor-**reh**ee / vor-**ray**-moh
Where can I buy...?	*Dove posso comprare...?*	**doh**-vay **poh**-soh kohm-**prah**-ray
Where can we buy...?	*Dove possiamo comprare...?*	**doh**-vay poh-see**ah**-moh kohm-**prah**-ray
How much is it?	*Quanto costa?*	**kwahn**-toh **koh**-stah
I'm / We're...	*Sto / Stiamo...*	stoh / stee**ah**-moh
...just browsing.	*...solo guardando.*	**soh**-loh gwar-**dahn**-doh
Do you have something...?	*Avete qualcosa di...?*	ah-**vay**-tay kwahl-**koh**-zah dee
...cheaper	*...meno caro*	**may**-noh **kah**-roh
...better	*...miglior qualità*	**meel**-yor kwah-lee-**tah**
Better quality, please.	*Qualcosa di migliore qualità, per favore.*	kwahl-**koh**-zah dee **meel**-yoh-ray kwah-lee-**tah** pehr fah-**voh**-ray
genuine / imitation	*autentico / imitazione*	ow-**tehn**-tee-koh / ee-mee-taht-see**oh**-nay

Can I / Can we see more?	Posso / Possiamo vederne ancora?	**poh**-soh / poh-see**ah**-moh vay-**dehr**-nay ahn-**koh**-rah
This one.	Questo qui.	**kweh**-stoh kwee
Can I try it on?	Lo posso provare?	loh **poh**-soh proh-**vah**-ray
Do you have a mirror?	Ha uno specchio?	ah **oo**-noh **spay**-keeoh
Too...	Troppo...	**troh**-poh
...big.	...grande.	**grahn**-day
...small.	...piccolo.	**pee**-koh-loh
...expensive.	...caro.	**kah**-roh
It's too...	È troppo...	eh **troh**-poh
...short / long.	...corto / lungo.	**kor**-toh / **loon**-goh
...tight / loose.	...stretto / largo.	**streht**-toh / **lar**-goh
...dark / light.	...scuro / chiaro.	**skoo**-roh / kee**ah**-roh
What is it made of?	Di che cosa è fatto?	dee kay **koh**-zah eh **fah**-toh
Is it machine washable?	Si può lavare in lavatrice?	see pwoh lah-**vah**-ray een lah-vah-**tree**-chay
Will it shrink?	Si ritira?	see ree-**tee**-rah
Will it fade in the wash?	Scolora quando si lava?	skoh-**loh**-rah **kwahn**-doh see **lah**-vah
Credit card O.K.?	Carta di credito è O.K.?	**kar**-tah dee **kray**-dee-toh eh "O.K."
Can you ship this?	Può spedirmelo?	pwoh spay-**deer**-may-loh
Tax-free?	Esente da tasse?	ay-**zehn**-tay dah **tah**-say
I'll think about it.	Ci penserò.	chee pehn-say-**roh**
What time do you close?	A che ora chiudete?	ah kay **oh**-rah keeoo-**day**-tay
What time do you open tomorrow?	A che ora aprite domani?	ah kay **oh**-rah ah-**pree**-tay doh-**mah**-nee

Street Markets

Did you make this?	L'avete fatto voi questo?	lah-**vay**-tay **fah**-toh **voh**ee **kweh**-stoh
Is that your final price?	È questo il prezzo finale?	eh **kweh**-stoh eel **prehd**-zoh fee-**nah**-lay
Cheaper?	Me lo dà a meno?	may loh dah ah **may**-noh
My last offer.	La mia ultima offerta.	lah **mee**-ah **ool**-tee-mah oh-**fehr**-tah
Good price.	Buon prezzo.	bwohn **prehd**-zoh
I'll take it.	Lo prendo.	loh **prehn**-doh
We'll take it.	Lo prendiamo.	loh prehn-dee**ah**-moh
I'm nearly broke.	Sono quasi al verde.	**soh**-noh **kwah**-zee ahl **vehr**-day
We're nearly broke.	Siamo quasi al verde.	see**ah**-moh **kwah**-zee ahl **vehr**-day
My male friend...	Il mio amico...	eel **mee**-oh ah-**mee**-koh
My female friend...	La mia amica...	lah **mee**-ah ah-**mee**-kah
My husband...	Mio marito...	**mee**-oh mah-**ree**-toh
My wife...	Mia moglie...	**mee**-ah **mohl**-yay
...has the money.	...ha i soldi.	ah ee **sohl**-dee

At street markets, it's common to bargain.

Clothes

For...	Per...	pehr
...a male / a female baby.	...un neonato / una neonata.	oon nay-oh-**nah**-toh / **oo**-nah nay-oh-**nah**-tah
...a male / a female child.	...un bambino / una bambina.	oon bahm-**bee**-noh / **oo**-nah bahm-**bee**-nah
...a male / a female teenager.	...un ragazzo / una ragazza.	oon rah-**gahd**-zoh / **oo**-nah rah-**gahd**-zah
...a man.	...un uomo.	oon **woh**-moh
...a woman.	...una donna.	**oo**-nah **doh**-nah
bathrobe	accappatoio	ah-kah-pah-**toh**-yoh
bib	bavaglino	bah-vahl-**yee**-noh
belt	cintura	cheen-**too**-rah
bra	reggiseno	ray-jee-**zay**-noh

clothing	vestiti	vehs-**tee**-tee
dress	vestito	vehs-**tee**-toh
	da donna	dah **doh**-nah
flip-flops	ciabatte da	chah-**bah**-tay dah
	piscina	pee-**shee**-nah
gloves	guanti	**gwahn**-tee
hat	cappello	kah-**pehl**-loh
jacket	giacca	**jah**-kah
jeans	jeans	"jeans"
nightgown	vestaglia	vehs-**tahl**-yah
nylons	collant	koh-**lahnt**
pajamas	pigiama	pee-**jah**-mah
pants	pantaloni	pahn-tah-**loh**-nee
raincoat	impermeabile	eem-pehr-may-**ah**-bee-lay
sandals	sandali	sahn-**dah**-lee
scarf	sciarpa, foulard	**shar**-pah, foo-**lard**
shirt...	camicia...	kah-**mee**-chah
...long-sleeved	...a maniche	ah mah-**nee**-kay
	lunghe	**loong**-gay
...short-sleeved	...a maniche corte	ah mah-**nee**-kay **kor**-tay
...sleeveless	...senza maniche	**sehn**-sah mah-**nee**-kay
shoelaces	lacci da scarpe	**lah**-chee dah **skar**-pay
shoes	scarpe	**skar**-pay
shorts	pantaloni corti	pahn-tah-**loh**-nee **kor**-tee
skirt	gonna	**goh**-nah
sleeper (for baby)	tutina (da	too-**tee**-nah (dah
	neonato)	nay-oh-**nah**-toh)
slip	sottoveste	soh-toh-**vehs**-tay
slippers	ciabatte,	chah-**bah**-tay,
	pantofole	pahn-**toh**-foh-lay
socks	calzini	kahlt-**see**-nee
sweater	maglione	mahl-yee**oh**-nay
swimsuit	costume	kohs-**too**-may
	da bagno	dah **bahn**-yoh
tennis shoes	scarpe da	**skar**-pay dah
	ginnastica	jee-**nah**-stee-kah
T-shirt	maglietta	mahl-**yay**-tah
underwear	mutande	moo-**tahn**-day
vest	gilet	jee-**lay**

Colors

black	nero	**nay**-roh
blue	azzurro	ahd-**zoo**-roh
brown	marrone	mah-**roh**-nay
gray	grigio	**gree**-joh
green	verde	**vehr**-day
orange	arancio	ah-**rahn**-choh
pink	rosa	**roh**-zah
purple	viola	vee**oh**-lah
red	rosso	**roh**-soh
white	bianco	bee**ahn**-koh
yellow	giallo	**jah**-loh
dark / light	scuro / chiaro	**skoo**-roh / kee**ah**-roh
lighter	più chiaro	pew kee**ah**-roh
brighter	più brillante	pew bree-**lahn**-tay
darker	più scuro	pew **skoo**-roh

Materials

brass	ottone	oh-**toh**-nay
bronze	bronzo	**brohnt**-soh
ceramic	ceramica	chay-**rah**-mee-kah
copper	rame	**rah**-may
cotton	cotone	koh-**toh**-nay
glass	vetro	**vay**-troh
gold	oro	**oh**-roh
lace	pizzo	**peed**-zoh
leather	cuoio / pelle	**kwoh**-yoh / **pehl**-lay
linen	lino	**lee**-noh
marble	marmo	**mar**-moh
metal	metallo	may-**tah**-loh
nylon	nylon	**nee**-lohn
paper	carta	**kar**-tah
pewter	peltro	**pehl**-troh
plastic	plastica	**plah**-stee-kah
polyester	polyestere	poh-lee-ehs-**tay**-ray
porcelain	porcellana	por-chay-**lah**-nah

silk	seta	**say**-tah
silver	argento	ar-**jehn**-toh
velvet	velluto	vay-**loo**-toh
wood	legno	**layn**-yoh
wool	lana	**lah**-nah

Jewelry

bracelet	bracciale	brah-chee**ah**-lay
brooch	spilla	**spee**-lah
earrings	orecchini	oh-ray-**kee**-nee
jewelry	gioielli	joh-**yeh**-lee
necklace	collana	koh-**lah**-nah
ring	anello	ah-**nehl**-loh
Is this...?	Questo è...?	**kwehs**-toh eh
...sterling silver	...argento sterling	ar-**jehn**-toh **stehr**-leeng
...real gold	...oro zecchino	**oh**-roh tseh-**kee**-noh
...stolen	...rubato	roo-**bah**-toh

Sports

Bicycling

bicycle	bicicletta	bee-chee-**klay**-tah
mountain bike	mountain bike	"mountain bike"
I'd like to rent a bicycle.	Vorrei noleggiare una bicicletta.	vor-**reh**ee noh-leh-**jah**-ray **oo**-nah bee-chee-**klay**-tah
We'd like to rent two bicycles.	Vorremmo noleggiare due biciclette.	vor-**ray**-moh noh-leh-**jah**-ray **doo**-ay bee-chee-**klay**-tay
How much...?	Quanto...?	**kwahn**-toh
...per hour	...all'ora	ah-**loh**-rah
...per half day	...per mezza giornata	pehr **mehd**-zah jor-**nah**-tah
...per day	...al giorno	ahl **jor**-noh
Is a deposit required?	Ci vuole un deposito?	chee **vwoh**-lay oon day-**poh**-zee-toh

deposit	*deposito*	day-**poh**-zee-toh
helmet	*casco*	**kahs**-koh
lock	*lucchetto*	loo-**keht**-toh
air / no air	*aria /*	**ah**-reeah /
	senza aria	**sehn**-sah **ah**-reeah
tire	*gomma*	**goh**-mah
pump	*pompa*	**pohm**-pah
map	*cartina*	kar-**tee**-nah
How many gears?	*Quante marce?*	**kwahn**-tay **mar**-kay
What is a...route	*Mi può*	mee pwoh
of about ___	*indicare un*	een-dee-**kah**-ray oon
kilometers?	*percorso... di*	pehr-**kor**-soh... dee
	circa ___	**cheer**-kah ___
	chilometri?	kee-**loh**-may-tree
...good	*...bello*	**behl**-loh
...scenic	*...panoramico*	pah-noh-**rah**-mee-koh
...interesting	*...interessante*	een-tay-ray-**sahn**-tay
...easy	*...facile*	**fah**-chee-lay
How many	*Quanti minuti /*	**kwahn**-tee mee-**noo**-tee /
minutes / How	*Quante ore*	**kwahn**-tay **oh**-ray
many hours by	*in bicicletta?*	een bee-chee-**klay**-tah
bicycle?		
I (don't) like hills.	*(Non) mi*	(nohn) mee
	piacciono le	peeah-**choh**-noh lay
	salite.	sah-**lee**-tay
I brake for	*Mi fermo*	mee **fehr**-moh
bakeries.	*ad ogni*	ahd **ohn**-yee
	pasticceria.	pah-stee-chay-**ree**-ah

For more on route-finding, see "Finding Your Way," beginning on page 50 in the Traveling chapter.

Swimming and Boating

Where can I /	*Dove posso /*	**doh**-vay **poh**-soh /
can we rent...?	*possiamo*	poh-seeah-moh
	noleggiare...?	noh-leh-**jah**-ray
...a paddleboat	*...un pedalò*	oon pay-dah-**loh**

...a rowboat	...una barca a remi	**oo**-nah **bar**-kah ah **ray**-mee
...a boat	...una barca	**oo**-nah **bar**-kah
...a sailboat	...una braca a vela	**oo**-nah **bar**-kah ah **vay**-lah
How much...?	Quanto...?	**kwahn**-toh
...per hour	...all'ora	ah-**loh**-rah
...per half day	...per mezza giornata	pehr **mehd**-zah jor-**nah**-tah
...per day	...al giorno	ahl **jor**-noh
beach	spiaggia	speeah-jah
nude beach	spiaggia nudista	speeah-jah noo-**dee**-stah
Where's a good beach?	Mi può indicare una bella spiaggia?	mee pwoh een-dee-**kah**-ray **oo**-nah **behl**-lah speeah-jah
Is it safe for swimming?	È sicura per nuotare?	eh see-**koo**-rah pehr nwoh-**tah**-ray
flip-flops	ciabatte da piscina	chah-**bah**-tay dah pee-**shee**-nah
pool	piscina	pee-**shee**-nah
snorkel and mask	boccaglio e maschera	boh-**kahl**-yoh ay mahs-**kay**-rah
sunglasses	occhiali da sole	oh-keeah-lee dah **soh**-lay
sunscreen	protezione solare	proh-teht-seeoh-nay soh-**lah**-ray
surfboard	tavola da surf	**tah**-voh-lah dah soorf
surfer	surfer	**soorf**-er
swimsuit	costume da bagno	kohs-**too**-may dah **bahn**-yoh
towel	asciugamano	ah-shoo-gah-**mah**-noh
waterskiing	sci acquatico	shee ah-**kwah**-tee-koh
windsurfing	windsurf	**weend**-soorf

In Italy, nearly any beach is topless, but if you want a nude beach, keep your eyes peeled for a *spiaggia nudista*.

Sports Talk

sports	gli sport	**lee**yee sport
game	partita	par-**tee**-tah
championship	campionato	kahm-peeoh-**nah**-toh
soccer	football, calcio	**foot**-bahl, **kahl**-choh
basketball	basket	**bah**-skeht
hockey	hockey	**oh**-kee
American football	football Americano	**foot**-bahl ah-may-ree **kah**-noh
baseball	baseball	**bahs**-bahl
tennis	tennis	**tehn**-nees
golf	golf	gohlf
skiing	sci	shee
gymnastics	ginnastica	jee-**nah**-stee-kah
jogging	jogging	**joh**-geeng
Olympics	le Olimpiadi	lay oh-leem-peeah-dee
medal...	medaglia...	may-**dahl**-yah
...gold / silver / bronze	...oro / argento / bronzo	**oh**-roh / ar-**jehn**-toh / **brohnt**-soh
Which is your favorite sport / athlete?	Qual'è il suo sport / giocatore?	kwah-**leh** eel **soo**-oh sport / joh-kah-**toh**-ray
Which is your favorite team?	Qual'è la sua squadra?	kwah-**leh** lah **soo**-ah **skwah**-drah
Where can I see a game?	Dove posso vedere una partita?	**doh**-vay **poh**-soh vay-**day**-ray **oo**-nah par-**tee**-tah
Where's a good place to jog?	Dov'è un buon luogo per fare jogging?	doh-**veh** oon bwohn loo**oh**-goh pehr **fah**-ray **joh**-geeng

Entertainment

What's happening tonight?	Che cosa succede stasera?	kay **koh**-zah soo-**chay**-day stah-**zay**-rah
What do you recommend?	Che cosa raccomanda?	kay **koh**-zah rah-koh-**mahn**-dah
Where is it?	Dov'è?	doh-**veh**
How do you get there?	Come ci si arriva?	**koh**-may chee see ah-**ree**-vah
Is it free?	È gratis?	eh **grah**-tees
Are there seats available?	Ci sono ancora dei posti?	chee **soh**-noh ahn-**koh**-rah **deh**ee **poh**-stee
Where can I buy a ticket?	Dove si comprano i biglietti?	**doh**-vay see kohm-**prah**-noh ee beel-**yay**-tee
Do you have tickets for today / tonight?	Ha dei biglietti per oggi / stasera?	ah **deh**ee beel-**yay**-tee pehr **oh**-jee / stah-**zay**-rah
When does it start?	A che ora comincia?	ah kay **oh**-rah koh-**meen**-chah
When does it end?	A che ora finisce?	ah kay **oh**-rah fee-**nee**-shay
Where's the best place to dance nearby?	Qual'è il posto migliore per ballare qui vicino?	kwah-**leh** eel **poh**-stoh meel-**yoh**-ray pehr bah-**lah**-ray kwee vee-**chee**-noh
Where do people stroll?	Dov'è la passeggiata?	doh-**veh** lah pah-say-**jah**-tah

Entertaining Words

movie...	cinema...	**chee**-nay-mah
...original version	...versione originale	vehr-see**oh**-nay oh-ree-jee-**nah**-lay
...in English	...in inglese	een een-**glay**-zay
...with subtitles	...con sottotitoli	kohn soh-toh-**tee**-toh-lee

...dubbed	...doppiato	doh-pee**ah**-toh
music...	musica...	**moo**-zee-kah
...live	...dal vivo	dahl **vee**-voh
...classical	...classica	**klah**-see-kah
...folk	...folk	fohlk
...opera	...lirica	**lee**-ree-kah
...symphony	...sinfonica	seen-**foh**-nee-kah
...choir	...corale	koh-**rah**-lay
...traditional	...tradizionale	trah-deet-seeoh-**nah**-lay
old rock	rock vecchio stile	rohk **vehk**-eeoh **stee**-lay
jazz / blues	jazz / blues	jahz / "blues"
singer	cantante	kahn-**tahn**-tay
concert	concerto	kohn-**chehr**-toh
show	spettacolo	speht-**tah**-koh-loh
dancing	ballare	bah-**lah**-ray
folk dancing	danze	**dahnt**-say
	popolari	poh-poh-**lah**-ree
disco	discoteca	dee-skoh-**tay**-kah
bar with	locale con	loh-**kah**-lay kohn
live music	musica dal	**moo**-zee-kah dahl
	vivo	**vee**-voh
nightclub	locale notturno	loh-**kah**-lay noh-**toor**-noh
no cover charge	ingresso libero	een-**gray**-soh **lee**-bay-roh
sold out	tutto esaurito	**too**-toh ay-zow-**ree**-toh

For cheap entertainment, join the locals and take a *passeggiata* (stroll) through town. As you bump shoulders in the crowd, you'll know why it's also called *struscio* (rubbing). On workdays, Italians stroll between work and dinner. On holidays, they hit the streets after lunch. This is Italy on parade. People are strutting. If ever you could enjoy being forward, this is the time. Whispering a breathy *bella* (cute girl) or *bello* (cute guy) feels natural.

CONNECT

Phoning

I'd like to buy a...	*Vorrei comprare una...*	voh-**reh**ee kohm-**prah**-ray **oo**-nah
...telephone card.	*...carta telefonica.*	**kar**-tah tay-lay-**foh**-nee-kah
...cheap international telephone card.	*...carta telefonica prepagate internazionali.*	**kar**-tah tay-lay-**foh**-nee-kah pray-pah-**gah**-tay een-tehr-naht-seeoh-**nah**-lee
Where is the nearest phone?	*Dov'è il telefono più vicino?*	doh-**veh** eel tay-**lay**-foh-noh pew vee-**chee**-noh
It doesn't work.	*Non funziona.*	nohn foont-seeoh-nah
May I use your phone?	*Posso usare il telefono?*	**poh**-soh oo-**zah**-ray eel tay-**lay**-foh-noh
Can you talk for me?	*Può parlare per me?*	pwoh par-**lah**-ray pehr may
It's busy.	*È occupato.*	eh oh-koo-**pah**-toh
Will you try again?	*Può riprovare?*	pwoh ree-proh-**vah**-ray
Hello. (on phone)	*Pronto.*	**prohn**-toh
My name is ___.	*Mi chiamo ___.*	mee kee**ah**-moh

Sorry, I speak only a little Italian.	*Mi dispiace, parlo solo un po' italiano.*	mee dee-spee**ah**-chay **par**-loh **soh**-loh oon poh dee-tah-lee**ah**-noh
Speak slowly and clearly.	*Parli lentamente e chiaramente.*	**par**-lee layn-tah-**mayn**-tay ay keeah-rah-**mayn**-tay
Wait a moment.	*Un momento.*	oon moh-**mayn**-toh

In this book, you'll find the phrases you need to reserve a hotel room (page 55) or a table at a restaurant (page 74). To spell your name over the phone, refer to the code alphabet on page 59.

Make your calls using handy phone cards sold at post offices, train stations, *tabacchi* (tobacco shops), and from machines near phone booths. There are two kinds:

1) an insertable card (*carta telefonica*) that you slide into a phone in a phone booth (tear the corner off your phone card before using), and...

2) a cheaper-per-minute international phone card (with a scratch-off PIN code) that you can use from any phone, usually even from your hotel room. If a phone balks, change its setting from pulse to tone. To get a PIN card, ask for a *carta telefonica prepagate internazionali.*

You can also make phone calls from post offices, telephone offices, and metered phones in cafés and bars.

At phone booths, you'll encounter these words on the phone's message display: *sganciare* (which means either hang onto the phone...or hang up), *inserire una carta* (insert a card), *carta telefonica* (the phone acknowledges that you've inserted a phone card), then *selezionare* or *digitare numero* (dial your number). *Occupato* means busy. You'll see the *credito* (monetary value of your card) tick down after you connect. When you hang up, you'll see *attendere prego* (please wait), *ritirare la carta* (retrieve your card), and again *sganciare* (you're done or you can start again). There are some regional differences in the various messages, but the sequence is the same.

Italian phones are temperamental. At any time while you're dialing, you may hear a brusque recording:

"*Telecom Italia informazione gratuita: Il numero selezionato
è inesistente*" (Telecom Italia free information: The number
you're dialing is nonexistent). If you get this message,
try dialing again, slowly, as though the phone doesn't
understand numbers very well. For more tips, see "Let's Talk
Telephones" on page 282 in the Appendix.

Telephone Words

telephone	*telefono*	tay-**lay**-foh-noh
telephone card	*carta*	**kar**-tah
	telefonica	tay-lay-**foh**-nee-kah
cheap	*carta*	**kar**-tah
international	*telefonica*	tay-lay-**foh**-nee-kah
telephone card	*prepagate in-*	pray-pah-**gah**-tay een-
	ternazionali	tehr-naht-seeoh-**nah**-lee
PIN code	*PIN*	peen
phone booth	*cabina*	kah-**bee**-nah
	telefonica	tay-lay-**foh**-nee-kah
out of service	*guasto*	goo**ah**-stoh
metered phone	*telefono a*	tay-**lay**-foh-noh ah
	scatti	**skah**-tee
phone office	*posto*	**poh**-stoh
	telefonico	tay-lay-**foh**-nee-koh
	pubblico	**poob**-lee-koh
operator	*centralinista*	chayn-trah-lee-**nee**-stah
international	*assistenza per*	ah-see-**stehnt**-sah pehr
assistance	*chiamate inter-*	keeah-**mah**-tay een-tehr-
	nazionali	naht-seeoh-**nah**-lee
international call	*telefonata inter-*	tay-lay-foh-**nah**-tah een-tehr-
	nazionale	naht-seeoh-**nah**-lay
collect call	*telefonata a*	tay-lay-foh-**nah**-tah ah
	carico del	**kah**-ree-koh dayl
	desinatario	dehs-tee-nah-**tah**-reeoh
credit card call	*telefonata con*	tay-lay-foh-**nah**-tah kohn
	la carta di	lah **kar**-tah dee
	credito	**kray**-dee-toh
toll-free	*numero verde*	**noo**-may-roh **vehr**-day

fax	*fax*	fahks
country code	*prefisso per*	pray-**fee**-soh pehr
	il paese	eel pah-**ay**-zay
area code	*prefisso*	pray-**fee**-soh
extension	*numero interno*	**noo**-may-roh een-**tehr**-noh
telephone book	*elenco*	ay-**lehn**-koh
	telefonico	tay-lay-**foh**-nee-koh
yellow pages	*pagine gialle*	**pah**-jee-nay **jah**-lay

Cell Phones

Where is a cell phone shop?	*Dov'è un negozio di cellulari?*	doh-**veh** oon nay-**goht**-seeoh dee chehl-loo-**lah**-ree
I'd like / We'd like...	*Vorrei / Vorremmo...*	vor-**reh**ee / vor-**ray**-moh
...a cell phone.	*...un telefono cellulare.*	oon tay-**lay**-foh-noh chehl-loo-**lah**-ray
...a chip.	*...una scheda.*	**oo**-nah **skay**-dah
...to buy more time.	*...una ricarica.*	**oo**-nah ree-**kah**-ree-kah
How do you...?	*Come si fa a...?*	**koh**-may see fah ah
...make calls	*...fare una chiamata*	**fah**-ray **oo**-nah keeah-**mah**-tah
...receive calls	*...ricevere una chiamata*	ree-**chay**-vay-ray **oo**-nah keeah-**mah**-tah
Will this work outside this country?	*Funziona anche all'estero?*	foont-see**oh**-nah **ahn**-kay ah-lehs-**tay**-roh
Where can I buy a chip for this service / phone?	*Dove posso comprare una scheda per questo gestore / telefono?*	**doh**-vay **poh**-soh kohm-**prah**-ray **oo**-nah **skay**-dah pehr **kweh**-stoh jehs-**toh**-ray / tay-**lay**-foh-noh

Many travelers now buy cell phones in Europe to make both local and international calls. You'll pay under $100 for a "locked" phone that works only in the country you buy it in

(includes about $20 worth of calls). You can buy additional
time at a newsstand or cell phone shop. An "unlocked"
phone is more expensive (over $100), but it works all over
Europe: when you cross a border, buy a SIM card at a cell
phone shop and insert the pop-out chip, which comes with
a new phone number. Pricier tri-band phones (*ttelefono tri-
banda*) also work in North America.

E-Mail and
the Web

E-Mail

My e-mail address is...	*Il mio indirizzo di posta elettronica è...*	eel **mee**-oh een-dee-**reed**-zoh dee **poh**-stah ay-leht-**troh**-nee-kah eh
What's your e-mail address?	*Qual è il suo indirizzo di posta elettronica?*	kwahl eh eel **soo**-oh een-dee-**reed**-zoh dee **poh**-stah ay-leht-**troh**-nee-kah
Can I use this computer to check my e-mail?	*Posso usare il computer per controllare mia posta elettronica?*	**poh**-soh oo-**zah**-ray eel kohm-**poo**-ter pehr kohn-troh-**lah**-ray **mee**-ah **poh**-stah ay-leht-**troh**-nee-kah
Where can I / can we access the Internet?	*C'è un posto dove posso / possiamo accedere a Internet?*	cheh oon **poh**-stoh **doh**-vay **poh**-soh / poh-see**ah**-moh ah-**chay**-day-ray ah **een**-tehr-neht
Where is an Internet café?	*Dov'è un` Internet café?*	doh-**veh** oon **een**-tehr-neht kah-**fay**

How much for...minutes?	Quanto costa per... minuti?	**kwahn**-toh **koh**-stah pehr... mee-**noo**-tee
...10	...dieci	deea**y**-chee
...15	...quindici	**kween**-dee-chee
...30	...trenta	**trayn**-tah
...60	...sessanta	say-**sahn**-tah
Help me, please.	Mi aiuti, per favore.	mee ah-**yoo**-tee pehr fah-**voh**-ray
How do I...	Come si fa a...	**koh**-may see fah ah
...start this?	...accendere questo?	ah-**chehn**-day-ray **kweh**-stoh
...send a file?	...mandare un file?	mahn-**dah**-ray oon **fee**-lay
...print out a file?	...stampare un file?	stahm-**pah**-ray oon **fee**-lay
...make this symbol?	...fare questo simbolo?	**fah**-ray **kweh**-stoh **seem**-boh-loh
...type @?	...fare la chiocciola?	fah-ray lah keeoh-choh-lah
This isn't working.	Non funziona.	nohn foont-see**oh**-nah

Web Words

e-mail	posta elettronica	**poh**-stah ay-leht-**troh**-nee-kah
e-mail address	indirizzo di posta elettronica	een-dee-**reed**-zoh dee **poh**-stah ay-leht-**troh**-nee-kah
Web site	sito Internet	**see**-toh **een**-tehr-neht
Internet	Internet	**een**-tehr-neht
surf the Web	navigare su Internet	nah-vee-**gah**-ray soo **een**-tehr-neht
download	scaricare	shah-ree-**kah**-ray
@ sign	chiocciola	keeoh-choh-lah
dot	punto	**poon**-toh
hyphen (-)	trattino	trah-**tee**-noh
underscore (_)	linea bassa	**lee**-nay-ah **bah**-sah
modem	modem	**moh**-dehm

KEY PHRASES: E-MAIL AND THE WEB

e-mail	*posta elettronica*	**poh**-stah ay-leht-**troh**-nee-kah
Internet	*Internet*	**een**-tehr-neht
Where is the nearest Internet access point?	*Dov'è l'Internet più vicino?*	doh-**veh** **leen**-tehr-neht pew vee-**chee**-noh
I'd like to check my e-mail.	*Vorrei controllare la mia posta elettronica.*	vor-**reh**ee kohn-troh-**lah**-ray lah **mee**-ah poh-stah ay-leht-**troh**-nee-kah

On Screen

aprire	open	**salvare**	save
cancellare	delete	**stampare**	print
documento	file	**scrivere**	write
inviare	send	**rispondere**	reply
messaggio	message		

Mailing

Where is the post office?	*Dov'è la Posta?*	doh-**veh** lah **poh**-stah
Which window for...?	*Qual'è lo sportello per...?*	kwah-**leh** loh spor-**tehl**-loh pehr
Is this the line for...?	*È questa la fila per...?*	eh **kweh**-stah lah **fee**-lah pehr
...stamps	...*francobolli*	frahn-koh-**boh**-lee
...packages	...*pacchi*	**pah**-kee
To the United States...	*Per Stati Uniti...*	pehr **stah**-tee oo-**nee**-tee
...by air mail.	...*per via aerea.*	pehr **vee**-ah ah-**ay**-ray-ah
...by surface mail.	...*via terra.*	**vee**-ah **tehr**-rah
...slow and cheap.	...*lento e economico.*	**lehn**-toh ay ay-koh-**noh**-mee-koh
How much is it?	*Quanto costa?*	**kwahn**-toh **koh**-stah

How much to send a letter / postcard to...?	Quanto costa mandare una lettera / una cartolina a...?	**kwahn**-toh **koh**-stah mahn-**dah**-ray **oo**-nah leht-**tay**-rah / **oo**-nah kar-toh-**lee**-nah ah
I need stamps for ___ postcards to...	Ho bisogno di francobolli per ___ cartoline per...	oh bee-**zohn**-yoh dee frahn-koh-**boh**-lee pehr ___ kar-toh-**lee**-nay pehr
...America / Canada.	...gli Stati Uniti / il Canada.	**lee**yee **stah**-tee oo-**nee**-tee / eel kah-nah-**dah**
Pretty stamps, please.	Dei bei francobolli, per favore.	**deh**ee **beh**ee frahn-koh-**boh**-lee pehr fah-**voh**-ray
I always choose the slowest line.	Scelgo sempre la fila più lenta.	**shehl**-goh **sehm**-pray lah **fee**-lah pew **lehn**-tah
How many days will it take?	Quanti giorni ci vogliono?	**kwahn**-tee **jor**-nee chee **vohl**-yoh-noh

In Italy, you can often get stamps at the corner *tabacchi* (tobacco shop). As long as you know which stamps you need, this is a great convenience. Unless you like to gamble, avoid mailing packages from Italy. The most reliable post offices are in the Vatican City.

KEY PHRASES: MAILING		
post office	ufficio postale	oo-**fee**-choh poh-**stah**-lay
stamp	francobollo	frahn-koh-**boh**-loh
postcard	lettera	**leht**-tay-rah
letter	cartolina	kar-toh-**lee**-nah
air mail	per via aerea	pehr **vee**-ah ah-**ay**-ray-ah
Where is the post office?	Dov'è la Posta?	doh-**veh** lah **poh**-stah
I need stamps for ___ postcards / letters to America.	Ho bisogno di francobolli per ___ cartoline / lettere per gli Stati Uniti.	oh bee-**zohn**-yoh dee frahn-koh-**boh**-lee pehr ___ kar-toh-**lee**-nay / **leht**-tay-ray pehr **lee**yee **stah**-tee oo-**nee**-tee

CONNECT

Licking the Postal Code

Post & Telegraph Office	Poste e Telegrafi	**poh**-stay ay tay-**lay**-grah-fee
post office	ufficio postale	oo-**fee**-choh poh-**stah**-lay
stamp	francobollo	frahn-koh-**boh**-loh
postcard	cartolina	kar-toh-**lee**-nah
letter	lettera	**leht**-tay-rah
envelope	busta	**boo**-stah
package	pacco	**pah**-koh
box...	scatola...	**skah**-toh-lah
...cardboard	...de cartone	day kar-**toh**-nay
string	filo	**fee**-loh
tape	scotch	"scotch"
mailbox	cassetta postale	kah-**say**-tah poh-**stah**-lay
air mail	per via aerea	pehr **vee**-ah ah-**ay**-ray-ah
express	espresso	eh-**sprehs**-soh
surface mail	via terra	**vee**-ah **tehr**-rah
slow and cheap	lento e economico	**lehn**-toh ay ay-koh-**noh**-mee-koh
book rate	prezzo di listino	**prehd**-zoh dee lee-**stee**-noh
weight limit	limite di peso	lee-**mee**-tay dee **pay**-zoh
registered	raccomandata	rah-koh-mahn-**dah**-tah
insured	assicurato	ah-see-koo-**rah**-toh
fragile	fragile	frah-**jee**-lay
contents	contenuto	kohn-tay-**noo**-toh
customs	dogana	doh-**gah**-nah
sender	mittente	mee-**tehn**-tay
destination	destinatario	dehs-tee-nah-**tah**-reeoh
to / from	da / a	dah / ah
address	indirizzo	een-dee-**reed**-zoh
zip code	codice postale	koh-**dee**-chay poh-**stah**-lay
general delivery	fermo posta	**fehr**-moh **poh**-stah

CONNECT

HELP!

Help!	Aiuto!	ah-**yoo**-toh
Call a doctor!	Chiamate un dottore!	keeah-**mah**-tay oon doh-**toh**-ray
Call...	Chiamate...	keeah-**mah**-tay
...the police.	...la polizia.	lah poh-leet-**see**-ah
...an ambulance.	...un'ambulanza.	oo-nahm-boo-**lahnt**-sah
...the fire department.	...i vigili del fuoco.	ee **vee**-jee-lee dehl **fwoh**-koh
I'm lost.	Mi sono perso[a].	mee **soh**-noh **pehr**-soh
We're lost.	Ci siamo persi[e].	chee seeah-moh **pehr**-see
Thank you for your help.	Grazie dell'aiuto.	**graht**-seeay dehl-ah-**yoo**-toh
You are very kind.	Lei è molto gentile.	**leh**ee eh **mohl**-toh jehn-**tee**-lay

In Italy, call 118 if you have a medical emergency.

Theft and Loss

| Stop, thief! | Fermatelo! Al ladro! | fehr-**mah**-tay-loh ahl **lah**-droh |
| I have been robbed. | Sono stato[a] derubato[a]. | **soh**-noh **stah**-toh day-roo-**bah**-toh |

174

We have been robbed.	Siamo stati[e] derubati[e].	seeah-moh stah-tee day-roo-bah-tee
A thief took...	Un ladro ha preso...	oon lah-droh ah pray-zoh
Thieves took...	I ladri hanno preso...	ee lah-dree ah-noh pray-zoh
I have lost my money.	Ho perso i soldi.	oh pehr-soh ee sohl-dee
We have lost our money.	Abbiamo perso i soldi.	ah-beeah-moh pehr-soh ee sohl-dee
I've lost my...	Ho perso il mio...	oh pehr-soh eel mee-oh
...passport.	...passaporto.	pah-sah-por-toh
...ticket.	...biglietto.	beel-yay-toh
...baggage.	...bagaglio.	bah-gahl-yoh
...wallet.	...portafoglio.	por-tah-fohl-yoh
I've lost...	Ho perso...	oh pehr-soh
...my purse.	...la mia borsa.	la mee-ah bor-sah
...my faith in humankind.	...la fiducia nel prossimo.	lah fee-doo-chah nayl proh-see-moh
We've lost our...	Abbiamo perso i nostri...	ah-beeah-moh pehr-soh ee noh-stree
...passports.	...passaporti.	pah-sah-por-tee
...tickets.	...biglietti.	beel-yay-tee
...baggage.	...bagagli.	bah-gahl-yee
I want to contact my embassy.	Vorrei contattare la mia ambasciata.	vor-rehee kohn-tah-tah-ray lah mee-ah ahm-bah-sheeah-tah
I need to file a police report for my insurance.	Devo fare una denuncia per la mia assicurazione.	day-voh fah-ray oo-nah day-noon-chah pehr lah mee-ah ah-see-koo-raht-seeoh-nay

Dialing 113 or 112 will connect you to English-speaking police help. See page 284 in the Appendix for U.S. embassies in Italy.

HELP!

KEY PHRASES: HELP

accident	*incidente*	een-chee-**dehn**-tay
emergency	*emergenza*	ay-mehr-**jehnt**-sah
police	*polizia*	poh-leet-**see**-ah
Help!	*Aiuto!*	ah-**yoo**-toh
Call a doctor / the police!	*Chiamate un dottore / la polizia!*	keeah-**mah**-tay oon doh-**toh**-ray / lah poh-leet-**see**-ah
Stop, thief!	*Fermatelo! Al ladro!*	fehr-**mah**-tay-loh ahl **lah**-droh

Helpful Words

ambulance	*ambulanza*	ahm-boo-**lahnt**-sah
accident	*incidente*	een-chee-**dehn**-tay
injured	*ferito*	fay-**ree**-toh
emergency	*emergenza*	ay-mehr-**jehnt**-sah
emergency room	*pronto soccorso*	**prohn**-toh soh-**kor**-soh
fire	*fuoco*	**fwoh**-koh
police	*polizia*	poh-leet-**see**-ah
smoke	*fumo*	**foo**-moh
thief	*ladro*	**lah**-droh
pickpocket	*borsaiolo*	bor-sah-**yoh**-loh

Help for Women

Leave me alone.	*Mi lasci in pace.*	mee **lah**-shee een **pah**-chay
I want to be alone.	*Voglio stare sola.*	**vohl**-yoh **stah**-ray **soh**-lah
I'm not interested.	*Non sono interessata.*	nohn **soh**-noh een-tay-ray-**sah**-tah
I'm married.	*Sono sposata.*	**soh**-noh spoh-**zah**-tah
I'm a lesbian.	*Sono lesbica.*	**soh**-noh **lehz**-bee-kah
I have a contagious disease.	*Ho una malattia contagiosa.*	oh **oo**-nah mah-lah-**tee**-ah kohn-tah-**joh**-zah

You are bothering me.	*Mi sta importunando.*	mee stah eem-por-too-**nahn**-doh
This man is bothering me.	*Questo uomo mi importuna.*	**kweh**-stoh **woh**-moh mee eem-por-**too**-nah
You are intrusive.	*Mi sta dando fastidio.*	mee stah **dahn**-doh fah-**stee**-deeoh
Don't touch me.	*Non mi tocchi.*	nohn mee **toh**-kee
You're disgusting.	*Tu sei disgustoso.*	too **seh**ee dees-goo-**stoh**-zoh
Stop following me.	*La smetta di seguirmi.*	lah **smay**-tah dee say-**gweer**-mee
Stop it!	*La smetta!*	lah **smay**-tah
Enough!	*Basta!*	**bah**-stah
Go away.	*Se ne vada.*	say nay **vah**-dah
Get lost!	*Sparisca!*	spah-**ree**-skah
Drop dead!	*Crepi!*	**kray**-pee
I'll call the police.	*Chiamo la polizia.*	kee**ah**-moh lah poh-leet-**see**-ah

HELP!

Whenever macho males threaten to make leering a contact sport, local women stroll arm-in-arm or holding hands. Wearing conservative clothes and avoiding smiley eye contact also convey a "don't hustle me" message.

SERVICES

Laundry

Is a... nearby?	*C'è una... qui vicino?*	cheh **oo**-nah... kwee vee-**chee**-noh
...self-service laundry	*...lavanderia self-service*	lah-vahn-day-**ree**-ah sehlf-**sehr**-vees
...full-service laundry	*...lavanderia*	lah-vahn-day-**ree**-ah
Help me, please.	*Mi aiuti, per favore.*	mee ah-**yoo**-tee pehr fah-**voh**-ray
How does this work?	*Come funziona?*	**koh**-may foont-see**oh**-nah
Where is the soap?	*Dov'è il detersivo?*	doh-**veh** eel day-tehr-**see**-voh
Are these yours?	*Sono suoi questi?*	**soh**-noh **swoh**-ee **kweh**-stee
This stinks.	*Questo puzza.*	**kweh**-stoh **pood**-zah
Smells...	*Sente...*	**sehn**-tay
...like spring time.	*...del profumo di primavera.*	dehl proh-**foo**-moh dee pree-mah-**vay**-rah
...like a locker room.	*...d'uno spogliatoio.*	**doo**-noh spohl-yah-**toh**-yoh
...like cheese.	*...del formaggio.*	dehl for-**mah**-joh

178

I need change.	Ho bisogno di moneta.	oh bee-**zohn**-yoh dee moh-**nay**-tah
Same-day service?	Servizio in giornata?	sehr-**veet**-seeoh een jor-**nah**-tah
By when do I need to drop off my clothes?	Quando devo portare qui i miei panni?	**kwahn**-doh **day**-voh por-**tah**-ray kwee ee mee-**ay**ee **pah**-nee
When will they be ready?	Quando saranno pronti?	**kwahn**-doh sah-**rah**-noh **prohn**-tee
Dried?	Asciutti?	ah-**shoo**-tee
Folded?	Piegati?	peeay-**gah**-tee
Hey there, what's spinning?	Salve, come gira?	**sahl**-vay **koh**-may **jee**-rah

Clean Words

wash / dry	lavare / asciugare	lah-**vah**-ray / ah-shoo-**gah**-ray
washer / dryer	lavatrice / asciugatrice	lah-vah-**tree**-chay / ah-shoo-gah-**tree**-chay
detergent	detersivo da bucato	day-tehr-**see**-voh dah boo-**kah**-toh
token	gettone	jeht-**toh**-nay
whites	il bianco	eel bee**ahn**-koh
colors	il colore	eel koh-**loh**-ray
delicates	delicato	day-lee-**kah**-toh
handwash	lavare a mano	lah-**vah**-ray ah **mah**-noh

Haircuts

Where is a barber / hair salon?	Dov'è un barbiere / parrucchiere?	doh-**veh** oon bar-bee**ay**-ray / pah-roo-kee**ay**-ray
I'd like...	Vorrei...	vor-**reh**ee
...a haircut.	...un taglio.	oon **tahl**-yoh
...a permanent.	...una permanente.	**oo**-nah pehr-mah-**nehn**-tay
...just a trim.	...solo una spuntatina.	**soh**-loh **oo**-nah spoon-tah-**tee**-nah

Cut about this much off.	*Tagli tanto cosi.*	**tahl**-yee **tahn**-toh **koh**-zee
Cut my bangs here.	*Mi tagli la frangia qui.*	mee **tahl**-yee lah **frahn**-jah kwee
Longer here.	*Più lunghi qui.*	pew **loong**-gee kwee
Shorter here.	*Più corti qui.*	pew **kor**-tee kwee
I'd like my hair...	*Vorrei...*	vor-**reh**ee
...short.	*...tagliarmi i capelli.*	tahl-**yar**-mee ee kah-**pay**-lee
...colored.	*...tingermi i capelli.*	teen-**jehr**-mee ee kah-**pay**-lee
...shampooed.	*...fare uno shampoo.*	**fah**-ray **oo**-noh **shahm**-poo
...blow dried.	*...una piega a phon.*	**oo**-nah pee**ay**-gah ah fohn
It looks good.	*Sta bene.*	stah **behn**-ay

Repair

These handy lines can apply to any repair, whether it's a ripped rucksack, bad haircut, or crabby camera.

This is broken.	*Questo è rotto.*	**kweh**-stoh eh **roh**-toh
Can you fix it?	*Lo può aggiustare?*	loh pwoh ah-joo-**stah**-ray
Just do the essentials.	*Faccia solamente le cose essenziali.*	**fah**-chah soh-lah-**mayn**-tay lay **koh**-zay ay-saynt-see**ah**-lee
How much will it cost?	*Quanto costa?*	**kwahn**-toh **koh**-stah
When will it be ready?	*Quando sarà pronta?*	**kwahn**-doh sah-**rah** **prohn**-tah
I need it by ___.	*Ne ho bisogno entro ___.*	nay oh bee-**zohn**-yoh **ayn**-troh
We need it by ___.	*Ci serve per___.*	chee **sehr**-vay pehr
Without it, I'm...	*Senza sono...*	**sehn**-sah **soh**-noh
...lost.	*...perso.*	**pehr**-soh
...ruined.	*...rovinato.*	roh-vee-**nah**-toh
...finished.	*...finito.*	fee-**nee**-toh

Filling out Forms

Signore / Signora / Signorina	Mr. / Mrs. / Miss
nome	first name
cognome	name
indirizzo	address
domicilio	address
strada	street
città	city
stato	state
paese	country
nazionalità	nationality
origine / destinazione	origin / destination
età	age
data di nascita	date of birth
luogo di nascita	place of birth
sesso	sex
sposato / sposata	married man / married woman
scapolo / nubile	single man / single woman
professione	profession
adulto	adult
bambino / ragazzo / ragazza	child / boy / girl
bambini	children
famiglia	family
firma	signature

When filling out dates, do it European-style:
day/month/year.

HEALTH

I am sick.	Sto male.	stoh **mah**-lay
I feel (very) sick.	Mi sento (molto) male.	mee **sehn**-toh (**mohl**-toh) **mah**-lay
My husband / My wife...	Mio marito / Mia moglie...	**mee**-oh mah-**ree**-toh / **mee**-ah **mohl**-yay
My son / My daughter...	Mio figlio / Mia figlia...	**mee**-oh **feel**-yoh / **mee**-ah **feel**-yah
My male friend / My female friend...	Il mio amico / La mia amica...	eel **mee**-oh ah-**mee**-koh / lah **mee**-ah ah-**mee**-kah
...feels (very) sick.	...si sente (molto) male.	see **sehn**-tay (**mohl**-toh) **mah**-lay
It's urgent.	È urgente.	eh oor-**jehn**-tay
I / We need a doctor...	Ho / Abbiamo bisogno di un dottore...	oh / ah-bee**ah**-moh bee-**zohn**-yoh dee oon doh-**toh**-ray
...who speaks English	...che parli inglese.	kay **par**-lee een-**glay**-zay
Please call a doctor.	Per favore, chiami un dottore.	pehr fah-**voh**-ray kee**ah**-mee oon doh-**toh**-ray
Could a doctor come here?	Puo venire qua un dottore?	pwoh vay-**nee**-ray kwah oon doh-**toh**-ray
I am...	Sono...	**soh**-noh
He / She is...	Lui / Lei è...	lwee / **leh**ee eh

...allergic to penicillin / sulfa.	...allergico[a] alla pennicillina / ai sulfamidici.	ah-**lehr**-jee-koh **ah**-lah pehn-nee-chee-**lee**-nah / **ah**ee sool-fah-mee-**dee**-chee
I am diabetic.	Ho il diabete.	oh eel deeah-**bay**-tay
I have cancer.	Ho il cancro.	oh eel **kahn**-kroh
I had a heart attack __ years ago.	Ho avuto un infarto ___ anni fa.	oh ah-**voo**-toh oon een-**far**-toh ___ **ah**-nee fah
It hurts here.	Fa male qui.	fah **mah**-lay kwee
I feel faint.	Mi sento svenire.	mee **sehn**-toh svay-**nee**-ray
It hurts to urinate.	Fa male urinare.	fah **mah**-lay oo-ree-**nah**-ray
I have body odor.	Puzzo.	**pood**-zoh
I'm going bald.	Perdo i capelli.	**pehr**-doh ee kah-**pay**-lee
Is it serious?	È grave?	eh **grah**-vay
Is it contagious?	È contagioso?	eh kohn-tah-**joh**-zoh
Aging sucks.	Che schifo, invecchiare!	kay **skee**-foh een-vehk-kee**ah**-ray
Take one pill every __ hours for __ days before meals / with meals.	Prenda una pillola ogni ___ ore per ___ giorni prima dei pasti / con i pasti.	**prehn**-dah oo-nah peel-**oh**-lah **ohn**-yee ___ **oh**-ray pehr ___ **jor**-nee **pree**-mah **de**hee **pah**-stee / kohn ee **pah**-stee
I need a receipt for my insurance.	Ho bisogno di una ricevuta per la mia assicurazione.	oh bee-**zohn**-yoh dee **oo**-nah ree-chay-**voo**-tah pehr lah **mee**-ah ah-see-koo-raht-see**oh**-nay

Ailments

I have...	Ho...	oh
He / She has...	Lui / Lei ha...	lwee / **leh**ee ah
I / We need medication for...	Ho / Abbiamo bisogno di un farmaco per...	oh / ah-bee**ah**-moh bee-**zohn**-yoh dee oon far-**mah**-koh pehr
...arthritis.	...l'artrite.	lar-**tree**-tay

...asthma.	...l'asma.	**lahz**-mah
...athelete's foot (fungus).	...piede d'atleta (fungo).	peeay-day daht-**lay**-tah (**foong**-goh)
...bad breath.	...l'alito cattivo.	lah-**lee**-toh kah-**tee**-voh
...blisters.	...vesciche.	vay-**shee**-kay
...bug bites.	...le punture d'insetto.	lay poon-**too**-ray deen-**seht**-toh
...a burn.	...una bruciatura.	**oo**-nah broo-chah-**too**-rah
...chest pains.	...dolore al petto.	doh-**loh**-ray ahl **peht**-toh
...chills.	...i brividi.	ee bree-**vee**-dee
...a cold.	...un raffreddore.	oon rah-fray-**doh**-ray
...congestion.	...una congestione.	**oo**-nah kohn-jehs-tee**oh**-nay
...constipation.	...la stitichezza.	lah stee-tee-**kayd**-zah
...a cough.	...la tosse.	lah **toh**-say
...cramps.	...i crampi	ee **krahm**-pee
...diabetes.	...il diabete.	eel dee-ah-**bay**-tay
...diarrhea.	...la diarrea.	lah dee-ah-**ray**-ah
...dizziness.	...capogiri.	kah-poh-**jee**-ree
...earache.	...il mal d'orecchi.	eel mahl doh-**ray**-kee
...epilepsy.	...l'epilessia.	lay-pee-**lay**-seeah
...a fever.	...la febbre.	lah **feh**-bray
...the flu.	...l'influenza.	leen-floo-**ehnt**-sah
...food poisoning.	...l'avvelenamento da cibo.	lah-vehl-ehn-ah-**mehn**-toh dah **chee**-boh
...the giggles.	...la ridarella.	lah ree-dah-**ray**-lah
...hay fever.	...il raffreddore da fieno.	eel rah-fray-**doh**-ray dah fee**ay**-noh
...a headache.	...un mal di testa.	oon mahl dee **tehs**-tah
...a heart condition.	...i disturbi cardiaci.	ee dee-**stoor**-bee kar-dee**ah**-chee
...hemorrhoids.	...le emorroidi.	lay ay-moh-roh**ee**-dee
...high blood pressure.	...la pressione alta.	lah pray-see**oh**-nay **ahl**-tah
...indigestion.	...una indigestione.	**oo**-nah een-dee-jay-stee**oh**-nay
...an infection.	...una infezione.	**oo**-nah een-feht-see**oh**-nay

HEALTH

...inflammation.	...una infiammazione.	**oo**-nah een-feeah-maht-see**oh**-nay
...a migraine.	...l'emicrania.	lay-mee-**krah**-nee-ah
...nausea.	...l nausea.	lah **now**-zee-ah
...pneumonia.	...la bronco-polmonite.	lah brohn-koh-pohl-moh-**nee**-tay
...a rash.	...un'irritazione della pelle.	oo-nee-ree-taht-see**oh**-nay **dehl**-lah **pehl**-lay
...sinus problems.	...disturbi sinusali.	dee-**stoor**-bee see-noo-**zah**-lee
...a sore throat.	...il mal di gola.	eel mahl dee **goh**-lah
...a stomach ache.	...il mal di stomaco.	eel mahl dee **stoh**-mah-koh
...sunburn.	...una scottatura solare.	**oo**-nah skoh-tah-**too**-rah soh-**lah**-ray
...swelling.	...un gonfiore.	oon gohn-fee**oh**-ray
...a toothache.	...mal di denti.	mahl dee **dehn**-tee
...a urinary infection.	...infezione urinaria.	een-feht-see**oh**-nay oo-ree-**nah**-reeah
...a venereal disease.	...una malattia venerea.	**oo**-nah mah-lah-**tee**-ah vay-**nay**-ray-ah
...vicious sunburn.	...una grave scottatura solare.	oo-nah **grah**-vay skoh-tah-**too**-rah soh-**lah**-ray
...vomiting.	...il vomito	eel **voh**-mee-toh
...worms.	...vermi.	**vehr**-mee

KEY PHRASES: HEALTH

doctor	dottore	doh-**toh**-ray
hospital	ospedale	oh-spay-**dah**-lay
pharmacy	farmacia	far-mah-**chee**-ah
medicine	medicina	may-dee-**chee**-nah
I am sick.	Mi sento male.	mee **sehn**-toh **mah**-lay
I need a doctor (who speaks English).	Ho bisogno di un dottore (che parli inglese).	oh bee-**zohn**-yoh dee oon doh-**toh**-ray (kay **par**-lee een-**glay**-zay)
It hurts here.	Fa male qui.	fah **mah**-lay kwee

HEALTH

Women's Health

menstruation, period	le mestruazioni	lay may-stroo-aht-see**oh**-nee
menstrual cramps	i dolori mestruali	ee doh-**loh**-ree may-stroo-**ah**-lee
pregnancy (test)	(test di) gravidanza	(tehst dee) grah-vee-**dahnt**-sah
miscarriage	aborto spontaneo	ah-**bor**-toh spohn-**tah**-nay-oh
abortion	aborto	ah-**bor**-toh
birth control pills	pillole anti-concezionali	peel-**oh**-lay ahn-tee-kohn-chayt-seeoh-**nah**-lee
diaphragm	diaframma	deeah-**frah**-mah
condoms	preservativi	pray-zehr-vah-**tee**-vee
I'd like to see...	Vorrei vedere...	vor-**reh**ee vay-**dehr**-ay
...a female doctor.	...una dottoressa.	**oo**-nah doh-toh-**ray**-sah
...a female gynecologist.	...una ginecologa.	oo-nah jee-nay-koh-**loh**-gah
I've missed a period.	Ho saltato il ciclo mestruale.	oh sahl-**tah**-toh eel **chee**-kloh may-stroo-**ah**-lay
My last period started on ___.	L'ultima mestruazione è cominciata il ___.	**lool**-tee-mah may-stroo-aht-see**oh**-nay eh koh-meen-**chah**-tah eel ___
I am / She is... pregnant.	Sono / È incinta...	**soh**-noh / eh een-**cheen**-tah
...___ months	...di ___ mesi.	dee ___ **may**-zee

Parts of the Body

ankle	caviglia	kah-**veel**-yah
arm	braccio	**brah**-choh
back	schiena	skee**ay**-nah
bladder	vescica	vay-**shee**-kah
breast	seno	**say**-noh
buttocks	glutei	**gloo**-tehee

HEALTH

chest	*petto*	**pay**-toh
ear	*orecchio*	oh-**ray**-keeoh
elbow	*gomito*	goh-**mee**-toh
eye	*occhio*	**oh**-keeoh
face	*faccia*	**fah**-chah
finger	*dito*	**dee**-toh
foot	*piede*	pee**ay**-day
hair (head / body)	*capelli / peli*	kah-**pay**-lee / **pay**-lee
hand	*mano*	**mah**-noh
head	*testa*	**tehs**-tah
heart	*cuore*	**kwoh**-ray
intestines	*intestino*	een-tehs-**tee**-noh
knee	*ginocchio*	jee-**noh**-keeoh
leg	*gamba*	**gahm**-bah
lung	*polmone*	pohl-**moh**-nay
mouth	*bocca*	**boh**-kah
neck	*collo*	**koh**-loh
nose	*naso*	**nah**-zoh
penis	*pene*	**pay**-nay
rectum	*retto*	**ray**-toh
shoulder	*spalla*	**spah**-lah
stomach	*stomaco*	**stoh**-mah-koh
teeth	*denti*	**dehn**-tee
testicles	*testicoli*	tehs-**tee**-koh-lee
throat	*gola*	**goh**-lah
toe	*alluce*	ah-**loo**-chay
urethra	*uretra*	oo-**reht**-rah
uterus	*utero*	**oo**-tay-roh
vagina	*vagina*	vah-**jee**-nah
waist	*vita*	**vee**-tah
wrist	*polso*	**pohl**-soh

HEALTH

Testa
(head)

Orecchio
(ear)

Mano
(hand)

Petto
(chest)

Gomito
(elbow)

Braccio
(arm)

Polso
(wrist)

Pene
(penis)

Gamba
(leg)

Dito
(finger)

Ginocchio
(knee)

Caviglia
(ankle)

Piede
(foot)

Alluce
(toe)

HEALTH

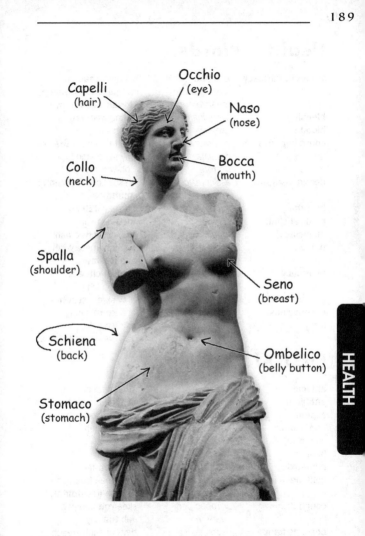

Capelli
(hair)

Occhio
(eye)

Naso
(nose)

Collo
(neck)

Bocca
(mouth)

Spalla
(shoulder)

Seno
(breast)

Schiena
(back)

Ombelico
(belly button)

Stomaco
(stomach)

HEALTH

Healthy Words

24-hour pharmacy	*farmacia aperta venti- quattro ore*	far-mah-**chee**-ah ah-**pehr**-tah vayn-tee- **kwah**-troh **oh**-ray
bleeding	*sanguinare*	sahn-gwee-**nah**-ray
blood	*sangue*	**sahn**-gway
contraceptives	*contraccettivi*	kohn-trah-chay-**tee**-vee
dentist	*dentista*	dayn-**tee**-stah
doctor	*dottore*	doh-**toh**-ray
health insurance	*assicurazione medica*	ah-see-koo-raht-see-**oh**-nay **mehd**-ee-kah
hospital	*ospedale*	oh-spay-**dah**-lay
medical clinic	*clinica*	**klee**-nee-kah
medicine	*medicina*	may-dee-**chee**-nah
nurse	*infermiera*	een-fehr-mee-**ay**-rah
pain	*dolore*	doh-**loh**-ray
pharmacy	*farmacia*	far-mah-**chee**-ah
pill	*pillola*	**pee**-loh-lah
prescription	*prescrizione*	pray-skreet-see-**oh**-nay
unconscious	*inconscio*	een-**kohn**-shoh
x-ray	*raggi x, radiografia*	**rah**-jee eeks, rah-dee-oh-grah-**fee**-ah

First-Aid Kit

antacid	*antiacido*	ahn-teeah-**chee**-doh
antibiotic	*antibiotici*	ahn-tee-beeoh-tee-chee
aspirin	*aspirina*	ah-spee-**ree**-nah
non-aspirin substitute	*Saridon*	**sah**-ree-dohn
bandage	*benda*	**behn**-dah
band-aids	*cerotti*	chay-**roh**-tee
cold medicine	*medicina per il raffreddore*	may-dee-**chee**-nah pehr eel rah-fray-**doh**-ray
cough drops	*sciroppo per la tosse*	skee-**roh**-poh pehr lah **toh**-say
decongestant	*decongestio- nante*	day-kohn-jehs-teeoh- **nahn**-tay

disinfectant	*disinfettante*	dee-seen-feht-**tahn**-tay
first-aid cream	*pomata*	proh-**mah**-tah
	antistaminica	ahn-tee-stah-**mee**-nee-kah
gauze / tape	*garza / nastro*	**gart**-sah / **nah**-stroh
laxative	*lassativo*	lah-sah-**tee**-voh
medicine for	*farmaco per*	far-**mah**-koh pehr
diarrhea	*la diarrea*	lah dee-ah-**ray**-ah
moleskin	*feltro, moleskin*	**fehl**-troh, "moleskin"
pain killer	*analgesico*	ah-nahl-**jehz**-ee-koh
Preparation H	*Preparazione*	pray-pah-raht-see**oh**-nay
	H	**ah**-kah
support bandage	*fascia di*	**fah**-shah dee
	sostegno	soh-**stehn**-yoh
thermometer	*termometro*	tehr-moh-**may**-troh
Vaseline	*vaselina*	vah-zay-**lee**-nah
vitamins	*vitamine*	vee-tah-**mee**-nay

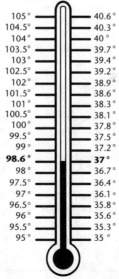

	Fahrenheit	Celsius
	105°	40.6°
	104.5°	40.3°
	104°	40°
	103.5°	39.7°
	103°	39.4°
	102.5°	39.2°
	102°	38.9°
	101.5°	38.6°
	101°	38.3°
	100.5°	38.1°
	100°	37.8°
	99.5°	37.5°
	99°	37.2°
	98.6°	**37°**
	98°	36.7°
	97.5°	36.4°
	97°	36.1°
	96.5°	35.8°
	96°	35.6°
	95.5°	35.3°
	95°	35°

Contacts and Glasses

glasses	*occhiali*	oh-kee**ah**-lee
sunglasses	*occhiali da sole*	oh-kee**ah**-lee dah **soh**-lay
prescription	*prescrizione*	pray-skreet-see**oh**-nay
contact lenses...	*lenti a contatto*	**lehn**-tee ah kohn-**tah**-toh
...soft	*...morbide*	**mor**-bee-day
...hard	*...dure*	**doo**-ray
cleaning solution	*liquido*	**lee**-kwee-doh
	disinfettante	dee-seen-feht-**tahn**-tay
soaking solution	*soluzione*	soh-loot-see**oh**-nay
	salina	sah-**lee**-nah
all-purpose solution	*liquido unico*	**lee**-kwee-doh **oo**-nee-koh
	per lenti a	pehr **lehn**-tee ah
	contatto	kohn-**tah**-toh
20/20 vision	*visione*	vee-zee**oh**-nay
	perfetto	pehr-**feht**-toh
I've... a contact	*Ho... una lente*	oh... **oo**-nah **lehn**-tay
lens.	*a contatto.*	ah kohn-**tah**-toh
...lost	*...perso*	**pehr**-soh
...swallowed	*...inghiottito*	een-goh-**tee**-toh

Toiletries

comb	*pettine*	pay-**tee**-nay
conditioner for hair	*balsamo*	**bahl**-sah-moh
condoms	*preservativi*	pray-zehr-vah-**tee**-vee
dental floss	*filo*	**fee**-loh
	interdentale	een-tehr-dayn-**tah**-lay
deodorant	*deodorante*	day-oh-doh-**rahn**-tay
facial tissue	*fazzoletto*	fahd-zoh-**lay**-toh
	di carta	dee **kar**-tah
hairbrush	*spazzola per*	spahd-**zoh**-lah pehr
	capelli	kah-**pay**-lee
hand lotion	*crema per*	**kray**-mah pehr
	le mani	lay **mah**-nee
lip salve	*burro di cacao*	**boo**-roh dee kah-**kah**-oh

HEALTH

mirror	*specchio*	**spay**-keeoh
nail clipper	*tagliaunghie*	tahl-yah-**oong**-gay
razor	*rasoio*	rah-**zoh**-yoh
sanitary napkins	*assorbenti*	ah-sor-**bayn**-tee
	igienici	ee-jay-**nee**-chee
scissors	*forbici*	for-**bee**-chee
shampoo	*shampoo*	**shahm**-poo
shaving cream	*crema da barba*	**kray**-mah dah **bar**-bah
soap	*sapone*	sah-**poh**-nay
sunscreen	*protezione*	proh-tayt-seeoh-nay
	solare	soh-**lah**-ray
suntan lotion	*crema*	**kray**-mah
	abbronzante	ah-brohnt-**sahn**-tay
tampons	*assorbenti*	ah-sor-**bayn**-tee
	interni	een-**tehr**-nee
tissues	*fazzoletti*	fahd-zoh-**leht**-tee
	di carta	dee **kar**-tah
toilet paper	*carta igienica*	**kar**-tah ee-**jay**-nee-kah
toothbrush	*spazzolino*	spahd-zoh-**lee**-noh
	da denti	dah **dayn**-tee
toothpaste	*dentifricio*	dayn-tee-**free**-choh
tweezers	*pinzette*	peent-**say**-tay

Makeup

blush	*fard*	fard
eye shadow	*ombretto*	ohm-**bray**-toh
eyeliner	*matita, eyeliner*	mah-**tee**-tah, "eyeliner"
face cleanser	*latte detergente*	**lah**-tay day-tehr-**jehn**-tay
face powder	*cipria*	**cheep**-reeah
foundation	*fondotinta*	fohn-doh-**teen**-tah
lipstick	*rossetto*	roh-**say**-toh
makeup	*trucco*	**troo**-koh
mascara	*mascara*	mah-**skah**-rah
moisturizer...	*crema*	**kray**-mah
	idratante...	ee-drah-**tahn**-tay
...with sun block	*...con protezione*	kohn proh-tayt-seeoh-nay
	solare	soh-**lah**-ray

nail polish	smalto per	**smahl**-toh pehr
	le unghie	lay **oong**-gay
nail polish remover	solvente per	sohl-**vehn**-tay pehr
	le unghie	lay **oong**-gay
perfume	profumo	proh-**foo**-moh

For Babies

baby	neonato	nay-oh-**nah**-toh
baby food	cibo per	**chee**-boh pehr
	neonati	nay-oh-**nah**-tee
bib	bavaglino	bah-vahl-**yee**-noh
bottle	biberon	**bee**-behr-ohn
diaper	pannolino	pah-noh-**lee**-noh
diapers	pannolini	pah-noh-**lee**-nee
diaper wipes	salviettine per	sahl-veeay-**tee**-nay pehr
	neonati	nay-oh-**nah**-tee
diaper ointment	olio per	**oh**-leeoh pehr
	neonati	nay-oh-**nah**-tee
formula...	formulazione...	for-moo-laht-see**oh**-nay
...powdered	...in polvere	een pohl-**vay**-ray
...liquid	...liquida	**lee**-kwee-dah
...soy	...di soia	dee **soh**-yah
medication for...	farmaco per la...	far-**mah**-koh pehr lah
...diaper rash	...dermatite da	dehr-mah-**tee**-tay dah
	pannolone	pah-noh-**loh**-nay
...teething	...dentizione	dehn-teet-see**oh**-nay
nipple	capezzolo	kah-pehd-**zoh**-loh
pacifier	ciucio	**choo**-choh
Will you	Può metterlo	pwoh meht-**tehr**-loh
refrigerate this?	in frigo?	een **free**-goh
Will you warm...	Può riscaldare...	pwoh ree-skahl-**dah**-ray...
for a baby?	per un neonato?	pehr oon nay-oh-**nah**-toh
...this	...questo	**kweh**-stoh
...some water	...un po' d'acqua	oon poh **dah**-kwah
...some milk	...un po' di latte	oon poh dee **lah**-tay
Not too hot, please.	Non troppo caldo,	nohn **troh**-poh **kahl**-doh
	per favore.	pehr fah-**voh**-ray

More Baby Things

backpack to carry baby	*zaino per portare i neonati*	tsah**ee**-noh pehr por-**tah**-ray ee nay-oh-**nah**-tee
booster seat	*seggiolino per neonati*	say-joh-**lee**-noh pehr nay-oh-**nah**-tee
car seat	*seggiolino per la macchina*	say-joh-**lee**-noh pehr lah **mah**-kee-nah
high chair	*seggiolone*	say-joh-**loh**-nay
playpen	*box*	bohks
stroller	*passeggino*	pah-say-**jee**-noh

CHATTING

English	Italian	Pronunciation
My name is ___.	Mi chiamo ___.	mee kee**ah**-moh
What's your name?	Come si chiama?	**koh**-may see kee**ah**-mah
This is...	Le presento...	lay pray-**zehn**-toh
Pleased to meet you.	Piacere.	peeah-**chay**-ray
How are you?	Come sta?	**koh**-may stah
Very well, thanks.	Molto bene, grazie.	**mohl**-toh **behn**-ay **graht**-seeay
Where are you from?	Di dove è?	dee **doh**-vay eh
What city?	Da che città?	dah kay chee-**tah**
What country?	Da che paese?	dah kay pah-**ay**-zay
What planet?	Da che pianeta?	dah kay peeah-**nay**-tah
I'm...	Sono...	**soh**-noh
...American.	...Americano[a].	ah-may-ree-**kah**-noh
...Canadian.	...Canadese.	kah-nah-**day**-zay
...a pest.	...una peste.	**oo**-nah **pehs**-tay
Where are you going? (singular / plural)	Dove va? / Dove andate?	**doh**-vay vah / **doh**-vay ahn-**dah**-tay
I'm going / We're going to ___.	Vado / Andiamo a ___.	**vah**-doh / ahn-dee**ah**-moh ah
Will you take my / our photo?	Mi / ci fa una foto?	mee / chee fah **oo**-nah **foh**-toh

196

| Can I take a photo of you? | Posso fare le una foto? | **poh**-soh **fah**-ray lay **oo**-nah **foh**-toh |
| Smile! (singular / plural) | Sorrida! / Sorridete! | soh-**ree**-dah / soh-ree-**day**-tay |

Nothing More Than Feelings...

I am / You are...	Sono / È...	**soh**-noh / eh
He / She is...	Lui / Lei è...	lwee / **leh**ee eh
...happy.	...felice.	fay-**lee**-chay
...sad.	...triste.	**tree**-stay
...tired.	...stanco[a].	**stahn**-koh
...lucky.	...fortunato[a].	for-too-**nah**-toh
I am / You are...	Ho / Ha...	oh / ah
He / She is...	Lui / Lei ha...	lwee / **leh**ee ah
...hungry.	...fame.	**fah**-may
...thirsty.	...sete.	**say**-tay
...homesick.	...nostalgia.	noh-**stahl**-jah
...cold.	...freddo.	**fray**-doh
...too warm.	...troppo caldo.	**troh**-poh **kahl**-doh

Who's Who

My... (m / f)	Mio / Mia...	**mee**-oh / **mee**-ah
...friend (m / f).	...amico / amica.	ah-**mee**-koh / ah-**mee**-kah
...boyfriend / girlfriend.	...ragazzo / ragazza.	rah-**gahd**-zoh / rah-**gahd**-zah
...husband / wife.	...marito / moglie.	mah-**ree**-toh / **mohl**-yay
...son / daughter.	...figlio / figlia.	**feel**-yoh / **feel**-yah
...brother / sister.	...fratello / sorella.	frah-**tehl**-loh / soh-**rehl**-lah
...father / mother.	...padre / madre.	**pah**-dray / **mah**-dray
...uncle / aunt.	...zio / zia.	**tsee**oh / **tsee**ah
...nephew or niece.	...nipote.	nee-**poh**-tay

CHATING

...male / female cousin.	...cugino / cugina.	koo-**jee**-noh / koo-**jee**-nah
...grandfather / grandmother.	...nonno / nonna.	**noh**-noh / **noh**-nah
...grandchild.	...nipote.	nee-**poh**-tay

Family

Are you married? (to a woman / a man)	È sposata? È sposato?	eh spoh-**zah**-tah eh spoh-**zah**-toh
Do you have children?	Ha bambini?	ah bahm-**bee**-nee
How many boys and girls?	Quanti maschi e femmine?	**kwahn**-tee **mahs**-kee ay fehm-**mee**-nay
Do you have photos?	Ha delle foto?	ah **dehl**-lay **foh**-toh
How old is your child?	Quanti anni ha il suo bambino?	**kwahn**-tee **ahn**-nee ah eel **soo**-oh bahm-**bee**-noh
Beautiful baby boy!	Bel bambino!	behl bahm-**bee**-noh
Beautiful baby girl!	Bella bambina!	**behl**-lah bahm-**bee**-nah
Beautiful children!	Bei bambini!	**beh**ee bahm-**bee**-nee

Work

What is your job?	Che lavoro fa?	kay lah-**voh**-roh fah
Do you like your work?	Le piace il suo lavoro?	lay pee**ah**-chay eel **soo**-oh lah-**voh**-roh
I work in...	Mi occupo...	mee oh-**koo**-poh
I'm studying to work in...	Studio per lavorare...	**stoo**-deeoh pehr lah-voh-**rah**-ray
I used to work in...	Lavoravo...	lah-voh-**rah**-voh
I want a job in...	Vorrei un lavoro...	vor-**reh**ee oon lah-**voh**-roh
...accounting.	...nella contabilità.	**nay**-lah kohn-tah-bee-lee-**tah**
...the medical field.	...nel campo medico.	nehl **kahm**-poh **may**-dee-koh

...social services.	...nell'assistenza sociale.	nay-lah-stee-**stehnt**-sah soh-**chah**-lay
...the legal profession.	...nel campo legale.	nehl **kahm**-poh lay-**gah**-lay
...banking.	...nel settore bancario.	nayl seht-**toh**-ray bahn-**kah**-reeoh
...business.	...in un'azienda.	een oo-naht-see**ehn**-dah
...government.	...nel governo.	nehl eel goh-**vehr**-noh
...engineering.	...nell'ingegneria.	nay-leen-jehn-**yay**-reeah
...public relations.	...nel relazioni pubbliche	nehl ray-laht-see**oh**-nee poo-**blee**-kay
...science.	...nel campo scientifico.	nehl **kahm**-poh shee-ehn-**tee**-fee-koh
...teaching.	...come insegnante.	**koh**-may een-sayn-**yahn**-tay
...the computer field.	...nel settore informatico.	nayl seht-**toh**-ray een-for-**mah**-tee-koh
...the travel industry.	...nel settore turistico.	nayl seht-**toh**-ray too-**ree**-stee-koh
...the arts.	...nel campo artistico.	nehl **kahm**-poh ar-**tee**-stee-koh
...journalism.	...nel giornalismo.	nayl jor-nahl-**ees**-moh
...a restaurant.	...in un ristorante.	een oon ree-stoh-**rahn**-tay
...a store.	...in un negozio.	een oon nay-**goht**-seeoh
...a factory.	...in una fabbrica.	een **oo**-nah fah-**bree**-kah
I'm a professional traveler.	Sono turista di professione.	**soh**-noh too-**ree**-stah dee proh-fay-see**oh**-nay
I am / We are...	Sono / Siamo...	**soh**-noh / see**ah**-moh
...unemployed.	...disoccupato[a].	dee-zoh-koo-**pah**-toh
...retired.	...in pensione.	een payn-see**oh**-nay
Do you have a...?	Ha un...?	ah oon
Here is my / our...	Ecco il mio / il nostro...	**ay**-koh eel **mee**-oh / eel **noh**-stroh
...business card	...biglietto da visita	beel-**yay**-toh dah **vee**-zee-tah
...e-mail address	...indirizzo di posta elettronica	een-dee-**reed**-zoh dee **poh**-stah ay-leht-**troh**-nee-kah

KEY PHRASES: CHATTING

My name is ___.	*Mi chiamo ___.*	mee kee**ah**-moh
What's your name?	*Come si chiama?*	**koh**-may see kee**ah**-mah
Pleased to meet you.	*Piacere.*	peeah-**chay**-ray
Where are you from?	*Di dove è?*	dee **doh**-vay eh
I'm from ___.	*Sono da ___.*	**soh**-noh dah
Where are you going? (singular / plural)	*Dove va? / Dove andate?*	**doh**-vay vah / **doh**-vay ahn-**dah**-tay
I'm going to ___.	*Vado a ___.*	**vah**-doh ah
I like...	*Mi piace...*	mee pee**ah**-chay
Do you like...?	*Le piace...?*	lay pee**ah**-chay
Thank you very much.	*Molte grazie.*	**mohl**-tay **graht**-seeay
Have a good trip!	*Buon viaggio!*	bwohn vee**ah**-joh

Chatting with Children

What's your name?	*Come ti chiami?*	**koh**-may tee kee**ah**-mee
My name is ___.	*Mi chiamo ___.*	mee kee**ah**-moh
How old are you?	*Quanti anni hai?*	**kwahn**-tee **ahn**-nee **ah**ee
Do you have brothers and sisters?	*Hai fratelli e sorelle?*	**ah**ee frah-**tehl**-lee ay soh-**rehl**-lay
Do you like school?	*Ti piace la scuola?*	tee pee**ah**-chay lah **skwoh**-lah
What are you studying?	*Che cosa stai studiando?*	kay **koh**-zah **stah**ee stoo-dee**ahn**-doh
I'm studying...	*Sto studiando...*	stoh stoo-dee**ahn**-doh
What's your favorite subject?	*Qual'è la tua materia preferita?*	kwah-**leh** lah **too**-ah mah-tay-**ree**-ah pray-fay-**ree**-tah
Do you have pets?	*Hai animali domestici?*	**ah**ee ah-nee-**mah**-lee doh-mehs-**tee**-chee
I have / We have a...	*Ho / Abbiamo un...*	oh / ah-bee**ah**-moh ah

...cat / dog / fish / bird.	...gatto / cane / pesce / uccello.	**gah**-toh / **kah**-nay / **peh**-shay / oo-**cheh**-loh
What is this / that?	Che cos'è questo / quello?	kay koh-**zeh kweh**-stoh / **kweh**-loh
Will you teach me / us...?	Mi / Ci insegni...?	mee / chee een-**sayn**-yee
...some Italian words	...delle parole in italiano	**dehl**-lay pah-**roh**-lay een ee-tah-leeah-noh
...a simple Italian song	...una canzone italiana facile	**oo**-nah kahnt-**soh**-nay ee-tah-leeah-nah **fah**-chee-lay
Guess which country I live in/ we live in.	Indovina in quale paese vivo / viviamo.	een-doh-**vee**-nah een **kwah**-lay pah-**ay**-zay **vee**-voh / vee-veeah-moh
How old am I?	Quanti anni ho?	**kwahn**-tee **ahn**-nee oh
I'm ___ years old.	Ho ___ anni.	oh ___ **ahn**-nee
Want to hear me burp?	Mi vuoi sentire ruttare?	mee **vwoh**ee sehn-**tee**-ray roo-**tah**-ray
Teach me a fun game.	Mi insegni un gioco divertente.	mee een-**sayn**-yee oon **joh**-koh dee-vehr-**tehn**-tay
Got any candy?	Hai una caramella?	**ah**ee **oo**-nah kah-rah-**mehl**-lah
Want to thumb-wrestle?	Vuoi fare la lotta con i pollici?	**vwoh**ee **fah**-ray lah **loh**-tah kohn ee poh-**lee**-chee
Gimme five. (hold up your hand)	Dammi un cinque.	**dah**-mee oon **cheeng**-kway

If you do break into song, try Happy Birthday (page 25) or Volare on page 277.

Travel Talk

I am / Are you...?	Sono / È...?	**soh**-noh / eh
...on vacation	...in vacanza	een vah-**kahnt**-sah
...on business	...qui per lavoro	kwee pehr lah-**voh**-roh
How long have you been traveling?	Da quanto tempo è in viaggio?	dah **kwahn**-toh **tehm**-poh eh een veeah-joh
day / week	giorno / settimana	**jor**-noh / say-tee-**mah**-nah

month / year	mese / anno	**may**-zay / **ahn**-noh
When are you going home?	Quando ritorna a casa?	**kwahn**-doh ree-**tor**-nah ah **kah**-zah
This is my first time in ___.	Questa è la mia prima volta in ___.	**kweh**-stah eh lah **mee**-ah **pree**-mah **vohl**-tah een
This is our first time in ___.	Questa è la nostra prima volta in ___.	**kweh**-stah eh lah **noh**-strah **pree**-mah **vohl**-tah een
It is (not) a tourist trap.	(Non) è una trappola per turisti.	(nohn) eh **oo**-nah trah-**poh**-lah pehr too-**ree**-stee
The Italians are friendly / boring / rude.	Gli italiani sono amichevoli / noiosi / maleducati.	**lee**yee ee-tah-lee**ah**-nee **soh**-noh ah-mee-kay-**voh**-lee / noh-**yoh**-zee / mah-lay-doo-**kah**-tee
Italy is fantastic.	L'Italia è fantastica.	lee-**tahl**-yah eh fahn-**tah**-stee-kah
So far...	Finora...	fee-**noh**-rah
Today...	Oggi...	**oh**-jee
...I have / we have seen ___ and ___.	...ho / abbiamo visto ___ e ___.	oh / ah-bee**ah**-moh **vee**-stoh ___ ay
Next...	Dopo...	**doh**-poh
Tomorrow...	Domani...	doh-**mah**-nee
...I will see / we will see ___.	...vedrò / vedremo ___.	vay-**droh** / vay-**dray**-moh
Yesterday...	Ieri....	**yay**-ree
...I saw / we saw ___.	...ho visto / abbiamo visto ___.	oh **vee**-stoh / ah-bee**ah**-moh **vee**-stoh
My / Our vacation is ___ days long. It began in ___ and finishes in ___ .	La mia / La nostra vacanza dura ___ giorni. Comincia a ___ e finisce a ___.	lah **mee**-ah / lah **noh**-strah vah-**kahnt**-sah **doo**-rah ___ **jor**-nee koh-**meen**-chah ah ___ ay fee-**nee**-shay ah
I'm happy here.	Sono felice qui.	**soh**-noh fay-**lee**-chay kwee
This is paradise.	Questo è il paradiso.	**kweh**-stoh eh eel pah-rah-**dee**-zoh
To travel is to live.	Viaggiare è vivere.	veeah-**jah**-ray eh vee-**vay**-ray

Travel is enlightening.	Viaggiare illumina.	veeah-**jah**-ray ee-**loo**-mee-nah
I wish all (American) politicians traveled.	Vorrei che tutti i politici (americani) viaggiassero.	vor-**reh**ee kay **too**-tee ee poh-**lee**-tee-chee (ah-may-ree-**kah**-nee) veeah-jah-**say**-roh
Have a good trip!	Buon viaggio!	bwohn veeah-joh

Map Musings

These phrases and maps will help you delve into family history and explore your travel dreams.

I live here.	Abito qui.	ah-**bee**-toh kwee
We live here.	Abitiamo qui.	ah-bee-teeah-moh kwee
I was born here.	Sono nato[a] qui.	**soh**-noh **nah**-toh kwee
My ancestors came from ___.	I miei antenati vennero da ___.	ee meeay-ee ahn-tay-**nah**-tee vay-**nay**-roh dah
I've traveled to ___.	Sono stato[a] a ___.	**soh**-noh **stah**-toh ah
We've traveled to ___.	Siamo stati[e] a ___.	seeah-moh **stah**-tee ah
Next I'll go to ___.	Poi andrò a ___.	**poh**ee ahn-**droh** ah
Next we'll go to ___.	Poi andremo a ___.	**poh**ee ahn-**dray**-moh ah
I'd like / We'd like to go to ___.	Vorrei / Vorremmo andare a ___.	vor-**reh**ee / vor-**ray**-moh ahn-**dah**-ray ah
Where do you live?	Dove abita?	**doh**-vay ah-**bee**-tah
Where were you born?	Dove è nato[a]?	**doh**-vay eh **nah**-toh
Where did your ancestors come from?	Da dove vennero i suoi antenati?	dah **doh**-vay vay-**nay**-roh ee **swoh**-ee ahn-tay-**nah**-tee
Where have you traveled?	Dove è stato[a]?	**doh**-vay eh **stah**-toh
Where are you going?	Dove va?	**doh**-vay vah
Where would you like to go?	Dove vorrebbe andare?	**doh**-vay voh-**ray**-bay ahn-**dah**-ray

CHATING

ITALY

EUROPE

THE UNITED STATES

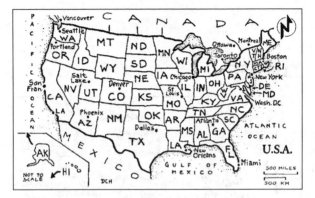

THE WORLD

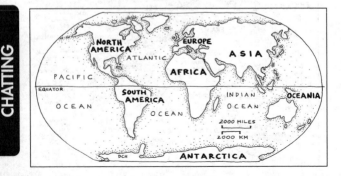

Favorite Things

What... do you like?	Qual'è il suo... preferito?	kwah-**leh** eel **soo**-oh... pray-fay-**ree**-toh
...art	...genere d'arte	**jay**-nay-ray **dar**-tay
...books	...genere di libri	**jay**-nay-ray dee **lee**-bree
...hobby	...passatempo	pah-sah-**tehm**-poh
...ice cream	...gelato	jay-**lah**-toh
...food	...cibo	**chee**-boh
...movie	...film	feelm
...music	...genere di musica	**jay**-nay-ray dee **moo**-zee-kah
...sport	...sport	sport
...vice	...vizio	**veet**-seeoh
...singer	...cantante	kahn-**tahn**-tay
...male movie star	...attore	ah-**toh**-ray
...male artist	...artista	ar-**tee**-stah
...male author	...autore	ow-**toh**-ray
...female movie star	...attrice	ah-**tree**-chay
...female artist	...artista	ar-**tee**-stah
...female author	...autrice	ow-**tree**-chay
Can you recommend a good...?	Può raccomandarmi un buon...?	pwoh rah-koh-mahn-**dar**-mee oon bwohn
...Italian CD	...CD italiano	chee-dee ee-tah-leeah-noh
...Italian book translated in English	...libro italiano in traduzione inglese	**lee**-broh ee-tah-leeah-noh een trah-doot-seeoh-nay een-**glay**-zay

Weather

What will the weather be like tomorrow?	Come sarà il tempo domani?	**koh**-may sah-**rah** eel **tehm**-poh doh-**mah**-nee
sunny / cloudy	bello / nuvoloso	**behl**-loh / noo-voh-**loh**-zoh

hot / cold	*caldo / freddo*	**kahl**-doh / **fray**-doh
muggy / windy	*umido /*	**oo**-mee-doh /
	ventoso	vehn-**toh**-zoh
rain / snow	*pioggia / neve*	peeoh-jah / **nay**-vay
Should I bring	*Devo portare*	**day**-voh por-**tah**-ray
a jacket?	*una giacca?*	**oo**-nah **jah**-kah

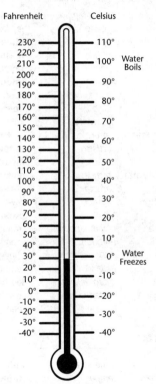

Thanks a Million

Thank you very much.	*Molte grazie.*	**mohl**-tay **graht**-seeay
A thousand thanks.	*Grazie mille.*	**graht**-seeay **mee**-lay
This is great fun.	*È un vero divertimento.*	eh oon **vay**-roh dee-vehr-tee-**mayn**-toh
You are...	*Lei è...*	**leh**ee eh
...helpful.	*...di aiuto.*	dee ah-**yoo**-toh
...wonderful.	*...meraviglioso[a].*	may-rah-veel-**yoh**-zoh
...generous.	*...generoso[a].*	jay-nay-**roh**-zoh
...kind.	*...gentile.*	jayn-**tee**-lay
You spoil me / us.	*Mi / Ci viziate.*	mee / chee veet-see**ah**-tay
You've been a great help.	*Lei è un grande aiuto.*	**leh**ee eh oon **grahn**-day ah-**yoo**-toh
You are a saint.	*Lei è un[a] santo[a].*	**leh**ee eh oon **sahn**-toh
I will remember you...	*Mi ricorderò di Lei...*	mee ree-kor-day-**roh** dee **leh**ee
We will remember you...	*Ci ricorderemo di Lei...*	chee ree-kor-day-**ray**-moh dee **leh**ee
...always.	*...sempre.*	**sehm**-pray
...till Tuesday.	*...fino a martedì.*	**fee**-noh ah mar-tay-**dee**

Responses for All Occasions

I like that.	*Mi piace.*	mee pee**ah**-chay
We like that.	*Ci piace.*	chee pee**ah**-chay
I like you.	*Lei mi piace.*	**leh**ee mee pee**ah**-chay
We like you.	*Lei ci piace.*	**leh**ee chee pee**ah**-chay
Great!	*Ottimo!*	**oh**-tee-moh
Fantastic!	*Fantastico!*	fahn-**tah**-stee-koh
What a nice place.	*Che bel posto.*	kay behl **poh**-stoh
Perfect.	*Perfetto.*	pehr-**feht**-toh
Funny.	*Divertente.*	dee-vehr-**tehn**-tay
Interesting.	*Interessante.*	een-tay-ray-**sahn**-tay
Really?	*Davvero?*	dah-**vay**-roh

Wow!	*Wow!*	"Wow"
Congratulations!	*Congratu-lazioni!*	kohn-grah-too-laht-see**oh**-nee
Well done!	*Bravo[a]!*	**brah**-voh
You're welcome.	*Prego.*	**pray**-goh
Bless you! (after sneeze)	*Salute!*	sah-**loo**-tay
What a pity.	*Che peccato.*	kay pehk-**kah**-toh
That's life.	*È la vita!*	eh lah **vee**-tah
No problem.	*Non c'è problema.*	nohn cheh proh-**blay**-mah
O.K.	*Va bene.*	vah **behn**-ay
This is the good life!	*Questa sì che è vita!*	**kweh**-stah see kay eh **vee**-tah
I feel like a pope! (happy)	*Sto come un papa!*	stoh **koh**-may oon **pah**-pah
Have a good day!	*Buona giornata!*	**bwoh**-nah jor-**nah**-tah
Good luck!	*Buona fortuna!*	**bwoh**-nah for-**too**-nah
Let's go!	*Andiamo!*	ahn-dee**ah**-moh

Smoking

Do you smoke?	*Fuma?*	**foo**-mah
Do you smoke pot?	*Fuma marijuana?*	**foo**-mah mah-ree-**wahn**-nah
I (don't) smoke.	*(Non) fumo.*	(nohn) **foo**-moh
We (don't) smoke.	*(Non) fumiano.*	(nohn) foo-mee**ah**-noh
I haven't any.	*Non ne ho.*	nohn nay oh
lighter	*accendino*	ah-chehn-**dee**-noh
cigarettes	*sigarette*	see-gah-**ray**-tay
marijuana	*marijuana*	mah-ree-**wahn**-nah
hash	*hashish*	hah-**sheesh**
joint	*canna*	**kah**-nah
stoned	*fumato, fatto*	foo-**mah**-toh, **fah**-toh
Wow!	*Wow!*	"Wow"

Conversing With Animals

rooster / cock-a-doodle-doo	gallo / chicchirichì	**gah**-loh / kee-kee-ree-**kee**
bird / tweet tweet	uccello / cip cip	oo-**chehl**-loh / cheep cheep
cat / meow	gatto / miao	**gah**-toh / **mee**-ow
dog / bark bark	cane / bau bau	**kah**-nay / bow bow
duck / quack quack	oca / quac quac	**oh**-kah / kwahk kwahk
cow / moo	mucca / muu	**moo**-kah / moo
pig / oink oink	maiale / oinc oinc	mah-**yah**-lay / oynk oynk

Profanity

People make animal noises, too. These words will help you understand what the more colorful locals are saying.

Go to hell!	Vai al diavolo!	**vah**ee ahl dee**ah**-voh-loh
Damn it.	Dannazione.	dah-naht-see**oh**-nay
bastard	bastardo	bah-**star**-doh
bitch	cagna, troia	**kahn**-yah, **troh**-yah
breasts (colloq.)	tete	**tay**-tay
penis (colloq.)	cazzo	**kahd**-zoh
butthole	stronzo	**strohnt**-soh
drunk	ubriaco	oo-bree**ah**-koh
idiot	idiota	ee-dee**oh**-tah
imbecile	imbecille	eem-bay-**chee**-lay
jerk	scemo	**shay**-moh
stupid	stupido	**stoo**-pee-doh
Did someone fart?	Ma qualcuno ha fatto una scoreggia?	mah kwahl-**koo**-noh ah **fah**-toh **oo**-nah skoh-**ray**-jah
I burped.	Ho ruttato.	oh roo-**tah**-toh
This sucks.	Questo fa schifo.	**kweh**-stoh fah **skee**-foh
Screw it.	Vaffanculo.	vah-fahn-**koo**-loh
Go take a shit.	Va'a cagare.	**vah**-ah kah-**gah**-ray

Shit.	*Merda.*	**mehr**-dah
Bullshit.	*Balle.*	**bah**-lay
Shove it up your ass.	*Mettitelo nel culo.*	meht-tee-**tay**-loh nayl **koo**-loh
Stick it between your teeth.	*Ficcatelo tra i denti.*	fee-kah-**tay**-loh trah ee **dayn**-tee
You are...	*Sei...*	seh**ee**
Don't be...	*Non essere...*	nohn ehs-**say**-ray
...a son of a whore.	*...un figlio di puttana.*	oon **feel**-yoh dee poo-**tah**-nah
...an asshole.	*...uno stronzo.*	**oo**-noh **strohnt**-soh
...an idiot.	*...un idiota.*	oon ee-dee**oh**-tah
...a creep.	*...un deficiente.*	oon day-fee-chee-**ehn**-tay
...a cretin.	*...un cretino.*	oon kray-**tee**-noh
...a pig.	*...un porco.*	oon **por**-koh

Sweet Curses

My goodness.	*Mamma mia.*	**mah**-mah **mee**-ah
Good heavens.	*Santo cielo.*	**sahn**-toh chee**ay**-loh
Shoot.	*Cavolo.*	**kah**-voh-loh
Darn it!	*Accidenti.*	ah-chee-**dehn**-tee

Create Your Own Conversation

You can mix and match these words into a conversation.
Make it as deep or silly as you want.

Who

I / you	*io / Lei*	**ee**oh / **leh**ee
he / she	*lui / lei*	lwee / **leh**ee
we / they	*noi / loro*	**noh**ee / **loh**-roh
my / your...	*mio / suo...*	**mee**-oh / **soo**-oh
...parents /	*...genitori /*	jay-nee-**toh**-ree /
children	*figli*	**feel**-yee
men / women	*uomini / donne*	woh-**mee**-nee / **doh**-nay
rich / poor	*ricchi / poveri*	**ree**-kee / **poh**-vay-ree
young /	*giovani /*	joh-**vah**-nee /
middle-aged / old	*di mezza età /*	dee **mehd**-zah ay-**tah** /
	anziani	ahnt-seeah-nee
Italians	*italiani*	ee-tah-leeah-nee
Austrians	*austriaci*	ow-stree**ah**-chee
Belgians	*belgi*	**bayl**-jee
Czech	*cechi*	**chay**-kee
French	*francesi*	frahn-**chay**-zee
Germans	*tedeschi*	tay-**dehs**-kee
Spanish	*spagnoli*	span-**yoh**-lee
Swiss	*svizzeri*	sveed-**zeh**-ree
Europeans	*europei*	ay-oo-roh-**pay**-ee
EU	*UE*	oo ay
(European Union)	*(Unione*	(oon-ee-**ohn**-ay
	Europeo)	ay-oo-roh-**pay**-oh)
Americans	*americani*	ah-may-ree-**kah**-nee
liberals	*liberali*	lee-bay-**rah**-lee
conservatives	*conservatori*	kohn-sehr-vah-**toh**-ree

radicals	radicali	rah-dee-**kah**-lee
terrorists	terroristi	tehr-roh-**ree**-stee
politicians	politici	poh-**lee**-tee-chee
big business	grande affare	**grahn**-day ah-**fah**-ray
multinational	multi-	mool-tee-
corporations	nazionale	naht-seeoh-**nah**-lay
military	militare	mee-lee-**tah**-ray
mafia	mafia	**mah**-feeah
refugees	profughi	proh-**foo**-gee
travelers	viaggiatori	veeah-jah-**toh**-ree
God	Dio	**dee**oh
Christian	cristiano	kree-stee**ah**-noh
Catholic	cattolico	kah-**toh**-lee-koh
Protestant	protestante	proh-tay-**stahn**-tay
Jew	ebreo	ay-**bray**-oh
Muslim	musulmano	moo-sool-**mah**-noh
everyone	tutti	**too**-tee

What

buy / sell	comprare / vendere	kohm-**prah**-ray / vehn-**day**-ray
have / lack	avere / non avere	ah-**vay**-ray / nohn ah-**vay**-ray
help / abuse	aiutare / abusare	ah-yoo-**tah**-ray / ah-boo-**zah**-ray
learn / fear	imparare / temere	eem-pah-**rah**-ray / tay-**may**-ray
love / hate	amare / odiare	ah-**mah**-ray / oh-dee**ah**-ray
prosper / suffer	prosperare / soffrire	proh-spay-**rah**-ray / soh-**free**-ray
take / give	prendere / dare	**prehn**-day-ray / **dah**-ray
want / need	volere / aver bisogno	voh-**lay**-ray / **ah**-vehr bee-**zohn**-yoh
work / play	lavorare / giocare	lah-voh-**rah**-ray / joh-**kah**-ray

Why

(anti-) globalization	(anti-) globalizzazione	(**ahn**-tee-)gloh-bah-leed-zaht-see**oh**-nay
class warfare	conflitto di classe	kohn-**flee**-toh dee **klah**-say
corruption	corruzione	koh-root-see**oh**-nay
democracy	democrazia	day-moh-kraht-**see**-ah
education	istruzione	een-stroot-see**oh**-nay
family	famiglia	fah-**meel**-yah
food	cibo	**chee**-boh
guns	armi	**ar**-mee
happiness	felicità	fay-lee-chee-**tah**
health	salute	sah-**loo**-tay
hope	speranza	spay-**rahnt**-sah
imperialism	imperialismo	eem-pehr-eeahl-**ees**-moh
lies	bugie	boo-**jee**-ay
love / sex	amore / sesso	ah-**moh**-ray / **sehs**-soh
marijuana	marijuana	mah-ree-**wahn**-nah
money / power	denaro / potere	day-**nah**-roh / poh-**tay**-ray
pollution	inquinamento	een-kwee-nah-**mayn**-toh
racism	razzismo	rahd-**zeez**-moh
regime change	cambio di regime	**kahm**-beeoh dee ray-**jee**-may
relaxation	rilassamento	ree-lah-sah-**mayn**-toh
religion	religione	ray-lee-**joh**-nay
respect	rispetto	ree-**spay**-toh
taxes	tasse	**tah**-say
television	televisione	tay-lay-vee-zee**oh**-nay
violence	violenza	vee-oh-**lehnt**-sah
work	lavoro	lah-**voh**-roh
war / peace	guerra / pace	**gwehr**-rah / **pah**-chay
global perspective	prospettiva globale	proh-spay-**tee**-vah gloh-**bah**-lay

You Be the Judge

(no) problem	(non c'è) problema	(nohn cheh) proh-**blay**-mah
(not) good	(non) bene	(nohn) **behn**-ay
(not) dangerous	(non) pericoloso	(nohn) pay-ree-koh-**loh**-zoh
(not) fair	(non) giusto	(nohn) **joo**-stoh
(not) guilty	(non) colpevole	(nohn) kohl-pay-**voh**-lay
(not) powerful	(non) potente	(nohn) poh-**tehn**-tay
(not) stupid	(non) stupido	(nohn) **stoo**-pee-doh
(not) happy	(non) felice	(nohn) fay-**lee**-chay
because / for	perchè / per	pehr-**keh** / pehr
and / or / from	e / o / da	ay / oh / dah
too much	troppo	**troh**-poh
(never) enough	(mai) abbastanza	(**mah**ee) ah-bah-**stahnt**-sah
same	stesso	**stay**-soh
better / worse	meglio / peggio	**mehl**-yoh / **peh**-joh
here / everywhere	qui / ovunque	kwee / oh-**voon**-kway

Beginnings and Endings

I like...	Mi piace...	mee pee**ah**-chay
We like...	Ci piace...	chee pee**ah**-chay
I don't like...	Non mi piace...	nohn mee pee**ah**-chay
We don't like...	Non ci piace...	nohn chee pee**ah**-chay
Do you like...?	Le piace...?	lay pee**ah**-chay
In the past...	In passato...	een pah-**sah**-toh
When I was younger,	Quando ero più giovane,	**kwahn**-doh **ay**-roh pew joh-**vah**-nay
I thought...	credevo...	cray-**day**-voh
Now, I think...	Ora penso...	**oh**-rah **pehn**-soh
I am / Are you...?	Sono / È...?	**soh**-noh / eh
...an optimist / pessimist	...ottimista / pessimista	oh-tee-**mee**-stah / pay-see-**mee**-stah
I believe...	Credo...	**kray**-doh
I don't believe...	Non credo...	nohn **kray**-doh
Do you believe...?	Lei crede...?	**leh**ee **kray**-day

CHATING

...in God	*...in Dio*	een **dee**oh
...in life after death	*...nella vita*	**nay**-lah **vee**-tah
	ultraterrena	ool-trah-tay-**ray**-nah
...in extraterrestrial	*...negli*	**nayl**-yee
life	*extraterrestri*	ehk-strah-tehr-**rehs**-tree
...in Santa Claus	*...in Babbo Natale*	een **bah**-boh nah-**tah**-lay
Yes. / No.	*Sì. / No.*	see / noh
Maybe. /	*Forse. /*	**for**-say /
I don't know.	*Non lo so.*	nohn loh soh
What's most	*Qual'è la cosa*	kwah-**leh** lah **koh**-zah
important in life?	*più importante*	pew eem-por-**tahn**-tay
	nella vita?	**nay**-lah **vee**-tah
The problem is...	*Il problema è...*	eel proh-**blay**-mah eh
The answer is...	*La risposta è...*	lah ree-**spoh**-stah eh
We have solved	*Abbiamo*	ah-bee**ah**-moh
the world's	*risolto i*	ree-**zohl**-toh ee
problems.	*problemi del*	proh-**blay**-mee dayl
	mondo.	**mohn**-doh

An Italian Romance

Words of Love

I / me / you / we	*io / mi /*	**ee**oh / mee /
	ti / noi	tee / **noh**ee
flirt	*flirtare*	fleer-**tah**-ray
kiss	*bacio*	**bah**-choh
hug	*abbraccio*	ah-**brah**-choh
love	*amore*	ah-**moh**-ray
make love	*fare l'amore*	**fah**-ray lah-**moh**-ray
condom	*preservativo*	pray-zehr-vah-**tee**-voh
contraceptive	*contraccetivo*	kohn-trah-chay-**tee**-voh
safe sex	*sesso sicuro*	**sehs**-soh see-**koo**-roh

sexy	*sensuale*	sayn-soo**ah**-lay
cozy	*accogliente*	ah-kohl-**yehn**-tay
romantic	*romantico*	roh-**mahn**-tee-koh
honey bunch	*dolce come*	**dohl**-chay **koh**-may
	il miele	eel mee**ay**-lay
cupcake	*pasticcino*	pah-stee-**chee**-noh
sugar pie	*zuccherino*	tsoo-kay-**ree**-noh
pussy cat	*gattino[a]*	gah-**tee**-noh

Ah, Amore

What's the matter?	*Qual'è il*	kwah-**leh** eel
	problema?	proh-**blay**-mah
Nothing.	*Niente.*	nee**ehn**-tay
I am / Are you...?	*Sono / È...?*	**soh**-noh / eh
...straight	*...normale*	nor-**mah**-lay
...gay	*...gay*	gay
...bisexual	*...bisessuale*	bee-sehs-soo**ah**-lay
...undecided	*...indeciso[a]*	een-day-**chee**-zoh
...prudish	*...pudico[a]*	**poo**-dee-koh
...horny	*...allupato[a]*	ah-loo-**pah**-toh
We are on our	*Siamo in luna*	see**ah**-moh een **loo**-nah
honeymoon.	*di miele.*	dee mee**ay**-lay
I have...	*Ho...*	oh
...a boyfriend.	*...il ragazzo.*	eel rah-**gahd**-zoh
...a girlfriend.	*...la ragazza.*	lah rah-**gahd**-zah
I'm married.	*Sono sposato[a].*	**soh**-noh spoh-**zah**-toh
I'm married	*Sono sposato[a]*	**soh**-noh spoh-**zah**-toh
(but...).	*(ma...).*	(mah)
I'm not married.	*Non sono*	nohn **soh**-noh
	sposato[a].	spoh-**zah**-toh
Do you have a	*Ha il ragazzo /*	ah eel rah-**gahd**-zoh /
boyfriend /	*la ragazza?*	lah rah-**gahd**-zah
a girlfriend?		
I'm	*Sono*	**soh**-noh
adventurous.	*avventuroso.*	ah-vehn-too-**roh**-zoh
I'm lonely.	*Sono solo[a].*	**soh**-noh **soh**-loh

CHATING

I'm lonely tonight.	*Sono solo[a] stasera.*	**soh**-noh **soh**-loh stah-**zay**-rah
I'm rich and single.	*Sono ricco[a] e single.*	**soh**-noh **ree**-koh ay **seeng**-glay
Do you mind if I sit here?	*Le dispiace se mi siedo qui?*	lay dee-spee**ah**-chay say mee see**ay**-doh kwee
Would you like a drink?	*Vuole qualcosa da bere?*	**vwoh**-lay kwahl-**koh**-zah dah **bay**-ray
Will you go out with me?	*Vuole uscire con me?*	**vwoh**-lay oo-**shee**-ray kohn may
Would you like to go out tonight for...?	*Vuole uscire stasera per...?*	**vwoh**-lay oo-**shee**-ray stah-**zay**-rah pehr
...a walk	*...una passeggiata*	**oo**-nah pah-say-**jah**-tah
...dinner	*...cena*	**chay**-nah
...a drink	*...qualcosa da bere*	kwahl-**koh**-zah dah **bay**-ray
Where's the best place to dance nearby?	*C'è un bel locale da ballo qui vicino?*	cheh oon behl loh-**kah**-lay dah **bah**-loh kwee vee-**chee**-noh
Do you want to dance?	*Vuole ballare?*	**vwoh**-lay bah-**lah**-ray
I have no diseases.	*Non ho malattie.*	nohn oh mah-lah-**tee**-ay
I have many diseases.	*Ho molte malattie.*	oh **mohl**-tay mah-lah-**tee**-ay
I have only safe sex.	*Faccio solo sesso sicuro.*	**fah**-choh **soh**-loh **sehs**-soh see-**koo**-roh
Let's have a wild and crazy night!	*Passiamo una notte di fuoco!*	pah-see**ah**-moh **oo**-nah **noh**-tay dee **fwoh**-koh
Can I take you home?	*Posso accompagnarti a casa?*	**poh**-soh ah-kohm-pahn-**yar**-tee ah **kah**-zah
Why not?	*Perché no?*	pehr-**kay** noh
How can I change your mind?	*Posso farti cambiare idea?*	**poh**-soh **far**-tee kahm-bee**ah**-ray ee-**day**-ah
Kiss me.	*Baciami.*	bah-chee**ah**-mee
May I kiss you?	*Posso baciarti?*	**poh**-soh bah-chee-**ar**-tee

Can I see you again?	*Ti posso rivedere?*	tee **poh**-soh ree-vay-**day**-ray
Your place or mine?	*A casa tua o a casa mia?*	ah **kah**-zah **too**-ah oh ah **kah**-zah **mee**-ah
How does this feel?	*Ti piace questo?*	tee pee**ah**-chay **kweh**-stoh
Is this an aphrodisiac?	*È un afrodisiaco questo?*	eh oon ah-froh-dee-**zee**-ah-koh **kweh**-stoh
This is (not) my first time.	*Questa (non) è la mia prima volta.*	**kweh**-stah (nohn) eh lah **mee**-ah **pree**-mah **vohl**-tah
You are my most beautiful souvenir.	*Sei il mio più bel ricordo.*	**seh**ee eel **mee**-oh pew behl ree-**kor**-doh
Do you do this often?	*Lo fai spesso?*	loh **fah**ee **speh**-soh
How's my breath?	*Com'è il mio alito?*	koh-**meh** eel **mee**-oh ah-**lee**-toh
Let's just be friends.	*Solo amici.*	**soh**-loh ah-**mee**-chee
I'll pay for my share.	*Pago per la mia parte.*	**pah**-goh pehr lah **mee**-ah **par**-tay
Would you like a massage...?	*Vorresti un massaggio...?*	vor-**ray**-stee oon mah-**sah**-joh
...for your back	*...alla schiena*	**ah**-lah shee**ay**-nah
...for your feet	*...ai piedi*	**ah**ee pee**ay**-dee
Why not?	*Perchè no?*	pehr-**keh** noh
Try it.	*Provalo.*	**proh**-vah-loh
It tickles.	*Fa solletico.*	fah soh-**lay**-tee-koh
Oh my God!	*Oh mio Dio!*	oh **mee**-oh **dee**-oh
I love you.	*Ti amo.*	tee **ah**-moh
Darling, will you marry me?	*Cara, mi vuoi sposare?*	**kah**-rah mee **vwoh**ee spoh-**zah**-ray

DICTIONARY

Italian/English

You'll see some of the words in the dictionary listed like this: aggressivo[a]. Use the *a* ending (pronounced "ah") if you're talking about a woman.

A

a	to; at	acerbo	sour
abbastanza	enough	acqua	water
abbigliamento, boutique di	clothing boutique	acqua del rubinetto	tap water
		acqua minerale	mineral water
abbronzarsi	sunbathe	acqua potabile	drinkable water
abbronzatura	suntan (n)	adattatore elettrico	electrical adapter
aborto	abortion		
aborto spontaneo	miscarriage	adesso	now
abusare	abuse (v)	adolescente	teenager
accappatoio	bathrobe	adulto	adult
accendino	lighter (n)	aeroplano	plane
accessibile con la sedia a rotelle	wheelchair-accessible	aeroporto	airport
		affamato	hungry
accesso a Internet	Internet access	affari	business
		affascinante	charming

affittare	rent (v)	**ancora**	more, again
Africa	Africa	**andare**	go
agenzia di viaggi	travel agency	**andata**	one way (ticket)
aggiustare	fix (v)	**andicappato**	handicapped
aggressivo[a]	aggressive	**anello**	ring (n)
agnello	lamb	**angolo**	corner
agnostico[a]	agnostic	**animale**	animal
ago	needle	**animale domestico**	pet (n)
agosto	August	**anno**	year
AIDS	AIDS	**annullare**	cancel
aiutare	help (v)	**antenato[a]**	ancestor
aiuto	help (n)	**antiacido**	antacid
aiuto, di	helpful	**antibiotico**	antibiotic
ala	wing	**antichità**	antiques
alba	sunrise	**antico**	ancient
albero	tree	**antipasti**	appetizers
alcool	alcohol	**anziani**	seniors
alimentari	grocery store	**aperto**	open (adj)
aliscafo	hydrofoil	**appartamento**	apartment
alito	breath	**appendiabiti**	coat hanger
all'aria aperta	outdoors	**appuntamento**	appointment
allergico[a]	allergic	**aprile**	April
allergie	allergies	**aprire**	open (v)
alt	stop (n, sign)	**apriscatola**	can opener
altare	altar	**arancia**	orange (fruit)
alto	tall; high	**arancione**	orange (color)
altro	other	**arcobaleno**	rainbow
altro, un	another	**argento**	silver
amante	lover	**aria**	air
amare	love (v)	**aria condizionata**	air-conditioned
ambasciata	embassy		
ambulanza	ambulance	**armadietti**	lockers
amicizia	friendship	**aroma**	flavor (n)
amico	friend	**arrabbiato[a]**	angry
amore	love (n)	**arrivare**	arrive
anabbaglianti	headlights	**arrivederci**	goodbye
analgesico	pain killer	**arrivi**	arrivals

arte	art; crafts	**autostrada**	highway
Arte Nouveau	Art Nouveau	**autunno**	autumn
artificiale	artificial	**avere**	have
artigianato	handicrafts	**avere bisogno di**	need
artista	artist	**avere fretta**	hurry (v)
artrite	arthritis	**avvelenamento da cibo**	food
ascensore	elevator		poisoning
asciugamano	towel	**avvocato**	lawyer
asciugare	dry (v)		
asciugatrice	dryer	**B**	
asciutto	dry (adj)	**Babbo Natale**	Santa Claus
ascoltare	listen	**bacio**	kiss
asino	donkey	**baffi**	moustache
asma	asthma	**bagaglio**	luggage
aspettare	wait	**bagaglio a mano**	carry-on
aspirina	aspirin		luggage
assaggiare	taste (v)	**bagnato**	wet
assegno	check (n)	**bagno**	bathroom; bath
assetato	thirsty	**balcone**	balcony
assicurato	insured	**ballare**	dance (v)
assicurazione	insurance	**balsamo**	conditioner (hair)
assicurazione medica	health	**bambinaia**	babysitter
	insurance	**bambini**	children
assolato	sunny	**bambino[a]**	child
assonnato[a]	sleepy	**bambola**	doll
assorbenti igienici	sanitary	**banca**	bank
	napkins	**bancomat**	cash machine
assorbenti interni	tampons	**bandiera**	flag
Astratto	abstract	**bar**	coffee shop
ateo[a]	atheist	**barba**	beard
attraente	handsome	**barbiere**	barber, barber shop
attraversare	go through	**barca**	boat
attraverso	through	**barca a remi**	rowboat
audioguida	audioguide	**basket**	basketball
autista	driver	**Bassi, Paesi**	Netherlands
autobus	bus (city)	**basso**	low
autostop	hitchhike	**batteria**	battery

battito cardiaco	pulse	**bottone**	button
bavaglino	bib	**boutique di**	clothing
Belgio	Belgium	**abbigliamento**	boutique
bello[a]	beautiful; nice	**box**	playpen
benda	bandage	**braca a vela**	sailboat
bene	fine (good)	**braccialetto**	bracelet
benvenuto	welcome	**braccio**	arm
benzina	gas	**Britannia**	Britain
benzinaio	gas station	**brividi**	chills
bere	drink (v)	**broncopolmonite**	pneumonia
berretto	cap	**bronzo**	bronze
bevanda	drink (n)	**bruciatura**	burn (n)
bianchetto	white-out	**bruciatura del sole**	sunburn
bianco	white	**brutto[a]**	ugly
biblioteca	library	**buco**	hole
bicchiere	glass	**bugie**	lies
bicicletta	bicycle	**bulbo**	bulb
biglietto	ticket	**buon giorno**	good day
biglietto da visita	business card	**buono**	good
		burro di cacao	lip salve
binario	platform; track (train)	**busta**	envelope
		busta de plastica sigillabile	Ziplock bag
biondo[a]	blond		
birra	beer		
bisogno di, avere	need (v)	**C**	
blocco note	notebook		
blu	blue	**cabina telefonica**	phone booth
bocca	mouth	**cacciaviti**	screwdriver
boccaglio	snorkel	**cadere**	fall (v)
boccia	bowl	**caffè**	coffee
bollito	boiled	**calcio**	soccer
bollitore	kettle	**caldo**	hot
bomba	bomb	**calendario**	calendar
borotalco	talcum powder	**calorie**	calorie
borsa	purse	**calzini**	socks
borsaiolo	pickpocket	**camare libere**	vacancy (hotel)
bottiglia	bottle	**cambiare**	change (v); transfer (v)

cambio	change (n); exchange (n)	**carne**	meat
camera	room	**caro**	expensive
camera da letto	bedroom	**carro attrezzi**	tow truck
camerata	dormitory	**carrozza letto**	sleeper car (train)
cameriera	waitress		
cameriere	waiter	**carrozza ristorante**	dining car (train)
camicetta	blouse	**carta**	paper
camicia	shirt	**carta di credito**	credit card
camminare	walk (v)	**carta igienica**	toilet paper
campagna	countryside	**carta telefonica**	telephone card
campane	bells		
campeggio	camping	**carte**	cards (deck)
camper	R.V.	**cartina**	card; map
campionato	championship	**cartoleria**	office supplies store
campo	field	**cartolina**	postcard
canale	canal	**casa**	house
cancellare	delete	**casalingo**	homemade
candela	candle	**cascata**	waterfall
candele	sparkplugs	**caseficio**	cheese shop
cane	dog	**cassetta**	tape (cassette)
canna	joint (marijuana)	**cassiere**	cashier
canoa	canoe	**castello**	castle
cantante	singer	**cattedrale**	cathedral
cantare	sing	**cattivo**	bad
cantina	cellar	**cattolico[a]**	Catholic (adj)
canzone	song	**cavalieri**	knights
capelli	hair	**cavallo**	horse
capire	understand	**cavatappi**	corkscrew
capitano	captain	**caviglia**	ankle
capo	boss	**cena**	dinner
capogiri	dizziness	**centralinista**	operator, receptionist
cappella	chapel		
cappello	hat	**centro**	center; downtown
caraffa	carafe	**centro commerciale**	shopping mall
caramella	candy		
carino[a]	pretty	**ceramica**	ceramic

cerotto	band-aid	**colazione**	breakfast
cestino	basket	**collana**	necklace
che cosa	what	**collant**	nylons (panty hose)
che peccato	it's a pity	**collina**	hill
check-in bagagli	baggage check	**collo**	neck
chi	who	**colori**	colors
chiaro	clear	**colpevole**	guilty
chiave	key	**coltello**	knife
chiesa	church	**combattere**	fight (v)
chiocciola	at sign (@)	**come**	how
chiostro	cloister	**cominciare**	begin
chitarra	guitar	**commercialista**	accountant
chiudere	lock (v)	**compleanno**	birthday
chiuso	closed	**completo**	no vacancy
chiusura lampo	zipper	**complicato**	complicated
ciabatte	slippers	**comprare**	buy
ciabatte da piscina	flip-flops	**con**	with
ciao	hello	**concerto**	concert
cibo	food	**conchiglia**	shell
cibo per neonati	baby food	**conduttore**	conductor
cielo	sky	**confermare**	confirm
cinese	Chinese (adj)	**confortevole**	comfortable
cinghia del ventilatore	fan belt	**congestione**	congestion (sinus)
cintura	belt	**congratulazioni**	congratulations
cioccolato	chocolate	**coniglio**	rabbit
cipria	face powder	**contadino[a]**	farmer
città	city, town	**contagioso**	contagious
classe	class	**contante**	cash
classe, prima	first class	**contento[a]**	happy
classe, secondo	second class	**conto**	bill (payment)
Classico	classical	**contraccettivi**	contraceptives
clinica	medical clinic	**coperta**	blanket
coda	tail	**copia**	copy
codice postale	zip code	**copisteria**	photocopy shop
coincidenza	connection (train)	**corda**	rope
		coro	choir

corpo	body
corrente	stream (n)
correre	run (v)
corridoio	aisle
corriera	long-distance bus
corruzione	corruption
corto[a]	short
cosa	thing
cosa, che	what
coscia	thigh
costa	coast
costare	cost (v)
costruzioni	construction (sign)
costume da bagno	swimsuit
cotone	cotton
crampi	cramps
crema da barba	shaving cream
crema idratante	moisturizer
crema per il sole	suntan lotion
crema per le mani	hand lotion
cripta	crypt
cristiano[a]	Christian (adj)
croce	cross
crudo	raw
cuccetta	berth (train)
cucchiaio	spoon
cucina	kitchen
cucinare	cook (v)
cugino[a]	cousin
cuore	heart
cupola	dome
cuscino	pillow

D

d'accordo	agree, OK
da	from
dare	give
decongestionante	decongestant
delizioso	delicious
democrazia	democracy
dente	tooth
denti	teeth
denti, mal di	toothache
dentifricio	toothpaste
dentista	dentist
dentizione	teething (baby)
dentro	inside
deodorante	deodorant
deposito	deposit
dermatite da pannolone	diaper rash
derubato	robbed
desiderare	wish (v)
destra	right (direction)
detersivo da bucato	laundry detergent
deviazione	detour
di	of
di aiuto	helpful
di sopra	upstairs
diabete	diabetes
diabetico[a]	diabetic
diaframma	diaphragm (birth control)
diamante	diamond
diapositiva	slide (photo)
diarrea	diarrhea
dicembre	December
dichiarare	declare (customs)
dietro	behind
difficile	difficult
dimenticare	forget
Dio	God

diretto	direct
direttore	manager
direzione	direction
dirupo	cliff
disinfettante	disinfectant
disoccupato[a]	unemployed
dispiace, mi	sorry
disturbare	disturb
disturbi cardiaci	heart condition
disturbi sinusali	sinus problems
dito	finger
dito del piede	toe
divertente	funny
divertimento	fun
divertirsi	enjoy
divorziato[a]	divorced
dizionario	dictionary
doccia	shower
dogana	customs
dolce	sweet
dolci	dessert
dolore	pain
dolore al petto	chest pains
dolori mestruali	menstrual cramps
domanda	question (n)
domandare	ask
domani	tomorrow
domenica	Sunday
donne	women
dopo	after
dopobarba	aftershave
dopodomani	day after tomorrow
doppio	double

dormire	sleep (v)
dottore	doctor
dove	where
dozzina	dozen
dritto	straight
duro	hard

E

e	and
è	is
ebreo	Jewish
eccellente	excellent
eccetto	except
economico	cheap
edificio	building
emergenza	emergency
emicrania	migraine
emorroidi	hemorrhoids
entrata	entry
epilessia	epilepsy
equitazione	horse riding
errore	mistake
esattamente	exactly
esausto	exhausted
esempio	example
est	east
estate	summer
età	age
Europa	Europe

F

fabbrica	factory
faccia	face
facile	easy
falso	false
famiglia	family
famoso[a]	famous

fantastico[a]	fantastic
fard	blush (makeup)
fare	make (v)
fare spese	shopping
fare una gita	hike
farmacia	pharmacy
farmaco per la diarrea	diarrhea medicine
fascia di sostegno	support bandage
fatto	stoned
fattoria	farm
fazzoletto di carta	facial tissue
febbraio	February
febbre	fever
felicità	happiness
feltro	moleskin
femmina	female
fermare	stop (v)
fermata	stop (n, train or bus)
ferramenta	hardware store
festa	party
fettina	slice
fiammiferi	matches
figlia	daughter
figlio	son
film	movie
filo	string
filo interdentale	dental floss
finestra	window
finire	finish (v)
finito	over (finished)
fiore	flower
firma	signature
fiume	river
folla	crowd (n)
fondo	bottom
fondotinta	foundation (makeup)
fontana	fountain
football	soccer
football Americano	American football
footing	jogging
forbici	scissors
forchetta	fork
formaggio	cheese
formulazione	baby formula
forno	oven
forse	maybe
forte	strong; loud
fortuna	luck
fossato	moat
foto	photo
fotocopia	photocopy
foto-ottica	camera shop
fragile	fragile
Francia	France
francobolli	stamps
fratello	brother
freccia	turn signal
freddo	cold (adj)
freni	brakes
fresco	fresh; cool
fretta, avere	hurry (v)
frizzante	fizzy
frontiera	border
frutta	fruit
frutti di mare	seafood
fumare	smoking
fumato	stoned
fumo	smoke (n)
funerale	funeral

fuochi d'artificio	fireworks
fuoco	fire
fusibili	fuses
futuro	future

G

galleria	gallery
galleria d'arte	art gallery
gamba	leg
garantito	guarantee
garza	gauze
gatto	cat
gelato	ice cream
gemelli	twins
generoso[a]	generous
genitori	parents
gennaio	January
gentile	kind
genuino	genuine
Germania	Germany
gettone	token
ghiaccio	ice
già	already
giallo	yellow
giardinaggio	gardening
giardino	garden
ginecologa	gynecologist
ginnastica	gymnastics
ginocchio	knee
giocare	play (v)
giocatore	athlete
giocattolo	toy
giochi, parco	playground
gioco	game
gioielli	jewelry
gioielliera	jewelry shop
giornalaio	newsstand

giornale	newspaper
giorno	day
giorno festivo	holiday
giorno, buon	good day (hello)
giovane	young
giovani	youths
giovedì	Thursday
gioventù, ostello della	youth hostel
giro	tour
gita, fare una	hike
giù	down
giubbotto	jacket
giugno	June
giusto	fair (just)
glutei	buttocks
gola	throat
gola, mal di	sore throat
gomito	elbow
gomma	tire (n)
gomma da cancellare	eraser
gomma da masticare	gum
gommone	raft
gonfiore	swelling (n)
gonna	skirt
Gotico	Gothic
graffetta	paper clip
grammatica	grammar
Gran Bretagna	Great Britain
grande	big
grande magazzino	department store
grassi	fat (n)
grasso[a]	fat (adj); greasy
gratis	free (no cost)

gravidanza	pregnancy
grazie	thanks
Grecia	Greece
grigio	gray
grotta	cave
guaio	trouble
guanti	gloves
guardare	look, watch (v)
guerra	war
guida	guide; guidebook
guidare	drive (v)
gusto	taste (n)

I

ieri	yesterday
il migliore	best
imbarazzante	embarrassing
immediatamente	immediately
imparare	learn
impermeabile	raincoat
importante	important
importato	imported
impossibile	impossible
Impressionista	Impressionist
improvvisamente	suddenly
in	in; by (via)
in pensione	retired
incartare	wrap
incastrato	stuck
incidente	accident
incinta	pregnant
incluso	included
incomprensione	misunder-standing
inconscio	unconscious
incredibile	incredible
incrocio	intersection

indicare	point (v)
indigestione	indigestion
indipendente	independent
indirizzo	address
indirizzo di posta elettronica	e-mail address
industria	industry
infermiera	nurse
infezione	infection
infezione urinaria	urinary infection
infiammazione	inflammation
influenza	flu
informazioni	information
infortunato	injured
ingeniere	engineer
inglese	English
ingoiare	swallow (v)
ingresso	entrance
innocente	innocent
inquinamento	pollution
insegnante	teacher
insetto	insect
insieme	together
insolazione	sunstroke
intelligente	intelligent
interessante	interesting
intestino	intestines
invece	instead
inverno	winter
invito	invitation
io	I
iodio	iodine
Irlanda	Ireland
irritazione della pelle	rash
isola	island

isolato	block
istante	instant
istruzione	education
Italia	Italy

L

labbro	lip
lacci da scarpe	shoelaces
ladro	thief
lago	lake
lampadina	light bulb
lana	wool
lassativo	laxative
latte detergente	face cleanser
lattina	can (n)
lavanderia	launderette
lavandino	sink
lavare	wash
lavatrice	washer
lavorare	work (v)
lavoro	work (n); occupation
legno	wood
lei	she
Lei	you (formal)
lenti a contatto	contact lenses
lento	slow
lenzuolo	sheet
lettera	letter
letti a castello	bunk beds
lettino	cot
letto	bed
letto, camera da	bedroom
letto, carrozza	sleeper car (train)
libere, camare	vacancy (hotel)
libero	vacant
libreria	book shop

libro	book
linea aerea	airline
linea bassa	underscore (_)
lingua	language
lino	linen
liquidazione	sale
liquido della trasmissione	transmission fluid
lista	list
litro	liter
locale	local
lontano	far
lotta	fight (n)
lozione anti-zanzare	insect repellant
luce	light (n)
luci posteriori	tail lights
luglio	July
lui	he
luna	moon
luna di miele	honeymoon
lunedì	Monday

M

macchina	car
macchina fotografica	camera
macho	macho
madre	mother
maggio	May
maglietta	T-shirt
maglione	sweater
magro[a]	skinny
mai	never
maiale	pig
mal d'orecchi	earache
mal di denti	toothache
mal di gola	sore throat

mal di stomaco	stomachache	**meno, più o**	approximately
mal di testa	headache	**menù**	menu
malato[a]	sick	**mercato**	market
malattia	disease	**mercato dei fiori**	flower market
malattia venerea	venereal disease	**mercato delle pulci**	flea market
mangiare	eat		
maniche	sleeves	**mercoledì**	Wednesday
manico	handle (n)	**merendina**	snack
mano	hand	**mese**	month
mano, bagaglio a	carry-on luggage	**messa**	church service
		messaggio	message
manzo	beef	**mestruazioni**	menstruation; period (woman's)
marca	clothesline		
marcio	rotten	**metallo**	metal
mare	sea	**metropolitana**	subway
marito	husband	**mezzanotte**	midnight
marmo	marble (material)	**mezzogiorno**	noon
marrone	brown	**mi dispiace**	sorry
martedì	Tuesday	**mi scusi**	excuse me
marzo	March	**mia**	my
mascara	mascara	**migliore, il**	best
mascella	jaw	**militare**	military
maschio	male	**minerale, acqua**	mineral water
massimo	maximum	**minimo**	minimum
matita	pencil; eyeliner	**minuti**	minutes
matrimonio	wedding	**mio**	my
mattina	morning	**misto**	mix (n)
maturo	ripe	**mobili**	furniture
meccanico	mechanic	**moda**	fashion
medicina	medicine	**moderno**	modern
medicina per il raffreddore	cold medicine	**moglie**	wife
		molti	many
Medievale	medieval	**molto**	much; very
medio	medium	**momento**	moment
meglio	better	**monastero**	monastery
mela	apple	**mondo**	world

monete	coins
montagna	mountain
monumento	monument
morire	die
morso	bite (n)
morto	dead
moschea	mosque
mostrare	show (v)
motocicletta	motorcycle
motorino	motor scooter
mucca	cow
muri fortificati	fortified wall
muscolo	muscle
museo	museum
musica	music
mussulmano[a]	Muslim (adj)
mutande	underwear
mutandine	underpants
mutandoni	briefs

N

naso	nose
nastro adesivo	scotch tape
Natale	Christmas
natura	nature
naturale	natural
nave	ship (n)
nazionalità	nationality
nebbia	fog
necessario	necessary
negozio	shop (n)
negozio di antiquariato	antiques shop
negozio di cellulari	cell phone shop
negozio di dolciumi	sweets shop
negozio di giocattoli	toy store
negozio di souvenir	souvenir shop
negozio di vini	wine shop
Neoclassico	neoclassical
neonato[a]	baby
nero	black
nervoso[a]	nervous
niente	nothing
nipote	grandchild; nephew; niece
no	no
noi	we; us
nome	name
non	not
nonna	grandmother
nonno	grandfather
nord	north
normale	normal
nostalgico[a]	homesick
notte	night
novembre	November
nubile	single (female)
nudo[a]	naked
numero verde	toll-free
nuotare	swim
nuovo	new
nuvoloso	cloudy
nylon	nylon (material)

O

o	or
obliterare	validate
occhiali	glasses (eye)
occhiali da sole	sunglasses
occhio	eye
occupato	occupied

oceano	ocean	padrone	owner
odiare	hate (v)	paese	country
odore	smell (n)	Paesi Bassi	Netherlands
oggi	today	Paesi Scandinavi	Scandinavia
ogni	each; every	pagare	pay
Olimpiadi	Olympics	pagina	page
olio	oil (n)	palazzo	palace
ombrello	umbrella	palla	ball
ombretto	eye shadow	panciotto	vest
omosessuale	gay	pane	bread
onesto[a]	honest	panificio	bakery
ora	hour	panino	sandwich
orario	timetable	panna	cream;
orario d'apertura	opening		whipped cream
	hours	pannolino	diaper
orecchi, mal d'	earache	pantaloncini	shorts
orecchini	earrings	pantaloni	pants
orecchio	ear	pantofole	slippers
organo	organ	papà	dad
originale	original	paradiso	heaven
oro	gold	parcheggiare	park (v)
orologio	clock, watch (n)	parcheggio	parking lot
orribile	horrible	parco	park (garden)
ospedale	hospital	parco giochi	playground
ospite	guest	parlare	talk
ostello	youth	parola	word
della gioventù	hostel	parrucchiere	beauty salon
ottico	optician	partenze	departures
ottimo	great	partire	leave
ottobre	October	Pasqua	Easter
ottone	brass	passaporto	passport
ovest	west	passato	past
		passeggero[a]	passenger
P		passeggino	stroller
		pasticceria	pastry / sweets
pacco	package		shop
pace	peace		
padre	father	pastiglie per la gola	lozenges

pattinaggio	skating	**pianta**	plant
pattini a rotelle	roller skates	**piatto**	plate
peccato, che	it's a pity	**piazza**	square
pedaggio	toll	**piazzuola**	campsite
pedalò	paddleboat	**picchetti della tenda**	tent pegs
pedone	pedestrian	**piccolo[a]**	small
peggio	worse	**piede**	foot
peggiore	worst	**piede d'atleta**	athlete's foot
pelle	skin; leather	**pietra**	rock (n)
pelletteria	leather shop	**pigiama**	pajamas
peltro	pewter	**pigro[a]**	lazy
pene	penis	**pillola**	pill
penna	pen	**pillole anticoncezionali**	birth control pills
pensare	think		
pensione, in	retired	**PIN**	PIN code
pepe	pepper	**pinzatrice**	stapler
per	for	**pinzette**	pliers; tweezers
per favore	please	**pioggia**	rain (n)
percentuale	percent	**piscina**	swimming pool
perchè	why (question); because (answer)	**pistola**	gun
		più	more
perfetto	perfect (adj)	**più o meno**	approximately
pericolo	danger	**più tardi**	later; afterwards
pericoloso	dangerous	**pizzo**	lace
periodo	period (of time)	**plastica**	plastic
perso[a]	lost	**po', un**	some
persona	person	**poco**	few
persone	people	**politici**	politicians
pesante	heavy	**polizia**	police
pescare	fish (v)	**pollo**	chicken
pesce	fish (n)	**polmoni**	lungs
peso	weight	**polso**	wrist
pettine	comb (n)	**polyestere**	polyester
petto	chest	**pomata antistaminica**	first-aid cream
pezzo	piece		
piacere	like (v)	**pomeriggio**	afternoon
piangere	cry (v)	**pompa**	pump (n)

ponte	bridge	**previsioni del tempo**	weather forecast
porcellana	porcelain		
porco	pork	**prezzo**	price
porta	door	**prima**	before
portacenere	ashtray	**prima classe**	first class
portafoglio	wallet	**primavera**	spring
portar via	take out (food)	**primo**	first
portare	carry	**primo soccorso**	first aid
porto	harbor	**principale**	main
Portogallo	Portugal	**privato**	private
possedere	own (v)	**problema**	problem
possibile	possible	**professione**	profession
posta	mail (n)	**profughi**	refugees
posta elettronica	e-mail	**profumo**	perfume
poster	poster	**proibito**	prohibited
posto	seat	**pronto**	ready
posto in vagone letto	sleeper (train)	**pronto soccorso**	emergency room
potabile, acqua	drinkable water	**pronuncia**	pronunciation
		prosperare	prosper
potente	powerful	**prossimo**	next
potere	can (v); power	**protestante**	Protestant (adj)
		protestare	complain
povero	poor	**protezione solare**	sunscreen
pratico[a]	practical	**prudente**	careful
prendere	take; catch (v)	**prurito**	itch (n)
prendere in prestito	borrow	**pubblico**	public
prenotare	reserve	**pulce**	flea
prenotazione	reservation	**pulito[a]**	clean (adj)
Preparazione H	Preparation H	**pullman**	long-distance bus
prescrizione	prescription	**pulpito**	pulpit
preservativo	condom	**punto**	dot (computer)
pressione alta	high blood pressure	**puntuale**	on time
prestare	lend		
presto	early	**Q**	
prete	priest	**quadro**	painting
		qualcosa	something

qualità	quality
quando	when
quanti	how many
quanto costa	how much ($)
quarto	quarter (1/4)
qui	here

R

raccomandare	recommend
raccordo anulare	ring road
radiatore	radiator
radiografia	X-ray
raffreddore	cold (n)
raffreddore da fieno	hay fever
ragazza	girl
ragazzo	boy
raggi x	X-ray
ragno	spider
rame	copper
rasoio	razor
razzismo	racism
re	king
regalo	gift
reggiseno	bra
regina	queen
religione	religion
reliquie	relic
Repubblica Ceca	Czech Republic
resistente	sturdy
retto	rectum
ricco[a]	rich
ricetta	recipe
ricevere	receive
ricevuta	receipt
ricordare	remember
ridere	laugh (v)

riempire	refill (v)
rilassamento	relaxation
rimborso	refund (n)
Rinascimento	Renaissance
riparare	repair (v)
riposare	relax (v)
rispetto	respect
risposta	answer
ritardo	delay (n)
ritiro bagagli	baggage claim
ritornare	return
ritorno	round trip
rivista	magazine
Romanico	Romanesque
Romantico	Romantic
romantico[a]	romantic
rosa	pink
rossetto	lipstick
rosso	red
rotaie	railway
rotonda	roundabout
rotto	broken
rovine	ruins
rubinetto	faucet
rubinetto, acqua del	tap water
rumoroso[a]	noisy
ruota	wheel
russare	snore

S

sabato	Saturday
sacchetto	bag
sacchetto di plastica	plastic bag
sacco a pelo	sleeping bag
sala d'aspetto	waiting room
sala di attesa	waiting room

salone	hall (big room)	**scienziato[a]**	scientist
saltare	jump (v)	**sciopero**	strike (stop work)
salumeria	delicatessen	**sciroppo**	cough drop
salute	health	**scivoloso**	slippery
Salute!	Cheers!	**sconto**	discount
salvare	save (computer)	**scotch**	tape (adhesive)
salvietta	napkin	**scrivere**	write
sandali	sandals	**scultore**	sculptor
sandali infradito	thongs	**scultura**	sculpture
sangue	blood	**scuola**	school
sanguinare	bleeding	**scuro**	dark
sano	healthy	**scuse**	apology
santo[a]	saint	**scusi, mi**	excuse me
sapere	know	**se**	if
sapone	soap	**secchio**	bucket
Saridon	non-aspirin substitute	**secco**	dry (adj)
scala	ladder	**secolo**	century
scaldare	heat (v)	**secondo classe**	second class
scale	stairs	**sedia**	chair
scandaloso	scandalous	**sedia a rotelle,**	wheelchair-
Scandinavi, Paesi	Scandinavia	**accessibile con la**	accessible
scapolo	single (male)	**seggiolino per**	car seat (baby)
scarafaggi	cockroach	**la macchina**	
scaricare	download	**seggiolino per**	booster seat
scarpe	shoes	**neonati**	
scarpe da ginnastica	tennis shoes	**seggiolone**	highchair
scarpe da tennis	tennis shoes	**segno**	sign
scarpe, lacci da	shoelaces	**segrete**	dungeon
scatola	box	**segreto**	secret
scherzo	joke (n)	**selvaggio[a]**	wild
schiena	back	**semaforo**	stoplight
sci	skiing	**seminterrato**	basement
sci acquatico	waterskiing	**semplice**	simple, plain
sciare	ski (v)	**sempre**	always
sciarpa	scarf	**seno**	breast
scienza	science	**senso unico**	one way (street)
		senza	without

separato	separate (adj)	sole	sun; sunshine
sera	evening	sole, bruciatura del	sunburn
serio	serious	sole, occhiali da	sunglasses
serratura	lock (n)	solo	only
servizio	service	solo[a]	alone
servizio di	babysitting	solvente per	nail polish
baby sitter	service	le unghie	remover
sesso	sex	sopra	above
seta	silk	sopra, di	upstairs
settembre	September	soprannome	nickname
settimana	week	sorella	sister
sfortunatamente	unfortunately	sorpresa	surprise (n)
		sorriso	smile (n)
si	yes	sottile	thin
sicuro	safe	sotto	under, below
sigarette	cigarette	sottoveste	slip
Signora	Mrs.	Spagna	Spain
signore	gentleman (singular);	spalle	shoulder
	ladies (plural)	spaventato[a]	afraid
Signore	Mr.	spazzolino da denti	toothbrush
signore	sir	specchio	mirror
Signorina	Miss	specialità	specialty
silenzio	silence	specialmente	especially
simile	similar	spedire	send
sinagoga	synagogue	spendere	spend
sinistra	left (direction)	speranza	hope
sintetico	synthetic	spese, fare	shopping
sito Internet	Web site	spesso	thick
smalto per	nail polish	spettacolo	show (n)
le unghie		spiaggia	beach
soccorso, primo	first aid	spiegare	explain
soccorso, pronto	emergency	spilla	pin; brooch
	room	spilla da balia	safety pin
soffrire	suffer	spingere	push
sognare	dream (v)	sporco	dirty
sogno	dream (n)	sposato[a]	married
soldi	money	squadra	team

stampare	print	**sveglia**	alarm clock
stanco	tired	**svegliarsi**	wake up
stanotte	tonight	**Svizzera**	Switzerland
starnuto	sneeze (n)		
Stati Uniti	United States	**T**	
stato	state	**taglia**	size
stazione	station	**tagliaunghie**	nail clipper
stazione degli autobus	bus station	**taglio di capelli**	haircut
		tappeto	carpet; rug
stazione della metropolitana	subway station	**tappi per le orecchie**	earplugs
		tappo	cork; sink stopper
stella	star (in sky)	**tardi**	late
stesso	same	**tardi, più**	later; afterwards
stile	style	**tasca**	pocket
stitichezza	constipation	**tassametro**	taxi meter
stivali	boots	**tasse**	tax
stoffa	cloth	**tavola da surf**	surfboard
stomaco	stomach	**tavola**	table
stomaco, mal di	stomachache	**tavolo**	desk
storia	history; story (floor)	**tazza**	cup
strada	street	**teatro**	theater; play (n)
straniero	foreign	**telefono**	telephone
strano[a]	strange (odd)	**telefono cellulare**	cell phone
stretto	tight; narrow	**televisione**	television
studente	student	**temere**	fear (v)
stupido[a]	stupid	**temperatura**	temperature
stuzzicadenti	toothpick	**tempo**	weather
su	on; up	**tempo, previsioni del**	weather forecast
subito	soon		
succhiotto	pacifier	**temporale**	storm
succo	juice	**tenda**	tent
sud	south	**tenere**	keep
sudare	sweat (v)	**tenero**	tender
suocera	mother-in-law	**tennis**	tennis
supermercato	supermarket	**tergicristalli**	windshield wipers
supplemento	supplement	**termometro**	thermometer
surfer	surfer	**terra**	earth

terribile	terrible
terroristi	terrorists
tesoro	treasury
test di gravidanza	pregnancy test
testa	head
testa, mal di	headache
testicoli	testicles
tetto	roof
tiepido	lukewarm
timbrare	validate
timido[a]	shy
tirare	pull; throw
toilette	toilet
torcia	flashlight
torre	tower
tosse	cough (n)
tossire	cough (v)
totale	total
tour guidato	guided tour
tradizionale	traditional
tradurre	translate
traffico	traffic
traghetto	ferry
tramonto	sunset
tranquillo	quiet
trattino	hyphen (-)
treno	train
trepiede	tripod
triste	sad
troppo	too
trucco	makeup
tu	you (informal)
Turchia	Turkey
turista	tourist
tutto	everything

U

ubriaco	drunk
uccello	bird
uccidere	kill
udire	hear
ufficio	office
ultimo	last
umido	muggy
un altro	another
un po'	some
una volta	once
unghie	fingernail
unico, senso	one way (street)
università	university
uomini	men
uomo	man
uretra	urethra
urgente	urgent
usare	use
uscita	exit
uscita d'emergenza	emergency exit
utero	uterus

V

vacanza	vacation
vagone	train car
valido	valid
valigia	suitcase
valle	valley
vasca da bagno	bathtub
vaselina	Vaseline
vecchio[a]	old
vedere	see
vedova	widow

vedovo	widower
vegetariano[a]	vegetarian (n)
vela	sailing
velluto	velvet
velocità	speed
vendere	sell
venerdì	Friday
venire	come
vento	wind
ventoso	windy
verde	green
vescica	bladder
vesciche	blisters
vestaglia	nightgown
vestiti	clothes
vestito	dress (n)
via aerea	air mail
viaggi, agenzia di	travel agency
viaggiare	travel
viaggiatori	travelers
viaggio	trip
vicino	near
video registratore	video recorder
vietato	forbidden
vietato fumare	non-smoking
vigneto	vineyard
villaggio	village
vino	wine
viola	purple
violenza	violence
violenza carnale	rape (n)
visita	visit (n)
visita, biglietto da	business card
visitare	visit (v)

vista	view
vita	life; waist
vitamine	vitamins
vivere	live (v)
voce	voice
volare	fly (v)
volere	want
volo	flight
volta, una	once
vomitare	vomit (v)
vuoto	empty

Z

zainetto	backpack
zaino	rucksack
zanzara	mosquito
zia	aunt
zio	uncle

English/Italian

You'll see some of the words in the dictionary listed like this: aggressivo[a]. Use the *a* ending (pronounced "ah") if you're talking about a woman.

A

abortion	aborto	**airline**	linea aerea
above	sopra	**airplane**	aeroplano
abstract	Astratto	**airport**	aeroporto
abuse (v)	abusare	**aisle**	corridoio
accident	incidente	**alarm clock**	sveglia
accountant	commercialista	**alcohol**	alcool
adapter, electrical	adattatore	**allergic**	allergico[a]
	elettrico	**allergies**	allergie
address	indirizzo	**alone**	solo[a]
address,	indirizzo di	**already**	già
e-mail	posta elettronica	**altar**	altare
adult	adulto	**always**	sempre
afraid	spaventato[a]	**ambulance**	ambulanza
Africa	Africa	**ancestor**	antenato[a]
after	dopo	**ancient**	antico
afternoon	pomeriggio	**and**	e
aftershave	dopobarba	**angry**	arrabbiato[a]
afterwards	più tardi	**animal**	animale
again	ancora	**ankle**	caviglia
age	età	**another**	un altro
aggressive	aggressivo[a]	**answer**	risposta
agnostic	agnostico[a]	**antacid**	antiacido
agree	d'accordo	**antibiotic**	antibiotico
AIDS	AIDS	**antiques**	antichità
air	aria	**antiques shop**	negozio di
air mail	via aerea		antiquariato
air-conditioned	aria	**apartment**	appartamento
	condizionata	**apology**	scuse

appetizers	antipasti
apple	mela
appointment	appuntamento
approximately	più o meno
April	aprile
arm	braccio
arrivals	arrivi
arrive	arrivare
art	arte
art gallery	galleria d'arte
Art Nouveau	Arte Nouveau
arthritis	artrite
artificial	artificiale
artist	artista
ashtray	portacenere
ask	domandare
aspirin	aspirina
asthma	asma
at	a
at sign (@)	chiocciola
atheist	ateo[a]
athlete	giocatore
athlete's foot	piede d'atleta
attractive	bello[a]
audioguide	audioguida
August	agosto
aunt	zia
Austria	Austria
autumn	autunno

B

baby	neonato[a]
baby booster seat	seggiolino per neonati
baby car seat	seggiolino pe la macchina
baby food	cibo per neonati

baby formula	formulazione
babysitter	bambinaia
babysitting service	servizio di baby sitter
back	schiena
backpack	zainetto
bad	cattivo
bag	sacchetto
bag, plastic	sacchetto di plastica
bag, Ziplock	busta de plastica sigillabile
baggage	bagaglio
baggage check	check-in bagagli
baggage claim	ritiro bagagli
bakery	panificio
balcony	balcone
ball	palla
banana	banana
bandage	benda
bandage, support	fascia di sostegno
band-aid	cerotto
bank	banca
barber	barbiere
barber shop	barbiere
baseball	baseball
basement	seminterrato
basket	cestino
basketball	basket
bath	bagno
bathrobe	accappatoio
bathroom	bagno
bathtub	vasca da bagno
battery	batteria
beach	spiaggia

beard	barba
beautiful	bello[a]
beauty salon	parrucchiere
because	perchè
bed	letto
bedbugs	insetti
bedroom	camera da letto
bedsheet	lenzuolo
beef	manzo
beer	birra
before	prima
begin	cominciare
behind	dietro
Belgium	Belgio
bells	campane
below	sotto
belt	cintura
berth (train)	cuccetta
best	il migliore
better	meglio
bib	bavaglino
bicycle	bicicletta
big	grande
bill (payment)	conto
bird	uccello
birth control pills	pillole anticoncezionali
birthday	compleanno
bite (n)	morso
black	nero
bladder	vescica
blanket	coperta
bleeding	sanguinare
blisters	vesciche
block	isolato
blond	biondo[a]
blood	sangue

blood pressure, high	pressione alta
blouse	camicetta
blue	blu
blush (makeup)	fard
boat	barca
body	corpo
boiled	bollito
bomb	bomba
book	libro
book shop	libreria
booster seat	seggiolino per neonati
boots	stivali
border	frontiera
borrow	prendere in prestito
boss	capo
bottle	bottiglia
bottom	fondo
boutique, clothing	boutique di abbigliamento
bowl	boccia
box	scatola
boy	ragazzo
bra	reggiseno
bracelet	braccialetto
brakes	freni
brass	ottone
bread	pane
breakfast	colazione
breast	seno
breath	alito
bridge	ponte
briefs	mutandoni
Britain	Britannia
broken	rotto
bronze	bronzo

brooch	spilla	cancel	annullare
brother	fratello	candle	candela
brown	marrone	candy	caramella
bucket	secchio	canoe	canoa
building	edificio	cap	berretto
bulb	bulbo	captain	capitano
bulb, light	lampadina	car	macchina
bunk beds	letti a castello	car (train)	vagone
burn (n)	bruciatura	car seat (baby)	seggiolino per
bus	autobus		la macchina
bus station	stazione degli	car, dining (train)	carrozza
	autobus		ristorante
bus stop	fermata	car, sleeper (train)	carrozza
bus, city	autobus		letto
bus, long-distance	pullman,	carafe	caraffa
	corriera	card	cartina
business	affari	card, telephone	carta telefonica
business card	biglietto da	cards (deck)	carte
	visita	careful	prudente
buttocks	glutei	carpet	tappeto
button	bottone	carry	portare
buy	comprare	carry-on luggage	bagaglio a
by (via)	in		mano
		cash	contante

C

		cash machine	bancomat
calendar	calendario	cashier	cassiere
calorie	calorie	cassette	cassetta
camera	macchina fotografica	castle	castello
camera shop	foto-ottica	cat	gatto
camper	camper	catch (v)	prendere
camping	campeggio	cathedral	cattedrale
campsite	piazzuola	Catholic (adj)	cattolico[a]
can (n)	lattina	cave	grotta
can (v)	potere	cell phone	telefono cellulare
can opener	apriscatola	cell phone shop	negozio di
Canada	Canada		cellulari
canal	canale	cellar	cantina

center	centro	**clinic, medical**	clinica
century	secolo	**clock**	orologio
ceramic	ceramica	**clock, alarm**	sveglia
chair	sedia	**cloister**	chiostro
championship	campionato	**closed**	chiuso
change (n)	cambio	**cloth**	stoffa
change (v)	cambiare	**clothes**	vestiti
chapel	cappella	**clothes pins**	spilla
charming	affascinante	**clothesline**	marca
cheap	economico	**clothing boutique**	boutique di
check (n)	assegno		abbigliamento
Cheers!	Salute!	**cloudy**	nuvoloso
cheese	formaggio	**coast**	costa
cheese shop	caseficio	**coat hanger**	appendiabiti
chest	petto	**cockroach**	scarafaggi
chest pains	dolore al petto	**coffee**	caffè
chicken	pollo	**coffee shop**	bar
child	bambino[a]	**coins**	monete
children	bambini	**cold (adj)**	freddo
chills	brividi	**cold (n)**	raffreddore
Chinese (adj)	cinese	**cold medicine**	medicina per
chocolate	cioccolato		il raffreddore
choir	coro	**colors**	colori
Christian (adj)	cristiano[a]	**comb (n)**	pettine
Christmas	Natale	**come**	venire
church	chiesa	**comfortable**	confortevole
church service	messa	**compact disc**	compact disc
cigarette	sigarette	**complain**	protestare
cinema	cinema	**complicated**	complicato
city	città	**computer**	computer
class	classe	**concert**	concerto
class, first	prima classe	**conditioner (hair)**	balsamo
class, second	secondo classe	**condom**	preservativo
classical	Classico	**conductor**	conduttore
clean (adj)	pulito[a]	**confirm**	confermare
clear	chiaro	**congestion**	congestione
cliff	dirupo	**(sinus)**	

congratulations	congratulazioni	credit card	carta di credito
connection (train)	coincidenza	cross	croce
		crowd (n)	folla
constipation	stitichezza	cry (v)	piangere
construction (sign)	costruzioni	crypt	cripta
		cup	tazza
contact lenses	lenti a contatto	customs	dogana
contagious	contagioso	Czech	Repubblica
contraceptives	contraccettivi	Republic	Ceca
cook (v)	cucinare		

D

cool	fresco		
copper	rame	dad	papà
copy	copia	dance (v)	ballare
copy shop	copisteria	danger	pericolo
cork	tappo	dangerous	pericoloso
corkscrew	cavatappi	dark	scuro
corner	angolo	dash (-)	trattino
corridor	corridoio	daughter	figlia
corruption	corruzione	day	giorno
cost (v)	costare	day after tomorrow	dopodomani
cot	lettino		
cotton	cotone	dead	morto
cough (n)	tosse	December	dicembre
cough (v)	tossire	declare (customs)	dichiarare
cough drop	sciroppo	decongestant	deconges-
country	paese		tionante
countryside	campagna	delay (n)	ritardo
cousin	cugino[a]	delete	cancellare
cow	mucca	delicatessen	salumeria
cozy	confortevole	delicious	delizioso
crafts	arte	democracy	democrazia
cramps	crampi	dental floss	filo interdentale
cramps, menstrual	dolori mestruali	dentist	dentista
		deodorant	deodorante
cream	panna	depart	partire
cream, first-aid	pomata antistaminica	department store	grande magazzino

departures	partenze	**donkey**	asino
deposit	deposito	**door**	porta
dessert	dolci	**dormitory**	camerata
detergent	detersivo da bucato	**dot (computer)**	punto
detour	deviazione	**double**	doppio
diabetes	diabete	**down**	giù
diabetic	diabetico[a]	**download**	scaricare
diamond	diamante	**downtown**	centro
diaper	pannolino	**dozen**	dozzina
diaper rash	dermatite da	**dream (n)**	sogno
	pannolone	**dream (v)**	sognare
diaphragm	diaframma	**dress (n)**	vestito
(birth control)		**drink (n)**	bevanda
diarrhea	diarrea	**drink (v)**	bere
diarrhea	farmaco per	**drive (v)**	guidare
medicine	la diarrea	**driver**	autista
dictionary	dizionario	**drunk**	ubriaco
die	morire	**dry (adj)**	secco, asciutto
difficult	difficile	**dry (v)**	asciugare
dining car (train)	carrozza	**dryer**	asciugatrice
	ristorante	**dungeon**	segrete
dinner	cena	**duty free**	duty free
direct	diretto		
direction	direzione	**E**	
dirty	sporco	**each**	ogni
discount	sconto	**ear**	orecchio
disease	malattia	**earache**	mal d'orecchi
disease, venereal	malattia	**early**	presto
	venerea	**earplugs**	tappi per le orecchie
disinfectant	disinfettante	**earrings**	orecchini
disturb	disturbare	**earth**	terra
divorced	divorziato[a]	**east**	est
dizziness	capogiri	**Easter**	Pasqua
doctor	dottore	**easy**	facile
dog	cane	**eat**	mangiare
doll	bambola	**education**	istruzione
dome	cupola	**elbow**	gomito

electrical adapter	adattatore elettrico
elevator	ascensore
e-mail	posta elettronica
e-mail address	indirizzo di posta elettronica
embarrassing	imbarazzante
embassy	ambasciata
emergency	emergenza
emergency exit	uscita d'emergenza
emergency room	pronto soccorso
empty	vuoto
engineer	ingeniere
English	inglese
enjoy	divertirsi
enough	abbastanza
entrance	ingresso
entrance (road)	entrata
entry	entrata
envelope	busta
epilepsy	epilessia
eraser	gomma da cancellare
especially	specialmente
Europe	Europa
evening	sera
every	ogni
everything	tutto
exactly	esattamente
example	esempio
excellent	eccellente
except	eccetto
exchange (n)	cambio
excuse me	mi scusi
exhausted	esausto

exit	uscita
exit, emergency	uscita d'emergenza
expensive	caro
explain	spiegare
eye	occhio
eye shadow	ombretto
eyeliner	matita, eyeliner

F

face	faccia
face cleanser	latte detergente
face powder	cipria
facial tissue	fazzoletto di carta
factory	fabbrica
fair (just)	giusto
fall (v)	cadere
false	falso
family	famiglia
famous	famoso[a]
fan belt	cinghia del ventilatore
fantastic	fantastico[a]
far	lontano
farm	fattoria
farmer	contadino[a]
fashion	moda
fat (adj)	grasso[a]
fat (n)	grassi
father	padre
faucet	rubinetto
fax	fax
fear (v)	temere
February	febbraio
female	femmina
ferry	traghetto
fever	febbre
few	poco

field	campo	foot	piede
fight (n)	lotta	football (soccer)	football, calcio
fight (v)	combattere		
fine (good)	bene	football, American	football Americano
finger	dito		
fingernail	unghie	for	per
finish (v)	finire	forbidden	vietato
fire	fuoco	foreign	straniero
fireworks	fuochi d'artificio	forget	dimenticare
first	primo	fork	forchetta
first aid	primo soccorso	formula (for baby)	formulazione
first class	prima classe		
first-aid cream	pomata antistaminica	foundation (makeup)	fondotinta
fish (n)	pesce	fountain	fontana
fish (v)	pescare	fragile	fragile
fix (v)	aggiustare	France	Francia
fizzy	frizzante	free (no cost)	gratis
flag	bandiera	fresh	fresco
flash (camera)	flash	Friday	venerdì
flashlight	torcia	friend	amico
flavor (n)	aroma	friendship	amicizia
flea	pulce	frisbee	frisbee
flea market	mercato delle pulci	from	da
		fruit	frutta
flight	volo	fun	divertimento
flip-flops	ciabatte da piscina	funeral	funerale
floss, dental	filo interdentale	funny	divertente
flower	fiore	furniture	mobili
flower market	mercato dei fiori	fuses	fusibili
		future	futuro
flu	influenza		
fly (v)	volare	**G**	
fog	nebbia	gallery	galleria
food	cibo	game	gioco
food poisoning	avvelenamento da cibo	garage	garage
		garden	giardino

gardening	giardinaggio	**guide**	guida
gas	benzina	**guidebook**	guida
gas station	benzinaio	**guided tour**	tour guidato
gauze	garza	**guilty**	colpevole
gay	omosessuale	**guitar**	chitarra
generous	generoso[a]	**gum**	gomma da masticare
gentleman	signore	**gun**	pistola
genuine	genuino	**gymnastics**	ginnastica
Germany	Germania	**gynecologist**	ginecologa

H

gift	regalo		
girl	ragazza	**hair**	capelli
give	dare	**haircut**	taglio di capelli
glass	bicchiere	**hall (big room)**	salone
glasses (eye)	occhiali	**hand**	mano
gloves	guanti	**hand lotion**	crema per
go	andare		le mani
go through	attraversare	**handicapped**	andicappato
God	Dio	**handicrafts**	artigianato
gold	oro	**handle (n)**	manico
golf	golf	**handsome**	attraente
good	buono	**happiness**	felicità
good day	buon giorno	**happy**	contento[a]
goodbye	arrivederci	**harbor**	porto
Gothic	Gotico	**hard**	duro
grammar	grammatica	**hardware store**	ferramenta
grandchild	nipote	**hash (drug)**	hashish
grandfather	nonno	**hat**	cappello
grandmother	nonna	**hate (v)**	odiare
gray	grigio	**have**	avere
greasy	grasso	**hay fever**	raffreddore
great	ottimo		da fieno
Great Britain	Gran Bretagna	**he**	lui
Greece	Grecia	**head**	testa
green	verde	**headache**	mal di testa
grocery store	alimentari	**headlights**	anabbaglianti
guarantee	garantito	**health**	salute
guest	ospite		

health	assicurazione	horse	cavallo
insurance	medica	horse riding	equitazione
healthy	sano	hospital	ospedale
hear	udire	hot	caldo
heart	cuore	hotel	hotel
heart condition	disturbi	hour	ora
	cardiaci	house	casa
heat (n)	calore	how	come
heat (v)	scaldare	how many	quanti
heaven	paradiso	how much ($)	quanto costa
heavy	pesante	hungry	affamato
hello	ciao	hurry (v)	avere fretta
help (n)	aiuto	husband	marito
help (v)	aiutare	hydrofoil	aliscafo
helpful	di aiuto	hyphen (-)	trattino
hemorrhoids	emorroidi		
here	qui	**I**	
hi	ciao		
high	alto	I	io
high blood pressure	pressione	ice	ghiaccio
	alta	ice cream	gelato
highchair	seggiolone	if	se
highway	autostrada	ill	malato[a]
hike	fare una gita	immediately	immediatamente
hill	collina	important	importante
history	storia	imported	importato
hitchhike	autostop	impossible	impossibile
hobby	hobby	Impressionist	Impressionista
hockey	hockey	in	in
hole	buco	included	incluso
holiday	giorno festivo	incredible	incredibile
homemade	casalingo	independent	indipendente
homesick	nostalgico[a]	indigestion	indigestione
honest	onesto[a]	industry	industria
honeymoon	luna di miele	infection	infezione
hope	speranza	infection, urinary	infezione
horrible	orribile		urinaria
		inflammation	infiammazione

information	informazioni	**job**	lavoro
injured	infortunato	**jogging**	footing
innocent	innocente	**joint (marijuana)**	canna
insect	insetto	**joke (n)**	scherzo
insect repellant	lozione	**journey**	viaggio
	anti-zanzare	**juice**	succo
inside	dentro	**July**	luglio
instant	istante	**jump (v)**	saltare
instead	invece	**June**	giugno
insurance	assicurazione		
insurance, health	assicurazione	**K**	
	medica	**keep**	tenere
insured	assicurato	**kettle**	bollitore
intelligent	intelligente	**key**	chiave
interesting	interessante	**kill**	uccidere
Internet	Internet	**kind**	gentile
Internet access	accesso a	**king**	re
	Internet	**kiss**	bacio
Internet café	Internet café	**kitchen**	cucina
intersection	incrocio	**kitchenette**	cucina
intestines	intestino	**knee**	ginocchio
invitation	invito	**knife**	coltello
iodine	iodio	**knights**	cavalieri
Ireland	Irlanda	**know**	sapere
is	è		
island	isola	**L**	
Italy	Italia	**lace**	pizzo
itch (n)	prurito	**ladder**	scala
		ladies	signore
J		**lady**	signora
jacket	giubbotto	**lake**	lago
January	gennaio	**lamb**	agnello
jaw	mascella	**language**	lingua
jeans	jeans	**large**	grande
jewelry	gioielli	**last**	ultimo
jewelry shop	gioielliera	**late**	tardi
Jewish	ebreo	**later**	più tardi

laugh (v)	ridere	**look**	guardare
launderette	lavanderia	**lost**	perso[a]
laundry soap	detersivo	**lotion, hand**	crema per
	da bucato		le mani
lawyer	avvocato	**loud**	forte
laxative	lassativo	**love (n)**	amore
lazy	pigro[a]	**love (v)**	amare
learn	imparare	**lover**	amante
leather	pelle	**low**	basso
leather shop	pelletteria	**lozenges**	pastiglie
leave	partire		per la gola
left (direction)	sinistra	**luck**	fortuna
leg	gamba	**luggage**	bagaglio
lend	prestare	**luggage, carry-on**	bagaglio
lenses, contact	lenti a		a mano
	contatto	**lukewarm**	tiepido
letter	lettera	**lungs**	polmoni
library	biblioteca		
lies	bugie	**M**	
life	vita		
light (n)	luce	**macho**	macho
light bulb	lampadina	**mad**	arrabbiato[a]
lighter (n)	accendino	**magazine**	rivista
like (v)	piacere	**mail (n)**	posta
linen	lino	**main**	principale
lip	labbro	**make (v)**	fare
lip salve	burro di cacao	**makeup**	trucco
lipstick	rossetto	**male**	maschio
list	lista	**mall (shopping)**	centro
listen	ascoltare		commerciale
liter	litro	**man**	uomo
little (adj)	piccolo	**manager**	direttore
live (v)	vivere	**many**	molti
local	locale	**map**	cartina
lock (n)	serratura	**marble (material)**	marmo
lock (v)	chiudere	**March**	marzo
lockers	armadietti	**marijuana**	marijuana
		market	mercato

market, flea	mercato delle pulci	mistake	errore
market, flower	mercato dei fiori	misunderstanding	incomprensione
market, open-air	mercato	mix (n)	misto
married	sposato[a]	moat	fossato
mascara	mascara	modem	modem
matches	fiammiferi	modern	moderno
maximum	massimo	moisturizer	crema idratante
May	maggio	moleskin	feltro, moleskin
maybe	forse	moment	momento
meat	carne	monastery	monastero
mechanic	meccanico	Monday	lunedì
medicine	medicina	money	soldi
medicine for a cold	medicina per il raffreddore	month	mese
		monument	monumento
medicine, non-aspirin substitute	Saridon	moon	luna
		more	ancora
medieval	Medievale	morning	mattina
medium	medio	mosque	moschea
men	uomini	mosquito	zanzara
menstrual cramps	dolori mestruali	mother	madre
		mother-in-law	suocera
menstruation	mestruazioni	motor scooter	motorino
menu	menù	motorcycle	motocicletta
message	messaggio	mountain	montagna
metal	metallo	moustache	baffi
meter, taxi	tassametro	mouth	bocca
midnight	mezzanotte	movie	film
migraine	emicrania	Mr.	Signore
military	militare	Mrs.	Signora
mineral water	acqua minerale	much	molto
minimum	minimo	muggy	umido
minutes	minuti	muscle	muscolo
mirror	specchio	museum	museo
miscarriage	aborto spontaneo	music	musica
Miss	Signorina	Muslim (adj)	mussulmano[a]
		my	mio / mia

N

nail (finger)	unghie
nail clipper	tagliaunghie
nail polish	smalto per le unghie
nail polish remover	solvente per le unghie
naked	nudo[a]
name	nome
napkin	salvietta
narrow	stretto
nationality	nazionalità
natural	naturale
nature	natura
nausea	nausea
near	vicino
necessary	necessario
neck	collo
necklace	collana
need (v)	avere bisogno di
needle	ago
neoclassical	Neoclassico
nephew	nipote
nervous	nervoso[a]
Netherlands	Paesi Bassi
never	mai
new	nuovo
newspaper	giornale
newsstand	giornalaio
next	prossimo
nice	bello[a]
nickname	soprannome
niece	nipote
night	notte
nightgown	vestaglia
no	no
no vacancy	completo
noisy	rumoroso[a]
non-aspirin substitute	Saridon
non-smoking	vietato fumare
noon	mezzogiorno
normal	normale
north	nord
nose	naso
not	non
notebook	blocco note
nothing	niente
November	novembre
now	adesso
nurse	infermiera
nylon (material)	nylon
nylons (panty hose)	collant

O

occupation	lavoro
occupied	occupato
ocean	oceano
October	ottobre
of	di
office	ufficio
office supplies store	cartoleria
oil (n)	olio
OK	d'accordo
old	vecchio[a]
Olympics	Olimpiadi
on	su
on time	puntuale
once	una volta
one way (street)	senso unico
one way (ticket)	andata
only	solo

open (adj)	aperto	**park (garden)**	parco
open (v)	aprire	**park (v)**	parcheggiare
open-air market	mercato	**parking lot**	parcheggio
opening hours	orario	**party**	festa
	d'apertura	**passenger**	passeggero[a]
opera	opera	**passport**	passaporto
operator	centralinista	**past**	passato
optician	ottico	**pastry shop**	pasticceria
or	o	**pay**	pagare
orange (color)	arancione	**peace**	pace
orange (fruit)	arancia	**pedestrian**	pedone
organ	organo	**pen**	penna
original	originale	**pencil**	matita
other	altro	**penis**	pene
outdoors	all'aria aperta	**people**	persone
oven	forno	**pepper**	pepe
over (finished)	finito	**percent**	percentuale
own (v)	possedere	**perfect (adj)**	perfetto
owner	padrone	**perfume**	profumo
		period (of time)	periodo
P		**period (woman's)**	mestruazioni
		person	persona
pacifier	succhiotto	**pet (n)**	animale domestico
package	pacco	**pewter**	peltro
paddleboat	pedalò	**pharmacy**	farmacia
page	pagina	**phone**	telefono
pail	secchio	**phone booth**	cabina
pain	dolore		telefonica
pain killer	analgesico	**phone, mobile**	telefono
pains, chest	dolore al petto		cellulare
painting	quadro	**photo**	foto
pajamas	pigiama	**photocopy**	fotocopia
palace	palazzo	**photocopy shop**	copisteria
panties	mutande	**pickpocket**	borsaiolo
pants	pantaloni	**picnic**	picnic
paper	carta	**piece**	pezzo
paper clip	graffetta	**pig**	maiale
parents	genitori		

pill	pillola	power	potere
pillow	cuscino	powerful	potente
pills, birth control	pillole anticoncezionali	practical	pratico[a]
		pregnancy	gravidanza
pin	spilla	pregnancy test	test di gravidanza
PIN code	PIN		
pink	rosa	pregnant	incinta
pity, it's a	che peccato	Preparation H	Preparazione H
pizza	pizza	prescription	prescrizione
plain	semplice	present (gift)	regalo
plane	aeroplano	pretty	carino[a]
plant	pianta	price	prezzo
plastic	plastica	priest	prete
plastic bag	sacchetto di plastica	print	stampare
		private	privato
plate	piatto	problem	problema
platform (train)	binario	profession	professione
play (n)	teatro	prohibited	proibito
play (v)	giocare	pronunciation	pronuncia
playground	parco giochi	prosper	prosperare
playpen	box	Protestant (adj)	protestante
please	per favore	public	pubblico
pliers	pinzette	pull	tirare
pneumonia	broncopolmonite	pulpit	pulpito
pocket	tasca	pulse	battito cardiaco
point (v)	indicare	pump (n)	pompa
police	polizia	punctual	puntuale
politicians	politici	purple	viola
pollution	inquinamento	purse	borsa
polyester	polyestere	push	spingere
poor	povero		
porcelain	porcellana	**Q**	
pork	porco	quality	qualità
Portugal	Portogallo	quarter (1/4)	quarto
possible	possibile	queen	regina
postcard	cartolina	question (n)	domanda
poster	poster	quiet	tranquillo

R

R.V.	camper
rabbit	coniglio
racism	razzismo
radiator	radiatore
radio	radio
raft	gommone
railway	rotaie
rain (n)	pioggia
rainbow	arcobaleno
raincoat	impermeabile
rape (n)	violenza carnale
rash	irritazione della pelle
rash, diaper	dermatite da pannolone
raw	crudo
razor	rasoio
ready	pronto
receipt	ricevuta
receive	ricevere
receptionist	centralinista
recipe	ricetta
recommend	raccomandare
rectum	retto
red	rosso
refill (v)	riempire
refugees	profughi
refund (n)	rimborso
relax (v)	riposare
relaxation	rilassamento
relic	reliquie
religion	religione
remember	ricordare
Renaissance	Rinascimento
rent (v)	affittare
repair (v)	riparare

reservation	prenotazione
reserve	prenotare
respect	rispetto
retired	in pensione
return	ritornare
rich	ricco[a]
right (direction)	destra
ring (n)	anello
ring road	raccordo anulare
ripe	maturo
river	fiume
robbed	derubato
rock (n)	pietra
roller skates	pattini a rotelle
Romanesque	Romanico
Romantic	Romantico
romantic	romantico[a]
roof	tetto
room	camera
rope	corda
rotten	marcio
round trip	ritorno
roundabout	rotonda
rowboat	barca a remi
rucksack	zaino
rug	tappeto
ruins	rovine
run (v)	correre
Russia	Russia

S

sad	triste
safe	sicuro
safety pin	spilla da balia
sailboat	braca a vela
sailing	vela
saint	santo[a]

sale	liquidazione	shampoo	shampoo
same	stesso	shaving cream	crema
sandals	sandali		da barba
sandwich	panino	she	lei
sanitary napkins	assorbenti	sheet	lenzuolo
	igienici	shell	conchiglia
Santa Claus	Babbo Natale	ship (n)	nave
Saturday	sabato	shirt	camicia
save (computer)	salvare	shoelaces	lacci da scarpe
scandalous	scandaloso	shoes	scarpe
Scandinavia	Paesi Scandinavi	shoes, tennis	scarpe
scarf	sciarpa		da ginnastica
school	scuola	shop (n)	negozio
science	scienza	shop, antique	negozio di
scientist	scienziato[a]		antiquariato
scissors	forbici	shop, barber	barbiere
scotch tape	nastro adesivo	shop, camera	foto-ottica
screwdriver	cacciaviti	shop, cell phone	negozio di
sculptor	scultore		cellulari
sculpture	scultura	shop, cheese	caseficio
sea	mare	shop, coffee	bar
seafood	frutti di mare	shop, jewelry	gioielliera
seat	posto	shop, leather	pelletteria
second class	secondo classe	shop, pastry	pasticceria
secret	segreto	shop, photocopy	copisteria
see	vedere	shop, souvenir	negozio di
self-service	self-service		souvenir
sell	vendere	shop, sweets	pasticceria,
send	spedire		negozio di dolciumi
seniors	anziani	shop, wine	negozio di vini
separate (adj)	separato	shopping	fare spese
September	settembre	shopping mall	centro
serious	serio		commerciale
service	servizio	short	corto[a]
service, church	messa	shorts	pantaloncini
sex	sesso	shoulder	spalle
sexy	sexy	show (n)	spettacolo

show (v)	mostrare	**slide (photo)**	diapositiva
shower	doccia	**slip**	sottoveste
shy	timido[a]	**slippers**	ciabatte,
sick	malato[a]		pantofole
sign	segno	**slippery**	scivoloso
signature	firma	**slow**	lento
silence	silenzio	**small**	piccolo[a]
silk	seta	**smell (n)**	odore
silver	argento	**smile (n)**	sorriso
similar	simile	**smoke**	fumo
simple	semplice	**smoking**	fumare
sing	cantare	**snack**	merendina
singer	cantante	**sneeze (n)**	starnuto
single (m / f)	scapolo / nubile	**snore**	russare
sink	lavandino	**snorkel**	boccaglio
sink stopper	tappo	**soap**	sapone
sinus problems	disturbi	**soap, laundry**	detersivo
	sinusali		da bucato
sir	signore	**soccer**	calcio
sister	sorella	**socks**	calzini
size	taglia	**some**	un po'
skating	pattinaggio	**something**	qualcosa
ski (v)	sciare	**son**	figlio
skiing	sci	**song**	canzone
skin	pelle	**soon**	subito
skinny	magro[a]	**sore throat**	mal di gola
skirt	gonna	**sorry**	mi dispiace
sky	cielo	**sour**	acerbo
sleep (v)	dormire	**south**	sud
sleeper (train)	posto in	**souvenir shop**	negozio di
	vagone letto		souvenir
sleeper car (train)	carrozza	**Spain**	Spagna
	letto	**sparkplugs**	candele
sleeping bag	sacco a pelo	**speak**	parlare
sleepy	assonnato[a]	**specialty**	specialità
sleeves	maniche	**speed**	velocità
slice	fettina	**spend**	spendere

spider	ragno	stuck	incastrato
spoon	cucchiaio	student	studente
sport	sport	stupid	stupido[a]
spring	primavera	sturdy	resistente
square	piazza	style	stile
stairs	scale	subway	metropolitana
stamps	francobolli	subway entrance	entrata
stapler	pinzatrice	subway exit	uscita
star (in sky)	stella	subway map	cartina
state	stato	subway station	stazione della
station	stazione		metropolitana
stomach	stomaco	subway stop	fermata
stomachache	mal di stomaco	suddenly	improvvisamente
stoned	fumato, fatto	suffer	soffrire
stop (n, sign)	stop, alt	suitcase	valigia
stop (n, train or bus)	fermata	summer	estate
stop (v)	fermare	sun	sole
stoplight	semaforo	sunbathe	abbronzarsi
stopper, sink	tappo	sunburn	bruciatura del sole
store	negozio	Sunday	domenica
store, department	grande	sunglasses	occhiali da sole
	magazzino	sunny	assolato
store, hardware	ferramenta	sunrise	alba
store, office	cartoleria	sunscreen	protezione solare
supplies		sunset	tramonto
store, toy	negozio di	sunshine	sole
	giocattoli	sunstroke	insolazione
storm	temporale	suntan (n)	abbronzatura
story (floor)	storia	suntan lotion	crema
straight	dritto		per il sole
strange (odd)	strano[a]	supermarket	supermercato
stream (n)	corrente	supplement	supplemento
street	strada	surfboard	tavola da surf
strike (stop work)	sciopero	surfer	surfer
string	filo	surprise (n)	sorpresa
stroller	passeggino	swallow (v)	ingoiare
strong	forte	sweat (v)	sudare

sweater	maglione
sweet	dolce
sweets shop	pasticceria, negozio di dolciumi
swelling (n)	gonfiore
swim	nuotare
swim trunks	costume d a bagno
swimming pool	piscina
swimsuit	costume da bagno
Switzerland	Svizzera
synagogue	sinagoga
synthetic	sintetico

T

table	tavola
tail	coda
tail lights	luci posteriori
take	prendere
take out (food)	portar via
talcum powder	borotalco
talk	parlare
tall	alto
tampons	assorbenti interni
tape (adhesive)	scotch
tape (cassette)	cassetta
taste (n)	gusto
taste (v)	assaggiare
tax	tasse
taxi meter	tassametro
teacher	insegnante
team	squadra
teenager	adolescente
teeth	denti
teething (baby)	dentizione

telephone	telefono
telephone card	carta telefonica
television	televisione
temperature	temperatura
tender	tenero
tennis	tennis
tennis shoes	scarpe da ginnastica
tent	tenda
tent pegs	picchetti della tenda
terrible	terribile
terrorists	terroristi
testicles	testicoli
thanks	grazie
theater	teatro
thermometer	termometro
thick	spesso
thief	ladro
thigh	coscia
thin	sottile
thing	cosa
think	pensare
thirsty	assetato
thongs	sandali infradito
thread	filo
throat	gola
through	attraverso
throw	tirare
Thursday	giovedì
ticket	biglietto
tight	stretto
time, on	puntuale
timetable	orario
tire (n)	gomma
tired	stanco

tissue, facial	fazzoletto di carta
to	a
today	oggi
toe	dito del piede
together	insieme
toilet	toilette
toilet paper	carta igienica
token	gettone
toll	pedaggio
toll-free	numero verde
tomorrow	domani
tomorrow, day after	dopodomani
tonight	stanotte
too	troppo
tooth	dente
toothache	mal di denti
toothbrush	spazzolino da denti
toothpaste	dentifricio
toothpick	stuzzicadenti
total	totale
tour	giro
tour, guided	tour guidato
tourist	turista
tow truck	carro attrezzi
towel	asciugamano
tower	torre
town	città
toy	giocattolo
toy store	negozio di giocattoli
track (train)	binario
traditional	tradizionale
traffic	traffico
train	treno

train car	vagone
transfer (v)	cambiare
translate	tradurre
transmission fluid	liquido della trasmissione
travel	viaggiare
travel agency	agenzia di viaggi
traveler's check	traveler's check
travelers	viaggiatori
treasury	tesoro
tree	albero
trip	viaggio
tripod	trepiede
trouble	guaio
T-shirt	maglietta
Tuesday	martedì
tunnel	tunnel
Turkey	Turchia
turn signal	freccia
tweezers	pinzette
twins	gemelli

U

ugly	brutto[a]
umbrella	ombrello
uncle	zio
unconscious	inconscio
under	sotto
underpants	mutandine
underscore (_)	linea bassa
understand	capire
underwear	mutande
unemployed	disoccupato[a]
unfortunately	sfortunata-mente
United States	Stati Uniti

university	università	**vitamins**	vitamine
up	su	**voice**	voce
upstairs	di sopra	**vomit (v)**	vomitare
urethra	uretra		
urgent	urgente	**W**	
urinary infection	infezione	**waist**	vita
	urinaria	**wait**	aspettare
us	noi	**waiter**	cameriere
use	usare	**waiting room**	sala di attesa,
uterus	utero		sala d'aspetto
		waitress	cameriera
V		**wake up**	svegliarsi
vacancy (hotel)	camare libere	**walk (v)**	camminare
vacant	libero	**wall, fortified**	muri fortificati
vacation	vacanza	**wallet**	portafoglio
vagina	vagina	**want**	volere
valid	valido	**war**	guerra
validate	timbrare, obliterare	**warm (adj)**	caldo
valley	valle	**wash**	lavare
Vaseline	vaselina	**washer**	lavatrice
vegetarian (n)	vegetariano[a]	**watch (n)**	orologio
velvet	velluto	**watch (v)**	guardare
venereal disease	malattia	**water**	acqua
	venerea	**water, drinkable**	acqua
very	molto		potabile
vest	panciotto	**water, tap**	acqua del rubinetto
video	video	**waterfall**	cascata
video camera	video camera	**waterskiing**	sci acquatico
video recorder	video	**we**	noi
	registratore	**weather**	tempo
view	vista	**weather forecast**	previsioni
village	villaggio		del tempo
vineyard	vigneto	**Web site**	sito Internet
violence	violenza	**wedding**	matrimonio
virus	virus	**Wednesday**	mercoledì
visit (n)	visita	**week**	settimana
visit (v)	visitare	**weight**	peso

welcome	benvenuto	**work (n)**	lavoro
west	ovest	**work (v)**	lavorare
wet	bagnato	**world**	mondo
what	che cosa	**worse**	peggio
wheel	ruota	**worst**	peggiore
wheelchair-	accessibile con la	**wrap**	incartare
accessible	sedia a rotelle	**wrist**	polso
when	quando	**write**	scrivere
where	dove		
whipped cream	panna	**X**	
white	bianco	**X-ray**	raggi x, radiografia
white-out	bianchetto		
who	chi	**Y**	
why	perchè	**year**	anno
widow	vedova	**yellow**	giallo
widower	vedovo	**yes**	si
wife	moglie	**yesterday**	ieri
wild	selvaggio[a]	**you (formal)**	Lei
wind	vento	**you (informal)**	tu
window	finestra	**young**	giovane
windshield	tergicristalli	**youth hostel**	ostello della
wipers			gioventù
windsurfing	windsurf	**youths**	giovani
windy	ventoso		
wine	vino	**Z**	
wine shop	negozio di vini	**zero**	zero
wing	ala	**zip code**	codice postale
winter	inverno	**Ziplock bag**	busta de plastica
wipers,	tergicristalli		sigillabile
windshield		**zipper**	chiusura lampo
wish (v)	desiderare	**zoo**	zoo
with	con		
without	senza		
women	donne		
wood	legno		
wool	lana		
word	parola		

TIPS FOR HURDLING THE LANGUAGE BARRIER

Don't Be Afraid to Communicate

Don't be afraid to communicate. Even the best phrase book won't satisfy your needs in every situation. To really hurdle the language barrier, you need to leap beyond the printed page and dive into contact with the locals. Never allow your lack of foreign-language skills to isolate you from the people and cultures you traveled halfway around the world to experience. Remember that in every country you visit, you're surrounded by expert, native-speaking tutors. Spend bus and train rides letting them teach you.

Start conversations by asking politely in the local language, "Do you speak English?" When you speak English with someone from another country, talk slowly, clearly, and with carefully chosen words. Use what the Voice of America calls "simple English." You're talking to people who are wishing it was written down, hoping to see each letter as it tumbles out of your mouth. Pronounce each letter, avoiding all contractions and slang. For bad examples, listen to other tourists.

Keep things caveman-simple. Make single nouns work as entire sentences ("Photo?"). Use internationally-understood words ("Self-service" works in Rome). Butcher the language if you must. The important thing is to make the effort. To get air mail stamps, you can flap your wings and say "tweet, tweet." If you want milk, moo and pull two imaginary udders. Risk looking like a fool.

If you're short on words, make your picnic a potluck. Pull out a map and point out your journey. Draw what you mean. Bring photos from home and introduce your family. Play cards or toss a Frisbee. Fold an origami bird for kids or dazzle 'em with sleight-of-hand magic.

Go ahead and make educated guesses. Many situations are easy-to-fake multiple choice questions. Practice. Read timetables, concert posters, and newspapers. Listen to each language on a multilingual tour. Be melodramatic. Exaggerate the local accent. Self-consciousness is the deadliest communication-killer.

Choose multilingual people to communicate with, such as students, business people, urbanites, young well-dressed people, or anyone in the tourist trade. Use a small note pad to jot down handy phrases and to help you communicate more clearly with the locals by scribbling down numbers, maps, and so on. Some travelers carry important messages written on a small card: allergic to nuts, strict vegetarian, your finest ice cream.

International Words

As our world shrinks, more and more words hop across their linguistic boundaries and become international. Savvy travelers develop a knack for choosing words most likely to be universally understood ("auto" instead of "car," "kaput" instead of "broken," "photo" not "picture"). Internationalize your pronunciation. "University," if you play around with its sound (oo-nee-vehr-see-tay), will be understood anywhere. The average American is a real flunky in this area. Be creative.

Analogy communication is effective. Anywhere in Europe, "Attila" means "crude bully." When a bulky Italian crowds in front of you, say, *"Scusi*, Ah-tee-la" and retake your place. If you like your haircut and want to compliment your Venetian barber, put your hand sensually on your hair and say "Casanova." Nickname the hairstylist "Michelangelo" or "Rambo."

Here are a few internationally understood words. Remember, cut out the Yankee accent and give each word a pan-European sound.

Amigo	Communist	Mañana	Restaurant
Attila	Computer	McDonald's	Rock 'n' roll
(mean, crude)	Disco	Michael Jackson	Self-service
Auto	Disneyland	Michelangelo	Sex / Sexy
Autobus	(wonderland)	(artistic)	Sport
("booos")	Elephant	Moment	Stop
Bank	(big clod)	No	Super
Beer	English	No problem	Taxi
Bill Gates	("Engleesh")	Nuclear	Tea
Bon voyage	Europa	OK	Telephone
Bye-bye	Fascist	Oo la la	Toilet
Camping	Hello	Pardon	Tourist
Casanova	Hercules	Passport	U.S. profanity
(romantic)	(strong)	Photo	University
Central	Hotel	Photocopy	Vino
Chocolate	Information	Picnic	Yankee,
Ciao	Internet	Police	Americano
Coffee	Kaput	Post	
Coke, Coca-Cola	Mama mia	Rambo	

Italian Verbs

These conjugated verbs will help you construct a cave-man sentence in a pinch.

TO GO	*ANDARE*	ahn-**dah**-ray
I go	*io vado*	**ee**oh **vah**-doh
you go (formal)	*Lei va*	**leh**ee vah
you go (informal)	*tu vai*	too **vah**ee
he / she goes	*lui / lei va*	lwee / **leh**ee vah
we go	*noi andiamo*	**noh**ee ahn-deeah-moh
you go (plural formal)	*voi andate*	**voh**ee ahn-**dah**-tay
they go	*loro vanno*	**loh**-roh **vah**-noh
TO BE	*ESSERE*	ehs-**say**-ray
I am	*io sono*	**ee**oh **soh**-noh
you are (formal)	*Lei è*	**leh**ee eh
you are (informal)	*tu sei*	too **seh**ee
he / she is	*lui / lei è*	lwee / **leh**ee eh
we are	*noi siamo*	**noh**ee seeah-moh
you are (plural formal)	*voi siete*	**voh**ee see**ay**-tay
they are	*loro sono*	**loh**-roh **soh**-noh
TO DO	*FARE*	**fah**-ray
I do	*io faccio*	**ee**oh **fah**-choh
you do (formal)	*Lei fa*	**leh**ee fah
you do (informal)	*tu fai*	too **fah**ee
he / she does	*lui / lei fa*	lwee / **leh**ee fah
we do	*noi facciamo*	**noh**ee fah-chee**ah**-moh
you do (plural formal)	*voi fate*	**voh**ee **fah**-tay
they do	*loro fanno*	**loh**-roh **fah**-noh

TO HAVE	AVERE	ah-**vay**-ray
I have	io ho	**ee**oh oh
you have (formal)	Lei ha	**leh**ee ah
you have (informal)	tu hai	too **ah**ee
he / she has	lui / lei ha	lwee / **leh**ee ah
we have	noi abbiamo	**noh**ee ah-bee**ah**-moh
you have (plural formal)	voi avete	**voh**ee ah-**vay**-tay
they have	loro hanno	**loh**-roh **ah**-noh

TO SEE	VEDERE	vay-**day**-ray
I see	io vedo	**ee**oh **vay**-doh
you see (formal)	Lei vede	**leh**ee **vay**-day
you see (informal)	tu vedi	too **vay**-dee
he / she sees	lui / lei vede	lwee / **leh**ee **vay**-day
we see	noi vediamo	**noh**ee vay-dee**ah**-moh
you see (plural formal)	voi vedete	**voh**ee vay-**day**-tay
they see	loro vedono	**loh**-roh vay-**doh**-noh

TO SPEAK	PARLARE	par-**lah**-ray
I speak	io parlo	**ee**oh **par**-loh
you speak (formal)	Lei parla	**leh**ee **par**-lah
you speak (informal)	tu parli	too **par**-lee
he / she speaks	lui / lei parla	lwee / **leh**ee **par**-lah
we speak	noi parliamo	**noh**ee par-lee**ah**-moh
you speak (plural formal)	voi parlate	**voh**ee par-**lah**-tay
they speak	loro parlano	**loh**-roh par-**lah**-noh

TO LIKE	PIACERE	peeah-**chay**-ray
I like	mi piace	mee pee**ah**-chay
you like (formal)	Le piace	lay pee**ah**-chay
you like (informal)	ti piace	tee pee**ah**-chay
he / she likes	gli / le piace	**lee**yee / lay pee**ah**-chay
we like	ci piace	chee pee**ah**-chay
you like (plural formal)	vi piace	vee pee**ah**-chay
they like	gli piace	**lee**yee pee**ah**-chay

TO WANT	*VOLERE*	voh-**lay**-ray
I want	*io voglio*	**ee**oh **vohl**-yoh
you want (formal)	*Lei vuole*	**leh**ee **vwoh**-lay
you want (informal)	*tu vuoi*	too **vwoh**ee
he / she wants	*lui / lei vuole*	lwee / **leh**ee **vwoh**-lay
we want	*noi vogliamo*	**noh**ee vohl-**yah**-moh
you want (plural formal)	*voi volete*	**voh**ee voh-**lay**-tay
they want	*loro vogliono*	**loh**-roh vohl-**yoh**-noh

TO MAKE	*FARE*	**fah**-ray
I make	*io faccio*	**ee**oh **fah**-choh
you make (formal)	*Lei fa*	**leh**ee fah
you make (informal)	*tu fai*	too **fah**ee
he / she makes	*lui / lei fa*	lwee / **leh**ee fah
we make	*noi facciamo*	**noh**ee fah-chee**ah**-moh
you make (plural formal)	*voi fate*	**voh**ee **fah**-tay
they make	*loro fanno*	**loh**-roh **fah**-noh

TO NEED	*AVERE BISOGNO DI*	ah-**vay**-ray bee-**zohn**-yoh dee
I need	*io ho bisogno di*	**ee**oh oh bee-**zohn**-yoh dee
you need (formal)	*Lei ha bisogno di*	**leh**ee ah bee-**zohn**-yoh dee
you need (informal)	*tu hai bisogno di*	too **ah**ee bee-**zohn**-yoh dee
he / she needs	*lui / lei ha bisogno di*	lwee / **leh**ee ah bee-**zohn**-yoh dee
we need	*noi abbiamo bisogno di*	**noh**ee ah-bee**ah**-moh bee-**zohn**-yoh dee
you need (plural formal)	*voi avete bisogno di*	**voh**ee ah-**vay**-tay bee-**zohn**-yoh dee
they need	*loro hanno bisogno di*	**loh**-roh **ah**-noh bee-**zohn**-yoh dee

Italian Tongue Twisters

Tongue twisters are a great way to practice a language and break the ice with locals. Here are a few Italian tongue twisters (called *scioglilingue*, or "tongue melters") that are sure to challenge you—and amuse your hosts.

Trentatrè trentini arrivarono a Trento tutti e trentatrè trottorellando.	Thirty-three people from Trent arrived in Trent, all thirty-three trotting.
Chi fù quel barbaro barbiere che barberò così barbaramente a Piazza Barberini quel povero barbaro di Barbarossa?	Who was that barbarian barber in Barberini Square who shaved that poor barbarian Barbarossa?
Sopra la panca la capra canta, sotto la panca la capra crepa.	On the bench the goat sings, under the bench the goat dies.
Tigre contro tigre.	Tiger against tiger.

English Tongue Twisters

After your Italian friends have laughed at you, let them try these tongue twisters in English.

If neither he sells seashells, nor she sells seashells, who shall sell seashells? Shall seashells be sold?	Se ne lui ne lei vende conchiglie chi vende conchiglie? Saranno vendute le conchiglie?
Peter Piper picked a peck of pickled peppers.	Pietro Piper ha colto una misura di due galloni di peperoni sottaceto.
Rugged rubber baby buggy bumpers.	Forte paraurti di gomma di carrozzelle.
The sixth sick sheik's sixth sheep's sick.	La sesta pecora del sesto sciecco ammalato è ammalata.

Red bug's blood and black bug's blood.	Il sangue del insetto rosso e il sangue del insetto nero.
Soldiers' shoulders.	Le spalle dei soldati.
Thieves seize skis.	I ladri afferano gli sci.
I'm a pleasant mother pheasant plucker. I pluck mother pheasants. I'm the most pleasant mother pheasant plucker that ever plucked a mother pheasant.	Io sono uno/a spennatore/trice di fagiani femmine piacevole. Io spenno fagiani femmine. Sono il/la più piacevole spennatore/trice di fagiani femmine che abbia mai spennato un fagiano femmina.

Italian Songs

Songs provide a fun way to break down the language barrier. Here's one you might recognize. Get a friendly local to help you with the words and the tune.

Volare
—Domenico Modugno, 1958

Penso che un sogno così non ritorni mai più, mi dipingevo le mani e la faccia di blu. Poi d'improvviso venivo dal vento rapito, e incominciavo a volare nel cielo infinito.	I think a dream like this will never come again, I painted my hands and my face blue. When all of a sudden from an entrancing wind I came and began to fly in the the infinite sky.
Volare, oh oh, cantare, oh oh oh oh. Nel blu dipinto di blu, felice di stare lassù.	Fly, sing... In the blue painted blue, happy to be up there.
E volavo volavo felice più in alto del sole ed ancora più su	And I flew and I flew happily higher than the sun and higher still

mentre il mondo pian piano spariva lontano laggiù.	while the world slowly, slowly disappeared
Una musica dolce suonava soltanto per me.	Far down there a sweet music played only for me.
Volare, oh oh, cantare, oh oh oh oh.	Fly, sing...
Nel blu dipinto di blu, felice di stare lassù.	In the blue painted blue happy to be up there.
Ma tutti i sogni nell'alba svaniscon perchè	But all the dreams vanish at dawn because
quando tramonta la luna li porta con sè.	the setting moon takes them with it.
Ma io continuo a sognare negli occhi tuoi belli	But I continue to dream in your beautiful eyes
che sono blu come un cielo trapunto di stelle	That are blue like a sky embroidered with stars.
Volare, oh oh, cantare, oh oh oh oh.	Fly, sing...
Nel blu degli occhi tuoi blu felice di stare quaggiù.	In the blue of your blue eyes happy to stay down here.
E continuo a volare felice più in alto del sole ed ancora più su	And I continue to fly happily higher than the sun and higher still
mentre il mondo pian piano scompare	While the world slowly slowly disappeared
negli occhi tuoi blu	in your blue eyes.
La tua voce è una musica dolce che suona per me.	Your voice is sweet music that plays for me.
Volare, oh oh, cantare, oh oh oh oh.	Fly, sing...
Nel blu degli occhi tuoi blu felice di stare quaggiù.	In the blue of your blue eyes happy to stay down here.
Nel blu degli occhi tuoi blu felice di stare quaggiù.	In the blue of your blue eyes happy to stay down here.

Italian Gestures

Body language is an important part of communicating in Italy, especially hand gestures. Here are a few common gestures and their meanings:

Hand purse: Straighten the fingers and thumb of one hand, bringing them all together making an upward point about a foot in front of your face. Your hand can be held still or moved a little up and down at the wrist. This is a common and very Italian gesture for a query. It is used to say "What do you want?" or "What are you doing?" or "What is it?" or "What's new?" It can also be used as an insult to say "You fool."

Cheek screw: Make a fist, stick out your forefinger, and (without piercing the skin) screw it into your cheek. The cheek screw is used widely in Italy to mean good, lovely, beautiful. Many Italians also use it to mean clever.

Eyelid pull: Place your extended forefinger below the center of your eye and pull the skin downward. It means, "Be alert, that guy is clever."

Forearm jerk: Clench your right fist and jerk your forearm up as you slap your right bicep with your left palm. This is a rude phallic gesture that men throughout southern Europe often use the way many Americans "give someone the finger." This jumbo version of "flipping the bird" says "I'm superior."

Chin flick: Tilt your head back slightly and flick the back of your fingers forward in an arc from under your chin. In Italy this means "I'm not interested, you bore me," or "You bother me." In southern Italy it can mean "No."

Beckoning and Waving: To beckon someone in southern Europe, you wave your palm down; to summon someone in northern Europe you bring your palm up. While most people greet each other by waving with their palm out, you'll find many Italians wave "at themselves" as infants do, with their palm towards their face. Ciao-ciao.

Numbers and Stumblers

- Europeans write a few of their numbers differently than we do. 1 = 1 , 4 = 4 , 7 = 7 .
- Europeans write the date in this order: day/month/year.
- Commas are decimal points and decimals are commas. A dollar and a half is 1,50 and there are 5.280 feet in a mile.
- The European "first floor" isn't the ground floor, but the first floor up.
- When counting with your fingers, start with your thumb. If you hold up only your first finger, you'll probably get two of something.

APPENDIX

Let's Talk
Telephones

Making Calls within a European Country: About half of all European countries use area codes (like we do); the other half uses a direct-dial system without area codes.

To make calls within a country that uses a direct-dial system (Belgium, Czech Republic, Denmark, France, Italy, Portugal, Norway, Spain, and Switzerland), you dial the same number whether you're calling across the country or across the street.

In countries that use area codes (such as Austria, Britain, Finland, Germany, Ireland, the Netherlands, and Sweden), you dial the local number when calling within a city, and you add the area code if calling long-distance within the country.

Making International Calls: You always start with the international access code (011 if you're calling from America or Canada, or 00 from Europe), then dial the country code of the country you're calling.

What you dial next depends on the phone system of the country you're calling. If the country uses area codes, drop the initial zero of the area code, then dial the rest of the number.

Countries that use direct-dial systems (no area codes) vary in how they're accessed internationally by phone. You always start by dialing the international access code, followed by the country code. Then, if you're calling the Czech Republic, Denmark, Italy, Norway, Portugal, or Spain, simply dial the phone number in its entirety. But if you're calling Belgium, France, or Switzerland, drop the initial zero of the phone number.

APPENDIX

Country Codes

After you've dialed the international access code, dial the code of the country you're calling.

Austria—43	Belgium—32
Britain—44	Canada—1
Czech Rep.—420	Denmark—45
Estonia—372	Finland—358
France—33	Germany—49
Gibraltar—350	Greece—30
Ireland—353	Italy—39
Morocco—212	Netherlands—31
Norway—47	Portugal—351
Spain—34	Sweden—46
Switzerland—41	United States—1

Useful Phone Numbers

Emergency: 113 or 112
(English-speaking police help)
Ambulance: 118
Road Service: 116
Directory Assistance: 12
(for € 0.50, a message in Italian gives the number twice, very clearly)
Telephone help: 170 or 176
(in English; free directory assistance)

U.S. Embassy and Consulate

American Embassy
• Tel. 06-445-981
• Via Veneto 119, **Rome**

U.S. Consulate
• Tel. 02-290-351
• Via Principe Amedeo 2, **Milan**

Tear-Out Cheat Sheet

Keep these survival phrases in your pocket, handy to memorize or use if you're caught without your phrase book.

APPENDIX

Good day.	*Buon giorno.*	bwohn **jor**-noh
Do you speak English?	*Parla inglese?*	**par**-lah een-**glay**-zay
Yes. / No.	*Si. / No.*	see / noh
I don't understand.	*Non capisco.*	nohn kah-**pees**-koh
Please.	*Per favore.*	pehr fah-**voh**-ray
Thank you.	*Grazie.*	**graht**-seeay
You're welcome.	*Prego.*	**pray**-goh
I'm sorry.	*Mi dispiace.*	mee dee-speeah-chay
Excuse me. (to get attention)	*Mi scusi.*	mee **skoo**-zee
Excuse me. (to pass)	*Permesso.*	pehr-**may**-soh
(No) problem.	*(Non) c'è un problema.*	(nohn) cheh oon proh-**blay**-mah
It's good.	*Va bene.*	vah **behn**-ay
Goodbye.	*Arrivederci.*	ah-ree-vay-**dehr**-chee
How much is it?	*Quanto costa?*	**kwahn**-toh **koh**-stah
Write it?	*Me lo scrive?*	may loh **skree**-vay
euro (€)	*euro*	ay-**oo**-roh
one / two	*uno / due*	**oo**-noh / **doo**-ay
three / four	*tre / quattro*	tray / **kwah**-troh
five / six	*cinque / sei*	**cheeng**-kway / **seh**ee
seven / eight	*sette / otto*	**seht**-tay / **oh**-toh
nine / ten	*nove / dieci*	**noh**-vay / dee**ay**-chee
20	*venti*	**vayn**-tee
30	*trenta*	**trayn**-tah
40	*quaranta*	kwah-**rahn**-tah
50	*cinquanta*	cheeng-**kwahn**-tah
60	*sessanta*	say-**sahn**-tah
70	*settanta*	say-**tahn**-tah
80	*ottanta*	oh-**tahn**-tah
90	*novanta*	noh-**vahn**-tah
100	*cento*	**chehn**-toh

I would like...	*Vorrei....*	vor-**reh**ee
We would like...	*Vorremmo...*	vor-**ray**-moh
...this.	*...questo.*	**kweh**-stoh
...more.	*...di più.*	dee pew
...a ticket.	*...un biglietto.*	oon beel-**yay**-toh
...a room.	*...una camera.*	**oo**-nah **kah**-may-rah
...the bill.	*...il conto.*	eel **kohn**-toh
Is it possible?	*È possibile?*	eh poh-**see**-bee-lay
Where is the toilet?	*Dov'è la toilette?*	doh-**veh** lah twah-**leht**-tay
men	*uomini, signori*	**woh**-mee-nee, seen-**yoh**-ree
women	*donne, signore*	**doh**-nay, seen-**yoh**-ray
entrance / exit	*entrata / uscita*	ehn-**trah**-tah / oo-**shee**-tah
no entry	*non entrare, divieto d'accesso*	nohn ehn-**trah**-ray, dee-veeay-toh dahk-**sehs**-soh
open / closed	*aperto / chiuso*	ah-**pehr**-toh / kee**oo**-zoh
When does this open / close?	*A che ora apre / chiude?*	ah kay **oh**-rah **ah**-pray / kee**oo**-day
At what time?	*A che ora?*	ah kay **oh**-rah
Just a moment.	*Un momento.*	oon moh-**mayn**-toh
Now.	*Adesso.*	ah-**dehs**-soh
Soon.	*Presto.*	**prehs**-toh
Later.	*Più tardi.*	pew **tar**-dee
Today.	*Oggi.*	**oh**-jee
Tomorrow.	*Domani.*	doh-**mah**-nee
Monday	*lunedì*	loo-nay-**dee**
Tuesday	*martedì*	mar-tay-**dee**
Wednesday	*mercoledì*	mehr-koh-lay-**dee**
Thursday	*giovedì*	joh-vay-**dee**
Friday	*venerdì*	vay-nehr-**dee**
Saturday	*sabato*	**sah**-bah-toh
Sunday	*domenica*	doh-**may**-nee-kah

MAKING YOUR HOTEL RESERVATION

Most hotel managers know basic "hotel English." E-mailing or faxing are the preferred methods for reserving a room. They're clearer and more foolproof than telephoning. Photocopy and enlarge this form, or find it online at www.ricksteves.com/reservation.

One-Page Fax

To: _____ @ _____
            hotel   fax

From: _____ @ _____
            name   fax

Today's date: _____/_____/_____
              day month year

Dear Hotel_____

Please make this reservation for me:

Name: _____

Total # of people: _____ # of rooms: _____ # of nights: _____

Arriving: _____/_____/_____   Arrival time: (24-hr clock):_____
       day month year   (I will telephone if I will be late)

Departing: _____/_____/_____
          day month year

Room(s): Single____ Double____ Twin____ Triple____ Quad____ Quint____

With: Toilet____ Shower____ Bathtub____ Sink only____

Special needs: View____ Quiet____Cheapest____ Ground floor____

Credit card: Visa____ Mastercard____ American Express____

Please fax or e-mail your confirmation of my reservation, along with the type of room reserved and the price. Please also inform me of your cancellation policy. After I hear from you, I will quickly send my credit-card information as a deposit to hold the room. Thank you.

Signature _____

Name _____

Address _____

City _____State ____Zip Code _____Country _____

E-mail address _____

The perfect complement to your phrase book

Travel with Rick Steves' candid, up-to-date advice on the best places to eat and sleep, the must-see sights, getting off the beaten path—and getting the most out of every mile, minute and dollar while you're in Europe.

FREE-SPIRITED TOURS FROM

Rick Steves

Great Guides
Small Groups
No Grumps

Looking for a one, two, or three-week tour that travels in the Rick Steves style? Check out Rick Steves' educational, experiential tours of Europe.

Best of Europe •
Family Europe •
Eastern Europe •
Heart of France •
South of France •
Britain • Ireland •
Scotland • Italy • Village Italy
• Scandinavia • Turkey • London • Paris • Rome • Venice
• Spain/Portugal • Germany/Austria/Switzerland •
Florence • Prague • and more

Call (425) 771-8303 or visit www.ricksteves.com for a free copy of Rick Steves' tour catalog and DVD!

Rick Steves' Europe Through the Back Door
130 Fourth Avenue North, PO Box 2009, Edmonds, WA 98020 USA
Phone: (425) 771-8303 ■ Fax: (425) 771-0833 ■ www.ricksteves.com

Take a trip to ricksteves.com

Our website is bursting with free information to boost your Travel I.Q. and liven up your European adventure. Here's a sampling of what you'll find…

▼ The latest from Rick on where he's been and what's hot in Europe.

▼ Rick's comprehensive **Guide to European Railpasses**, complete with maps.

▼ Frequently asked travel questions and years of archived newsletter articles.

▼ Free podcasts of our **Travel with Rick Steves** radio shows.

▼ Full itineraries and seat availability for our free-spirited tours.

▼ A directory of the best travel websites.

▼ Our **Rick Steves Travel Store** features fast, secure, user-friendly online ordering for all your favorite travel bags, accessories, books and videos— with frequent money-saving specials.

Free, fresh travel tips from Rick.

Visit **www.ricksteves.com**
to get Rick's free
64-page newsletter... and more!